Modern Biology and
Natural Theology

Modern Biology and Natural Theology

Alan Olding

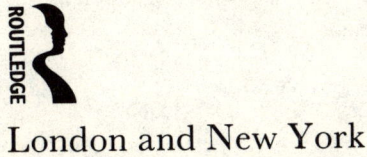

London and New York

First published 1991
by Routledge
11 New Fetter Lane, London EC4P 4EE

Simultaneously published in the USA and Canada
by Routledge
a division of Routledge, Chapman and Hall, Inc.
29 West 35th Street, New York, NY 10001

© 1991 Alan Olding

Typeset in 10/12 pt Monotype Baskerville, by Megaron,
Cardiff, Wales
Printed in England by T.J. Press, Padstow, Cornwall

All rights reserved. No part of this book may be reprinted or
reproduced or utilized in any form or by any electronic,
mechanical, or other means, now known or hereafter invented,
including photocopying and recording, or in any information
storage or retrieval system, without permission in writing from
the publishers.

British Library Cataloguing in Publication Data
Olding, Alan
  Modern biology and natural theology.
  1. Christian doctrine related to biology
  261.55

ISBN 0-415-04971-7

Library of Congress Cataloging in Publication Data
Olding, Alan, 1937–
   Modern biology and natural theology/Alan Olding.
      p. cm.
   Includes bibliographical references.
   ISBN 0-415-04971-7
   1. Biology–Religious aspects–Christianity. 2. Evolution–Religious aspects–Christianity. 3. Natural theology. 4. Teleology. I. Title.
BL225.043   1990
215'.74–dc20
                                        90–32960
                                        CIP

For my children Eleanor Fletcher Olding and Angus Anderson Olding.

And to the memories of my father and of Ken Cobb and Denise Reid.

Contents

Acknowledgements ix
Introduction x

Part I Biology

1   The decline of purposive explanations 3
    Purpose in physics and biology 3
    Paley and Darwin 6
    Biological functions 10
    Functions and accidents 15
    The teleological imagination 18
    Beyond tautology 22
    The quest for the wholly real 23

2   Biology and metaphysics 25
    Presuppositions 25
    Drawing teeth and blunting claws 30
    For reality 36

3   The stuff we are made of 47
    Behind appearances 47
    Atoms and their qualities 51
    Levels of discourse and levels of reality 53
    Ontological levels 57
    Polanyi's notion of levels 60
    The contradiction in the notion of levels 64
    Tensions 67

Part II Problems

4   Reductionism *or* Darwinism 71
    Ungrateful offspring 71
    Trouble in mind 74

5   Biology and knowledge 75
    Perception and survival 75
    Darwinism and scepticism 79

6   Consciousness and its objects 94
    Metaphysics again 94
    The argument developed 96
    The sensitive mind 102
    Perception as belief 106
    The perceiving self 112

Part III Natural theology

7   Biology and cosmology 117
    '*The fitness of the environment*' 117
    Anthropic answers 120
    The joker in the pack 122

8   From world to God 124
    Design 124
    An embodied god? 125
    Equivocation as analogy 130
    God willing 135

9   And back again 141
    The world willed 141
    Much ado out of nothing 146
    Science and theism 152
    The empirical content of theism 153
    Deism and the notion of 'the world' 154
    The agony of the world 162

Notes 165
Bibliography 170
Index 177

Acknowledgements

Special thanks are due to successive philosophy secretaries, Barbara Young and Judy Wolstenholme, for the skill, dedication and patience they showed in typing and retyping the manuscript. My thanks are also due to my desk editor at Routledge, Maria Stasiak, and to the copy editor, Sally Brooks, for the skill with which they have seen the manuscript through to publication, and to Peva Keane for the excellent index she compiled.

Several portions of the book have been previously published as articles in various philosophical journals and I wish to acknowledge permission to republish these as follows:

Part of Chapter 2 was orginally published as Part III of A. Olding (1984) 'On theories of evolution and their several natures', *Nature and System* 6, 2/3: 103–17.

Part of Chapter 3 was originally published as A. Olding (1980) 'Polanyi and the notion of hierarchies', *Religious Studies* 16: 19–102. Reprinted by permission of Cambridge University Press.

Part of Chapter 4 was originally published as A. Olding (1985) 'Reductionism and natural selection', *Synthese: An International Journal for Epistemology, Methodology and Philosophy of Science* 65: 407–10. Copyright © 1985 Kluwer Academic Publishers. Reprinted by permission of Kluwer Academic Publishers.

Chapter 5 was originally published as A. Olding (1985) 'Biology and knowledge', *Theoria: A Swedish Journal of Philosophy* IL, 1:1–22. It is reprinted by permission of the editors of *Theoria*.

Introduction

With sadness I closed Martin Gardner's recent collection of essays, *Whys of a Philosophical Scrivener* (Gardner 1985). In that volume he declares himself a fideist believing, for no reason whatsoever, in God's existence and, for good measure, immortality also. The fideism is not concealed and the God confessed is unmistakably that of old-fashioned theology, a person who made and keeps in order the universe in which we live. There is no attempt to avoid reproach by making out that God is, say, the feeling we have when tripping through a wood full of daffodils or that he is what lurks somewhere in or at the depths of being; nor does he, after the manner of the 'Wittgensteinian fideists', speak of the logic of the 'concept of God' and, thereby judiciously misusing the former term, logic, arrogate the authority of its name to a redefinition of the latter. And this is the man who not only has taught so many of us so much about logic, mathematics and science, particularly through his formerly regular series of articles in *Scientific American*, but who has ruthlessly and wittily exposed 'unreason' in field after field of enquiry.

But *why* will Gardner give no reasons for his belief in God? It is because, very honestly, he thinks that there are no good reasons for the giving. The argument from design for God's existence, the ontological argument, etc. are, all of them, irrevocably flawed. Is Gardner right and, in particular, is he justified in his poor view of natural theology, the kernel of which I take to be the argument from design?

Some of the issues involved, and which are taken up in detail in the body of this book, we can, in a preliminary way, get at by looking at a passage from a once influential seventeenth-century work of natural theology, the botanist John Ray's *The Wisdom of God Manifested in the Works of the Creation*:

> But the greatest of all the particular Phenomena is the Formation and Organisation of the Bodies of Animals, consisting of such vanity

and curiosity; that these mechanick Philosophers being no way able to give an account thereof from the necessary motion of matter, unguided by Mind for Ends, prudently therefore break off their System there, when they should come to Animals, and so leave it untoucht.

(Ray 1691:19)

We might smile indulgently at these supposed examples of 'Art and Contrivance' that Ray thinks should 'convince and silence all Atheistick Gainsayers' (Ray 1691:20). We now know, do we not?, that the mechanic philosophy *can* explain the formation and organisation of living things. Ray, himself, defended Harvey's conception of the heart as a pump against Descartes' theory that it was a sort of furnace – although, curiously, he thought that it was still necessary to postulate a 'plastic nature' for the full explanation of the heart-beat – and these days we have many readily accessible accounts of mechanistic explanations of the development, structure and functioning of organisms. Moreover, these explanations have gone beyond the pushes and pulls of everyday gross bodies to detailed biochemical accounts – of photosynthesis, respiration and the like – with hints of the strange world of quantum physics simmering beneath the biochemistry. We are not made merely of iron enough for a packet of tin-tacks or phosphorus for a box of matches as the older popular texts used to tell us. We are highly structured complexes, exquisitely tailored from material made possible by the ingenious chemistry of the carbon atom – yet, at the end of the day, that is what we *merely* are.

But from whence are we derived? The answer of modern science is as clear concerning our manufacture as our make-up. We are bits of complex chemistry evolved from less complex chemistry. According to one account, in an oceanic 'primordial soup' the trick of molecular replication was invented and this immediately made possible an evolutionary explosion of life-forms. On Earth the possibility set into actuality – life, in its complex variety, is the result of purely natural forces, its story told in terms of not quite perfect replications and how natural selection ceaselessly scrutinises offspring whose genetic plans stray from the normal. Almost three hundred years after the father of modern botany, John Ray, thought he could refute the mechanic philosophy and atheistic gainsayers we have a modern biologist, Richard Dawkins, who opens his own brilliant account of the complexities of life by telling us of his belief that the existence of humans 'once presented the greatest of all mysteries, but that it is a mystery no longer because it is solved. Darwin and Wallace solved it though we shall continue to add footnotes to their solution for a while yet' (Dawkins 1988:xiii).

Dawkins does not think that John Ray – and later William Paley – was wrong in stressing the explanatory shortcomings of the naturalistic science of his day. It is just that his challenge has been taken up, in particular by Darwin and Wallace and their successors, and a purely materialist explanation given of the evolution of life. Now just what is it about organisms that cries out for explanation according to both Dawkins and the more rational and scientifically learned of the earlier exponents of natural theology? It is, as has been hinted, their complexity and apparent design. 'The one thing that makes evolution such a neat theory', says Dawkins, 'is that it explains how organised complexity can arise out of primeval simplicity' (Dawkins 1988:viii). This raises the question of whether the issue of organised complexity is the only really important one in the discussion of the truth of Darwinism. It is a thesis of this book, taken up particularly in Part II, that it is not. There are other questions – a little 'metaphysical', perhaps, but none the less requiring more than a dismissive shrug of the shoulders – that need clear answers before the Darwinian theory can settle down contentedly in its nest of minor footnotes.

Old John Ray's challenge is with us still. I am not about to gnaw away at the theory of natural selection from the inside, as it were, by taking the popular line that it is statistically impossible for very complicated functional organs, such as eyes, to evolve by Darwinian processes – particularly after the drubbing given by Dawkins to Canon Montefiore on the issue (Dawkins 1988:37–41). But we might ask questions, in the spirit of Ray still although more cautiously than him, concerning the effectiveness of materialist theories of life. What of the origin of life? Peter Geach, whom we shall encounter again in Chapter 2, argues that it is a weakness in Darwinism that it presupposes the existence of a complicated reproductive apparatus before natural selection will get to work (Geach 1977:76–77). As a necessary presupposition of natural selection this reproductive system cannot, itself, be regarded as brought about by Darwinian forces. If, then, Darwinism cannot explain the origin of this particular complex system, the reproductive, why invoke it for other systems?

Conceivably, a biologist might take Geach's argument seriously. How would he answer it? There is, first, the logical point that however one thinks the first reproductive system appeared on the scene the postulation of it has explanatory priority. Reproduction explains the evolution of other organ systems in a way that no one of these other systems can account for the rest. But, second, our biologist may feel inclined to take up the question of the origin of reproduction. Is it the case that the first reproductive system had to be as complicated as Geach makes out? Suppose it were a short, replicating molecule of RNA. Is that so complex that we cannot imagine it resulting from early chemical evolution rather than conveniently put together by a final cause of some kind? If there are difficulties in imagining the direct emergence of organic replicators in this way then we might seriously consider the hypothesis that the first rough and ready replicators were inorganic, perhaps the clays composed largely of carbon's less-talented cousin, silicon, as A.G. Cairns-Smith has suggested (Cairns-Smith 1985).

There is, indeed, an interesting instance in the recent literature on natural theology where a philosopher finds a difficulty for theories of life's origin which is independently stated and taken up by a distinguished scientist. Anthony Kenny complains that the accounts of the origin of life which he has read all

> fail to make simultaneously plausible two elements which must both be explained if we are to account for the origin of life from the random motion of non-living molecules. To the extent that the random formation of groupings is made plausible, to explain the emergence of the first living cells, to the same extent the account makes less credible the origin of life from life alone which is the essence of reproduction of breeding.
>
> (Kenny 1987:81)

Freeman Dyson sees the same problem and, as a physicist much interested in life's beginnings, has moved towards its solution by hypothesising two origins for the modern cell. First on the biological scene was the metabolising, but only very roughly reproducing, cell. Only later, perhaps as a by-product of the cell's metabolism, did the much more accurate replicator, RNA, appear, first as a parasite but then by evolution becoming a symbiont and, finally, the cell's central information-bearing software package, directing with precision its metabolic machinery including that involved in reproduction (Dyson 1985).

These examples of speculative responses to very difficult questions about the origin of life illustrate well the metaphysical issues which underlie the hard science. Dyson remarks of Oparin's theory, as expressed in the latter's classic 1924 book, *The Origin of Life*, 'It was popular not because there was any evidence to support it but rather because it seemed to be the only alternative to biblical creationism' (Dyson 1985:31). The comment is not entirely fair to the theory but it does bring starkly to our attention that one of the major points at issue concerns the *kind* of explanation that is needed in this area of enquiry. Scientists working on the problem of the origin of life have, by and large, a stake in the metaphysical hypothesis that purely material causes rather than, say, the will of a disembodied biochemist, were at work in producing the first cellular complex. This, I take it, explains why S.L. Miller went to the trouble to discharge electrical sparks into his several plausible simulations of Earth's early atmosphere, obtaining thereby an interesting collection of amino acids. But it means, also, that scientific investigations, both theoretical and experimental, into how life began are also testing the metaphysical hypothesis of materialism. This, in turn, implies that, no matter what successes are accorded the scientific investigation and explanation of life's origin, the materialist theory, being testable, may be tested in other areas with no predetermined guarantee that it will there fare as brilliantly.

Although there are informed dissidents still, I should imagine that the majority of competent opinion is that science is a good way towards demonstrating the purely biochemical origin of life. I shall not, then, vacate my comfortable philosophical armchair to try to show the experts that there is something wrong with their chemistry. But although, in Australia as elsewhere, soon to be banished to odd dark and unfunded niches, armchair speculation in ivory towers may yet alight on issues that were once thought profoundly relevant to enquiry. One of these issues concerns what seems to me to be the uneasy relation between two features of modern biology. On the one hand we have the central theory of evolution by natural selection in which, despite the use of teleological looking language concerning functions, explanation is in terms of efficient causes; and, on the other hand, we have the increasing tendency towards scientifically reductionist accounts of organisms in terms of their basic chemical constituents. These two aspects I treat separately in Chapters 1 and 3. The question is: Are these two accounts of reality compatible? I briefly suggest in Chapter 4 that they are not.

There are many difficult problems surrounding the reductionist philosophy which, even at the inception of atomic theory in ancient Greece, pressed in upon those bold early thinkers in the guise of something like the distinction between the primary and secondary qualities of things. What, in one mood, may seem the simple and obvious move of explaining the properties of gross objects in terms of their tiny, invisible, impalpable constituents in fact stripped the common-sense things of the world of their colours and their stinks – in short, of all those characters commonly sensed – but in return indulgently gave us back two worlds: one, objective, mathematical, forever on the far side of consciousness and never reached by it; the other, the one in which we think we go about our business, never out of it. The mechanics of Galileo and Newton, as themselves descriptive of the 'everyday world', are often said to be approximate, but even this seems false if our interest is in the truth of the descriptions rather than in the 'good enough' value of the equations for manipulating things. Similarly, it is arguable, the Darwinian explanation of the evolution of life dissolves in the sea of fields and elementary particles that is said *really* to exist. The theologian or metaphysician might then tentatively ask why this strange reality lying beyond our ordinary, or even our scientifically skimming, ken should be such as to cast up an animal capable of wondering about it all – if, indeed, reductionism allows for that.

Questions cluster around this last hypothetical clause. In particular, what are the implications for the human condition of the reductionist philosophy if it is really thought through? Strangely enough – although perhaps not so strange when one detects the nervousness behind the levity – the 'minute philosophers', as Berkeley called them, often become quite jolly when questions with potentially ugly answers intrude themselves. Dawkins, for example, is a bundle of fun when he announces his own 'hierarchial reductionism' in contrast to the common or garden reductionism that (so he says) no one is actually common or garden enough to espouse on pain of being seen as morally equivalent to a baby-eater. What, then, is this virtuous hierarchial reductionism? After the laughter comes the reassurance.

> the hierarchial reductionist believes that carburettors are explained in terms of smaller units ... which are explained in terms of smaller units ... which are ultimately explained in terms of smaller fundamental particles. Reductionism, in this sense, is just another name for an honest desire to understand how things work.
>
> (Dawkins 1988:13)

Anxious neither to devour babies nor to throw them out with the bathwater, Dawkins swallows hierarchies whole so the logical bones do not stick in his throat – although a sharp and dangerous one labelled 'ultimately explained' only just slips past. The confusions involved in talk of 'hierarchies', 'levels', etc. I expose in Chapter 3.

Let us for now slide easily up and down the hierarchy of being, as Dawkins, Popper, Polanyi and others assure us we can, ignoring the immediate logical tension between Darwinism and the view, say, that the world is a collection of quarks and leptons. We know – or, let us say, in a certain mood we know – that it is such a collection. How can we, as particular gatherings of ultimate particles, know any such thing?

Part of the problem here stems directly from the acceptance of Darwinism as an explanation of our origin. We are, according to this theory, creatures that survive because natural selection has picked us out as fairly efficient survival machines. In particular, we have large, complex and, in some respects, clever brains. But then this cleverness, we assume, was selected by evolution because it had survival value, because, presumably, it allowed us to take control of complex situations. And this, as far as evolution is concerned, is the whole story: as long as our complex behaviour – manifested in our religious beliefs, in morality and so forth – aids the spread of our genes then evolution asks no more of it. The truth of our beliefs and our perceptions is irrelevant except as it may accidentally, as it were, promote survival. If we compare our perception of the world with the world as it is supposed really to be we get an idea of just how wrong – not just lackadaisical – our senses are. What of the intellect which, we might think, enables us to penetrate beyond the untrustworthy senses to the reality lying beyond? This, according to the familiar Darwinian story that threatens to make sceptics of us all, was not especially devised by God to attain the real. It will have its own human way of working, its own special logic and categories, put together in the interests of utility rather than truth. By what miracle, then – or, what in this context comes to the same thing, by what wholly improbable chance – have we twentieth-century apes in clothes grasped the truth of things?

This problem is a huge embarrassment for Darwinism for it means that the very rationality of our belief in the theory is at stake. Interestingly, Dawkins has given several Darwinian reasons for why it is difficult to understand Darwinism. For example, our minds, specifically adapted to pick out the likely exigencies of a short life, do not easily take in the aeons in which improbability becomes certainty (Dawkins 1988:xv). This argument which will, one hopes, aid the comprehension of Darwinism may also be a seed which, cultivated, will show the theory to be unbelievable. Dawkins, in fact, retains enough of a healthy realism to show how we are biologically constrained sometimes to go conceptually and perceptually astray. As mirrors of nature we are cracked and wanting but enough of the real is nevertheless reflected to show up the flaws. But now, once more, we have the question of why, on Darwinian principles, the mirror should not be utterly distorting if that best aids the production of viable progeny. As M.T. Ghiselin puts it: 'We are anything but a mechanism set up to perceive the truth for its own sake. Rather, we have evolved a nervous system that acts in the interests of our gonads, and one attuned to the demands of reproductive competition' (Ghiselin 1974:263). Our intellects, evolved to serve our gonads rather than verity, might not reasonably be expected to arrive at the truth of that fact.

After telling us that our organs of generation are masters or mistresses to our minds, Ghiselin sanguinely adds, 'Nevertheless, an ability to come to grips with the world as it really is can hardly be dismissed as maladaptive' (Ghiselin 1974:263). A reply to this is that how best adaptively a clever organism comes to grips with the world depends on how the world is. And certainly a determined Darwinist, taking seriously his theory that what really counts in the struggle for existence is how an organism *behaves* rather than what it truly believes, can bring havoc to a large portion of what we think we know. Michael Ruse, for instance, thinks that belief in an objective morality is an illusion wrought on our brains by the forces of selection.

> The Darwinian argues that morality simply does not work (from a biological perspective), unless we believe that it is objective. Darwinian theory shows that, in fact, morality is a function of (subjective) feelings; but it shows also that we have (and must have) the illusion of objectivity.
>
> (Ruse 1986a:253)

Morality, then, 'works' because it is caused to work by illusion – generating genes not because it has its *justification* in what there is. What of our other claims to knowledge?

Many have recently taken up this issue but it is still worth examining Korad Lorenz's 'Kant's doctrine of the a priori in the light of contemporary biology' (Lorenz 1975) because this classic, now near half-century old paper illustrates well the problems bristling in this area. In particular, in 'biologising Kant' Lorenz insists, contrary to the great German philosopher, that the 'a priori' forms and categories of perception are evolutionary adaptations to a 'real external world'. Now Kant, like Lorenz, confines the forms of space and time and the categories of causality etc. to experience as against the thing-in-itself; but whereas Kant obtains at least the show of respectability for his categories by ostensibly deriving them from the very general logical forms of judgement, while eschewing their application to things-in-themselves, Lorenz does not have this recourse. For the latter thinker the categories are in experience but experience is not directly *of* external reality although somehow related to it. The dilemma is that Lorenz thinks we know something of the 'external world', apart from the bare fact that it exists, but he is unable to explain how this is possible. What we get instead of real explanations are apparent ones in terms, for example, of different 'boundaries' between the experiences of various organisms and the 'transcendent' things of the world. In this instance we have no way of determining how deep, or if at all, our own boundary cuts into the world; and it is of no avail to appeal to a comparative study of animal perception, as Lorenz attempts, because this investigation will, itself, be contained within the limits of *our* perceptual and conceptual forms and we will necessarily interpret the *behaviour* of other beasts in terms of these forms and not theirs. Incidentally, I can make little of A.J. Clark's recent return to Kant in attempting to reconcile an anti-realist theory of meaning with the ontological realism of the evolutionary view. This unlikely concordance consists in rushing back to the comfort of thinkable but unknowable things-in-themselves of which, nevertheless, we can say we have 'the idea of an independent reality which makes minds which create concepts' (Clark 1984:488); and the reply is that, apart from the contradiction in saying of this *unknowable* reality not only that it is *independent* but that it *makes things* (so that the category of causality applies to it), Darwinian 'evolutionary epistemology' presupposes the truth of Darwinism which, in turn, presupposes a mass of knowable and known truths concerning the world which has cast up our minds.

It is, I think, true to say that Lorenz's basic position is that of representative realism whereby it is held that, in some sense, subjective experience represents external reality (classically by *copying* it). Indeed, he uses the word 'representation' but then, as if sensing the problems associated with the theory of perception it suggests, diverts the discussion into one concerning *adaptation*. In perception, and particularly in its formal 'a priori' features, the organism is adapted to real, physical features of the environment just as the streamlined shape and the fins of a fish are adaptations to the hydrodynamic properties of its watery situation. It is arguable that this so-called 'hypothetical realism' – which is really representative realism firmly asserted but barely and badly argued for – should be pushed in the direction of a fully-fledged direct realism such as that of John Anderson in which space and time are taken as the real, objective forms of occurrences and the categories as the general conditions of *existence* rather than knowledge (Anderson 1962; Baker 1986). However, I think that Lorenz would have resisted this move not only because direct realism does not accord easily with the general scientific picture of the world, but because his profound knowledge of animal behaviour made him distrust the idea that humans were especially privileged in their perception of reality.

Thorough discussion of the epistemological issues arising here would require another book. More modestly, what I want to bring out is that the epistemological question, whatever its solution, points up the fact that human, and probably other, animals are creatures that are aware – they are conscious. This comes out very clearly in a supplementary note appended to Lorenz's *Behind the Mirror*:

> From my standpoint of 'hypothetical realism' it is pointless to deny the patent reality of subjective experience. This primary experience, the initial datum, so to speak, is not only the basis of phenomenology and a large part of philosophy in general but also the source of all our indirect, transmitted knowledge about the material world around us . . . .
>
> (Lorenz 1977:246)

Whatever it is that we are directly aware of when, following Professor Price's advice (Price 1932), we gaze with full attention at a ripe tomato – whether our minds as it were, enclose private red sense-data to themselves or venture to embrace the tomato's red surface out there in its own right – it is an undeniable fact that we enter into the peculiar relation of being conscious of a coloured patch. And this fact of consciousness sits uneasily with Darwinism, inasmuch as this theory, itself, fits best with a mechanistic world view (see Chapter 1), and is absolutely inconsistent with a resolutely reductionist materialism (see Chapter 6). For these reasons strange manoeuvres have got underway to try to police this anarchistic, potentially unruly element, consciousness. As if in the belief that a reasonable naturalism is retained just by excluding miraculous interventions by God, the notion of emergence has emerged. Consciousness is a *fulguratio*, a metaphysical lightning flash not hurled by the hand of Zeus but sparking unannounced from nervous systems of a certain type and complexity; so that we are doubly lucky, the mental for no reason at all appearing in our evolutionary ancestry and our minds emerging from our waking brains every morning, just in time for breakfast. Other thinkers admit and then play down the awkward notion of consciousness. Thus

Gerhard Vollmer espouses what he calls an 'identity theory' although it is really a double-aspect theory in which a lick of mental paint is allowed here and there in the corridors of the brain. Anxious, on evolutionary grounds, to emphasise the efficacy of the mental, he, in fact, tells us that 'Physical processes *with* inner aspect rather differ even *physically* from processes *without* inner aspect' (Vollmer 1984:116) as if *that* will distinguish his theory from a patchy epiphenomenalism in which, to no avail, the light of consciousness occasionally shines in, but does not illuminate, the absolute night of material processes. Beyond such a view lies the identity theory proper of D.M. Armstrong in which the *name* consciousness is retained while the *notion* is subjected to a carefully judged 'analysis' that allows him to slip past the awkward *fact* to the neural potentiality it is now said to be identical with (Armstrong 1968). Here we come upon a fleet of Neurath-boats, simultaneously sailed and repaired by their crews and firing occasional shots at each other, but the whole constituting an armada under the common flag of reductive materialism. But the cause comes to grief on reefs of hard fact.

Having conceded an initial victory to materialism on the question of the origin of life we now claim a rout on the connected issues of knowledge and consciousness. The 'mechanic philosophers' have taken up Ray's challenge to explain complex organic form but, when they come up against the awkward fact of consciously knowing animals, yet still 'prudently therefore break off their System there'. The reductive materialism enthusiastically, and often aggressively, sponsored by some biologists is definitively falsified.

Other metaphysical options are once more open. The one which I explore in critical detail in Part III of this book is the hypothesis that, ultimately, a god is responsible for the universe. Here recognition of the human animal as a conscious existent may be brought in in several ways. First, it may be thought that, successful though naturalistic science is, it is spectacularly insufficient in explaining the origin of mind which is best accounted for by divine creative interventions. Second, one may be puzzled by the finely adjusted details of physical existence which seem just right for the evolution of conscious life – at least, in so far as they look like necessary conditions for that evolution – and a version of the design argument for a god's existence may be suggested. It is here that appeals to the so-called 'anthropic principle' may be made. But, third, it can be argued that the facts of mental life support mind–body dualism, which holds that the mind is a substance distinct from the body; and inasmuch as this is a plausible view so the dualist theory of a god distinct from the world gains in plausibility.

I shall have little to say about the first position, except to note that unlike fashionable theories of emergence it at least attempts to account for the origin of mind, but I shall take up the other two arguments which are closely connected. In considering the third position it seems clear that, regarded as an argument by analogy, the argument from design is strengthened if both terms of the analogy, human and the god's creative minds, are taken to be non-material spirits. There are several difficult issues here. First, it may be doubted that the notion of a non-embodied mind makes sense (Kenny 1987:84) and, of course, if it does not then the ordinary versions of the design argument cannot get started. In this book I assume, without argument, that the dualist concept of mind is coherent. Second, there is still the task, even given the fact of consciousness, of demonstrating that dualism is plausible and, once more, I shall assume that this has been accomplished.

The way seems clear for a straightforward exposition of the argument from design. As human minds produce their little bits of order in the world so the god produces the large-scale order of the universe. Unfortunately, things are not that simple. It is true that we have taken the terms at both ends of the analogy to be similar inasmuch as they are both non-material minds but closer examination reveals that the resemblance is bare indeed. This is particularly true if we look at the causal relations that are supposed to exist between minds and brains of humans and the designing god and the universe. The former are supposed to be in *interaction* with their little parcels of matter – even in willing something to happen there is first the willing and then the interaction with the nervous system which takes on the rest of the job of bringing about the action – whereas the god is supposed to bring order to the universe by mere willing, the order appearing directly out of his will. If this were not taken to be the case the argument would be one for animism rather than design and, pushed in this former direction, we would have no reason to attribute qualities of intelligence, knowledge, etc. to the god. The difference in the supposed modes of action of human minds and the god's mind – which, I shall argue, is often hidden from proponents of the design argument by equivocation on phrases such as 'direct action' – so weakens the analogical move from the one to the other that it is doubtful the goal can be reached.

John Anderson, in criticising David Hume's classic assault on the argument from design, made the following comment: 'Arguments like that of design, in fact, cannot be thoroughly gone into until attention is directed not merely to the illogicality of the proof offered but to the illogicality of what they are supposed to prove' (Anderson 1962:88). Following Anderson's advice, in Chapter 8 I examine the idea of a creator-god in its various forms and find several grave, if not actually fatal, difficulties for it. Thus, despite Professor Swinburne's efforts to persuade us that the concept of creation from nothing is coherent, I still find my own conceptual machinery sticking even when the notion is of human minds willing things like fountain pens into existence, let alone of God by fiat evoking universes. And here we must remember that, in discussing the relation between God and the universe, we have to do with *two* terms, that we should examine things from the side of the universe as well as from God's. When we do this, further problems arise, disguised by new subtle equivocations. Chapter 9 deals with these and it is argued that the only creation-hypothesis that makes much sense is that of deism. However, by this time the universe is assured of a robust independence while the argument for its design is left limp and halting by the wayside.

Part I
Biology

Chapter 1

The decline of purposive explanations

PURPOSE IN PHYSICS AND BIOLOGY

To make the great strides that it has in the last few centuries, physics had first to break free of the Aristotelian tradition. For Aristotle physical explanations include a purposive or teleological component. Things *strive* to attain their ends and ultimately, on the cosmological level, the activities of the world are to be explained in terms of things loving, and therefore attempting to imitate, the activity of the unmoved mover who, unaware of what he is elsewhere stirring up, calmly goes on thinking his own thoughts.

Physicists no longer think in terms of an immanent teleology in this way – at least, not in their non-metaphysical moments.[1] This is not to say that teleological thinking has no relevance at all for modern physics. A case can be made for the view that the Christian concept of God as creator of the universe provided the intellectual justification for the uprise of modern science. M.B. Foster (1934) has argued that Christianity, in contrast to an influential strand of Greek metaphysics, implied a concept of nature which is conducive to the empirical approach. In later Greek thought a thing, such as a tree, is regarded as a union of intelligible form and matter, the form of a thing being that which is grasped a priori by the intellect while the matter is that which is perceived. Matter was thought to be an imperfection and this led to Greek science playing down the importance of perception and emphasising an a priori deductive method. In Christianity the view is of things as freely created by God who is not now regarded, as Plato thought of him, as merely bringing together pre-existing form and matter; and matter, which still is what is perceived, is no longer thought of as contributing to the imperfection of things. This, Foster thinks, paved the way for the empirical approach of science.

It may be remarked of Foster's account of the origin of modern science that, even if true of the necessary *historical* precondition of that origin, it does not demonstrate that the Christian concept of the Creator is a necessary *metaphysical* foundation of science. The idea of a creator of the universe may have been essential if the harmful bifurcation of nature into form and matter were to be transcended; but the important thing for science just is the denial of such a dualism and this we can *now* have without also requiring the idea of God as an underpinning. We might go further and argue against thinkers, such as Stanley L. Jaki (1978), who wish still to hold out for the idea of God as the ground of intelligibility of the universe (and thus of the possibility of science), that their belief in such a creator in fact detracts from science. The ground of intelligibility is not, I take it, itself intelligible – for it would then require a further ground for *its* intelligibility and so on – and thus its postulation once more introduces unintelligibility into the very heart of things.

Even if the idea of a creative god does lie as the foundation of physics, this foundation does not usually erupt into the structure built upon it. Purpose maintains the universe in decent order and so can decently be ignored in the investigation of that order. An interesting exception to this way of seeing things appeared a few years ago in the *Scientific American*. In this article Sheldon Lee Glashow (1975) tells us that what at the moment seem to be the absolutely fundamental particles in the universe – the various quarks and leptons – can be divided into two sub-groups of four particles each. Only the particles in one of these sub-groups seem to be of much use: 'These four particles are the only ones needed to construct the world; they are sufficient to build all atoms and molecules, and even to keep the sun and the stars shining' (Glashow 1975:50).[2] The particles in the other sub-group are merely 'seen occasionally in cosmic rays, but mainly they are made in high-energy particle accelerators'(50). One response to this might be to say that this is just how things are: one lot of fundamental particles are capable of getting together to make atoms and molecules and stars while the other lot do not do very much at all. This is not Glashow's response. He wants to know *why* this is so:

> It would appear that nature could have made do with half as many fundamental things. Surely the second group was not created simply for the entertainment or edification of physicists, but what is the purpose of this grand doubling? At this point we have no answer.
> (Glashow 1975:50)

That Glashow raises this kind of question has to do with the fact that he is dealing with fundamental issues – cosmological issues – in physics. After all, he is talking about what it is that fundamentally exists, the ultimate particles that between them exhaust the contents of the universe. If he is not content to stay with principles discoverable within the universe then he has no choice but to seek them outwith it in the form of 'purposive principles' or whatever – in this case pre-eminently in what we might call the principle of cosmic tidiness. He does not believe that, despite appearances, there are types of fundamental particles which lie idly around and contribute nothing at all to important cosmic structures. He wants to find out what they are *for*.

Comparing this approach with the situation in biology, we are immediately struck by the fact that the biologist similarly asks questions with a teleological flavour. He also wants to know what certain things are *for*. However, for the biologist teleology does not come in only at the level of cosmological reflection, as it does for Glashow and for some of those theorists who speculate about the 'origin' of the universe, but stares him in the face as he investigates individual plants and animals. It is as if with life the purposive depth has burst the surface of contingent nature and bubbles in clear, bright streams in the open. Everywhere, with living things, there are ends, achieved and unachieved, and the means to those ends displayed.

It is true that, from the nineteenth century onwards, many biologists have sought to emulate the theories and methods of the physical sciences; but, unlike physicists, they have not been able easily to escape the use of teleological concepts, however much some of them regret this and even though they may try to excuse it as 'teleological shorthand'. A shorthand that has no longhand translation would seem to be the whole of the script. After all, one of the fathers of experimental biology, William Harvey, discovered the circulation of the blood because he was seeking the *purpose* served by the valves in the heart (Jaki 1978:82). Again, palaeontologists were not content merely to note the existence of peculiar depressions in the head shield of the Osteostraci – a group of now extinct fish-like ostracoderms – but they also speculated about their possible functions; and so, as Barbara Stahl tells us, one worker, Stensio, 'concluded that the depressed areas held electric organs, but other workers have guessed instead that they housed sense-receptor cells which detected disturbances in the water' (Stahl 1974:26).

PALEY AND DARWIN

What are we to make of this show of teleology, not even decently hidden away in the depths but glittering on the very surface of biological thought? Let us begin, where Darwin perhaps began, with William Paley's *Natural Theology*. According to R.E.D. Clark, in his hostile account of both Darwin and Darwinism, the last thing Darwin did as an undergraduate was actually study. Clark says of Darwin at Cambridge that 'He rarely studied or even attended lectures, except for a few which were compulsory, while most of his time was spent with a clique of riotous young men (Clark 1966:52–3).[3] As an exception to this life of dissipation Darwin made a careful study of Paley, not only that author's *Evidences of Christianity* and *Moral Philosophy* necessary for passing the BA examination, but also his *Natural Theology*.

The significance of this is that *Natural Theology* is a classic exposition of the so-called argument from design, which purports to demonstrate the existence of God from the fact of order in the world. 'In crossing a heath', says Paley in his famous opening lines,

> suppose I pitched my foot against a *stone*, and were asked how the stone came to be there; I might possibly answer that, for any thing I knew to the contrary, it had lain there for ever: nor would it perhaps be very easy to show the absurdity of this answer. But suppose I had found a *watch* upon the ground, and it should be inquired how the watch happened to be in that place; I should hardly think of the answer which I had before given – that, for anything I knew, the watch might have always been there.
>
> (Paley 1831:435)

And why not? 'For this reason, and for no other, viz. that, when we come to inspect the watch, we perceive (what we could not discover in the stone) that its several parts are framed and put together for a purpose' (Paley 1831:435). Paley has little difficulty in persuading us that 'the inference we think is inevitable, that the watch must have had a maker' (436).

Paley goes on to argue, with the use of many biological examples, that if we accept the inference that watches have makers then we must similarly believe that organisms and their parts are the result of design; for, even more than watches, organisms show 'marks of contrivance'. As Paley works out his argument he insists not only on the incredible complexity of organisms but also on the way this complexity serves the ends of animals and plants. The human eye, for example, is not only the most intricate of organs, it is also seemingly perfectly adapted to the end of seeing. In short, he points to the fact of adaptation.

A general logical remark that may be made here is that, as John Anderson put it in an article much neglected in discussions of the argument from design, 'there is no question of "marks of contrivance"' (Anderson 1962:250). That is, there is no such thing as a *quality* of 'contrivedness', or any set of qualities that have 'contrivedness' as a common feature, and to speak of contrivance is to speak of a *relation* between a contriver and what is contrived. If the question is not to be begged by assuming, from the beginning, such a relation, then the argument from design must be an argument from analogy. In this particular case the argument must be that living things so resemble the products of human manufacture that they require the supposition of an intelligent maker to explain their existence.

As with all arguments from analogy, the analogy may be denied or, even if admitted, it may nevertheless be argued that the things resembling each other also differ in some important respect and this may lead us to suggest differences in their supposed causes. In particular, when comparing machines with organisms, it should at least be noticed that they are made of different stuffs (except, of course, when the former are made of bits of the latter as in wooden instruments). This, in itself, might lead us to suspect that there might be differences in the causes when, for example, we compare the eye with a telescope.[4] The point is missed by Paley when he makes fun of the idea that presently existing organisms are the surviving examples of a variety of living things 'accidentally' produced by comparing it with the view 'that a mass of metals and other materials having run, when melted, into all possible forms, and shapes, and proportions, these things which we see, are what were left from the accident, as best worth preserving' (Paley 1831:449). Organic stuff, unlike metal, may be just the kind of stuff that, without the intervention of mind, can take on if not all possible, at least many 'forms and shapes and proportions'. This, of course, is a contention of modern biologists.

A case could be made for supposing that Paley's *Natural Theology*, besides providing an initial stimulus, was at least as important for the genesis of Darwin's theory of natural selection as Malthus's essay on population usually mentioned in this respect. If the latter work provided the final clue – which had only to be transformed from being a gloomy social theory about profligate breeding leading to competition for scarce resources into a similar all-embracing biological theory – Paley's *Natural Theology* not only from the beginning posed the general problem of organic adaptation but also unwittingly hinted at its naturalistic solution. For example, in Chapter 2 of *Natural Theology* he supposes that the watch he has compared with a living organism has the machinery to reproduce itself. This, he thinks, would be one more reason 'for referring the construction of the watch to design, and to supreme art' (Paley 1831:437). Yet he sees a problem here for he must now admit that the immediate cause of the second watch is the first one although he is quick to qualify this admission with the phrase 'in some sense'. What he is trying to do here is smuggle in, under the guise of 'marks of contrivance', extra properties over and above those the second watch is supposed to possess and which, by hypothesis, are fully accounted for by the existence of the first watch. That this is what is happening is shown by his discussion of the idea that we extend the chain of self-reproducing watches backwards. He argues that, even for an infinite chain, we still have to explain the marks of contrivance of the watches over and above the explanation we can now give of *any* watch in terms of the causal activity of a preceding one. What we have here is no longer the argument from design but the argument from contingency disguised as it; for if all the properties of all the watches are explained in terms of their efficient causes (and this the hypothesis of the infinite chain entails) then the only 'property' left to explain is the bare existence of the chain. And so Paley remarks, 'A chain, composed of an infinite number of links, can no more support itself, than a chain composed of a finite number of links' (Paley 1831:438).

Paley is struggling with the fact that organisms evidently do come as self-reproducing members of such (finite) chains. As David Hume put it:

> A tree bestows order and organisation on that tree which springs from it, without knowing the order; an animal, in the same manner, on its offspring.... And instances of this kind are even more frequent in the world, than those of order, which arise from reason and contrivance.
>
> (Hume 1962:179)

Given this commonly observed fact, the only place where Paley can plausibly seek evidence of design is at the very beginning of a finite chain of self-reproducing organisms. It is here, he might claim, that these firsts of a kind could not reasonably be said fortuitously to have sprung ready made into the world. But then we need only a slight modification of the idea of a chain of organisms – and one, moreover, that was very much in the air in Darwin's time – for even this doorway to design to be closed. The modification is to think of these chains of organisms not as consisting of identical members but as *evolutionary* chains where, bit by bit, the more complex emerges from the less. If we are successful in reconstructing such evolutionary chains, which may then be found to merge at various places like branches on a tree, then at no point between simplicity and complexity will there be a gap requiring a designing mind to venture in. It is still the case that, in these slowly evolving chains, one link fully explains the next even though the links differ in complexity.

We should be clear as to what it is that we have so far explained. Given that there is an evolving chain of Paley's reproducing watches – where we start, perhaps, with a heap of springs and cogs and so on and find evolved from it over the years the latest in digital bedside alarm clocks – then the structure of any one of these devices, including its own peculiarities, is explained by the reproductive capacity of the one immediately before it. But we know that, even with living things, such single strands of object succeeding object like beads on a string, would not, by themselves, show anything like a progressive evolution and, indeed, if there was a change from generation to generation this would certainly be deteriorative.[5] Part of the answer to this, as Darwin saw, is to think not in terms of single evolutionary strands of organisms but of *populations* succeeding populations.[6] Given this, plus the further assumption of heritable variations, then the clue to the mechanism of evolution is to be found in a theory which Paley very clearly states before rejecting it. This theory is

> that the eye, the animal to which it belongs, every other animal, every plant, indeed every organized body which we see, are only so many out of the possible varieties and combinations of beings, which the lapse of infinite ages has brought into existence – that the present world is the relic of that variety; millions of other bodily forms and other species have perished, being by the defect of their constitution incapable of preservation, or of continuance by generation.
>
> (Paley 1831:449)

One reason Paley did not see the power of this argument is that he did not consider it within an evolutionary context: he failed to connect it with his earlier discussion of chains of watches or organisms. We may surmise that this passage lay submerged in the depths of Darwin's mind, waiting its time before emerging at the centre of a fully-fledged naturalistic account of the origin of organic order. Evolution, he then saw, occurs because of a number of things. There is, first, the fact of heritable variation where changes in the parents are passed on to their offspring. There is also the fact that a population of organisms tends to produce far more offspring than will survive to maturity; from which it is inferred that there is a struggle for existence in which those better fitted to survive, i.e. better adapted to the environment, will be more likely to survive. It is, for Darwin, the interplay of these two things, heritable variation and the tendency of the fitter to survive, that drives evolution along. It is this theory, modified and clarified in many respects and with the details of inheritance, variation, environmental influence, etc. filled in, that is still the basis of the modern view. The universe is wrung dry of the last drops of purpose.

BIOLOGICAL FUNCTIONS

Darwinism has made the case for design, in so far as it is based on the complex structure of organisms, very shaky. As Norman Kemp Smith put it,

> The hinge of a door affords conclusive proof of the existence of an artificer: the hinge of the bivalve shell, though incomparably superior as a hinge, affords no such proof; it is as natural in its origin as anything in physical Nature can be known to be.[7]
>
> (Smith 1967:379)

This is not to say that the argument cannot still be grounded on more general considerations. For example, R.G. Swinburne (1968), in a defence of it, explicitly excludes, as evidence of design, such things as organic structures and instead concentrates his attention on very general 'laws of succession', e.g. the laws of dynamics, while Aquinas, as F.C. Copleston (1955:127) has pointed out, based his version of the argument on the achievement of overall order by disparate things. But whatever the merits of the more general forms of the argument from design, the god of its conclusion would seem to be remote from the remarkable organic structures that so impressed Paley – so much so as seriously to bring into question the propriety of functional concepts in biology. The postulate of such a god would be as relevant to the ascription of functions to the parts of organisms as the theory that life on Earth began because a passing friendly astronaut tipped a bucket or two of DNA molecules into our planet's primordial ocean. In fact, it has been argued that functional accounts of organic form etc. should be opposed just because they inevitably presuppose the notion of a more immediate design. Michael A. Simon has reported an argument of this kind as used by Jerome Schaffer:

> According to the view that the notion of functions is essentially linked to that of design, functional accounts are parasitic on purposive explanations. The reason why it is not ordinarily considered satisfactory to say that the function of water's expanding upon freezing is to make underwater life possible (even though it does have this effect) is, on this interpretation, that we do not have to conceive of the world as having been designed by a Creator. To ask why something is the case and to be prepared to accept a reply in terms of its function, so it is argued, is to assume that the phenomenon in question, if not actually the result of someone's intentions, is explicable in terms which indicate why it so appears.
> (Simon 1971:182–3)

This is the most common objection to the use of functional concepts in biology. Underlying it is the assumption that respectable functional accounts of items such as livers, cathode ray tubes, etc. presuppose a special teleological, causal account of how these items got to be where they are. On this assumption one can sensibly speak of the functional parts of artifacts because one can, in principle, tell a story of, for example, engineers designing and intending and putting these parts in place. The danger now is that someone who atheistically or agnostically wishes to retain functional explanations in biology will think still that he is committed to some kind of special, teleological, causal account of the origin of functional parts or systems. As intentions are ruled out as the special causes of livers or Kreb's cycles or whatever, appeal may be made to *final causes*, i.e. to the ends, taken as causally efficacious, which the functional parts subserve. And so it is sometimes thought that these ends to be attained are future states that act back in time as causes which drag preceding events in the direction of their own realisation. Such a concept of a final cause, with its implication of backward causation, might be thought objectionable in its own right; or objections might be raised concerning functional activity that fails to attain its proper end: how can an unrealised end possibly be a cause of anything? Marjorie Grene has remarked of the view that teleology is at home in evolutionary accounts, 'we can hardly hold that the speed of a future Derby winner induced his ancestor to run faster than the ones who didn't get away' (Grene 1974:221).

Some sense may be got in the work of Larry Wright of the logical tension which arises in insisting that, in supposed parallel to the case for artifacts, biological functional propositions involve reference to the aetiologies resulting in the presence of the functional items referred to. The problems for Wright's analysis are particularly revealing just because he does try to make it fit the orthodox, naturalistic, Darwinian account of the evolution of organisms while, at the same time, insisting on a unitary account both for what he calls 'conscious functions' (of artifacts) and 'natural functions' (of organisms). The claim is that to say, in paradigm cases, that something has a function is to give a certain kind of explanation for why that something is there. The explanation is a causal one but it is so in its own (functional-explanatory) way. '... functional explanations, although plainly not causal in the usual, restricted sense, do concern how the thing with the function got there. Hence they are aetiological, which is to say "causal" in an extended sense' (Wright 1976:227). Wright summarises his analysis of 'The function of X is Z' as follows:

(a) X is there because it does Z,
(b) Z is a consequence (or result) of X's being there.

(Wright 1976:232)

Here (a) is said to catch the 'aetiological form' of functional statements while (b) 'describes the convolution which distinguishes functional aetiologies from the rest' (232). This 'convolution' involves the 'forward orientation', i.e. reference to a future state, which, Wright thinks, is present in teleological explanations in general. Thus, for any functional part (e.g. the handle of a knife) the consequence of it being there is the reason for it being there (e.g. to make handling easier or throwing more effective).

Wright's account might seem easy enough to apply to artifacts. In particular, despite his talk of functional aetiologies involving a 'forward orientation' to the consequences of functional items, this can be interpreted in a non-mysterious way so as not to involve the action of future states somehow stretching out their tentacles against the stream of time and thereby *now* eliciting an appropriate action. If we say that the function of the screw is to adjust a certain valve then, on this account, we are saying something to the effect that the screw is where it is, in this particular machine, just because it has this consequence; where what this means is that the consequence is the engineer's *reason* for putting it there. As long as we do not closely scrutinise the use of intentional concepts as, indeed, J.R. Maze has recently done in his important book, *The Meaning of Behaviour* (Maze 1983), the supposedly peculiarly functional aetiology makes reference to a causal chain, involving the engineer's intentions, which does not mount an assault against the direction of time.

What now of natural functions, e.g. the functions of organs or organelles? Wright claims that his account is a unitary one in that it applies to both artifacts and organisms and this, indeed, he regards as one of its outstanding merits. He is, then, committed to the view that when we say that a certain organ, for example, has a function, we are implying that that function is the reason the organ is there. We might think that when we consider the aetiology of a natural functional item we should look for the intention – or whatever is analogous to an intention – that results in the item being there. But now we are lost because, as Wright admits, the way the functional parts of organisms come about is paradigmatically accidental – by means of chance mutations etc. To take up one of Wright's examples, there is no chemical engineer – or anything remotely resembling such an engineer – who works out the consequences of putting chlorophyll in plants and then puts it in them. His 'solution', which, in fact, depends on a massive equivocation, is to allow his 'unitary account' to split into two quite different sorts of aetiology and this has drastic consequences for its soundness as applied to natural functions. It is just here that Wright makes the appeal to the theory of natural selection. He now claims that there are important parallels between natural selection and what he calls 'conscious consequence-selection'. The latter involves choosing something X that does Z, 'where Z would be some possibility opened by, some advantage that would accrue from or some other result of having (using, and so forth) X' (Wright 1976:233). To use one of Wright's examples, I might say, 'I chose American Airlines because its five-across seating allows me to stretch out.' As he puts it, here 'the consequence *is* the function' (234). Natural selection is an 'extension' of this idea inasmuch as it similarly may be regarded as the selection of things (organisms) with characteristics having certain consequences – in this case consequences having to do with the way organisms 'fit' their environment. If it is objected that there still remains an important distinction between the two kinds of selection – because conscious consequence-selection involves choice whereas natural selection does not – then Wright replies that the gap is not as wide as first appears.

> For consequence-selection, by contrast with mere discrimination, de-emphasizes volition in just such a way as to blur its distinction from natural selection on precisely this point. Given our criteria, we might well say that X *does* select itself in conscious consequence-selection. By the very nature of X, Z, and our criteria (the

implementation of which may be considered the environment), X will automatically be selected. The cases are very close indeed.

(Wright 1976; 234)

I do not wish to deny that, for some purposes, a useful comparison may be made between natural selection and conscious consequence-selection. And it is true that these two kinds of selection involve causal sequences. Given the existence of products such as American Airlines or Watney's 'beer' we can explain their success or failure on the market by reference to customer acceptance or rejection; and given the existence of mutations, genetic recombination, etc. we can similarly explain the success or otherwise of organic 'products' by their 'acceptance' or 'rejection' by a demanding environment. Moreover, as with the earlier analysis of functional statements concerning artifacts, there is nothing temporally mysterious about the direction of the causal sequence – at least until we look closely at the present account as an analysis of biological functional propositions. When we do this we see that natural selection, even though it de-emphasises volition, is placed at the wrong end of the causal chain. What selection, either volitional or non-volitional, 'chooses' is a mechanical or organic piece of machinery just because it already has the relevant functional part. This is, or should be, perfectly clear with conscious consequence-selection because it is obvious that, in the relevant sense, consumers play no part in the aetiology of products. This part, the part played by the relevant intentions, belongs, for example, to the aeronautical engineers who design and put together aeroplanes. To think otherwise is to think that the present supply of products is explained by the future demand for them. Robert Cummins has put the point with regard to natural functions:

> To attempt to explain the heart's presence in vertebrates by appealing to its function in vertebrates is to attempt to explain the occurrence of the heart in vertebrates by appealing to factors which are causally irrelevant to its presence in vertebrates.
>
> (Cummins 1975:748)

The point is blurred in two ways by Wright in the paragraph immediately following the passage I quoted above. First, in claiming that he has a 'unifying analysis' of natural and conscious functions, in terms of the reason functional things are there, he once more argues that 'the differentiating feature is merely the *sort* of reason appropriate in either case: specifically whether a conscious agent was involved or not' (Wright 1976:234). This simply leaves out of consideration the different aetiologies involved in the conscious design of artifacts and the natural selection of organs; and that there are two different kinds of aetiology is further hidden when, a little later, he adds, with no distinction being made between artifacts and organisms, 'When we explain the presence or existence of X by appeal to a consequence Z, the overriding consideration is that Z must be or create conditions conducive to the survival or maintenance of X' (234). In other words, he is assuming, for *both* conscious and natural functional accounts, the same aetiology, i.e. the one that is supposed, through the notion of natural selection, to apply to natural functional accounts only.

Second, Wright, confusingly going now in the opposite direction, discusses the supposed aetiology of natural functions in terms which are really only applicable within the account he originally gave of conscious functions. In particular, he is led by his analysis to say that as with a useful but accidental modification of an artifact, we do not, *at first*, say it has a function but later may do; so when a new advantageous biological characteristic appears we cannot say, on its first appearance, that it is functional but later, when it becomes established in the population, we may say this. Wright is forced into this position because although mutations, in producing their consequences, occur in the same position in the causal sequence as intentions in producing theirs, there the similarity ends. As we have seen, he recognises that mutations are paradigmatically accidental, that they do not at all resemble the insights of engineers, so that there is no way we can determine the functions of natural items by what it is that mutations are trying to bring about. That is why, originally, he had to put the 'intention' for natural functions, in the form of environmental consequence-selection, at the wrong end of the causal chain. But, and this perhaps brings out the fundamental confusion, directly to compare natural mutations with happily useful accidental modifications of artifacts, which later become functions, only makes sense within an explanatory scheme where functions are paradigmatically determined by 'designers'.

FUNCTIONS AND ACCIDENTS

What Wright says about mutations is plainly contradicted by biological practice. Biologists do explain, in terms of their functions, why (the phenotypic effects of) some mutations become established. From the start, blackening of the wings of moths living in sooty woods acted as (functioned as) camouflage and that is why their owners survived at the expense, by and large, of their paler kin. But biologists also explain why other mutations, equally functionally advantageous, do not succeed, e.g. because of the statistical vagaries of the small populations in which they venture forth. It seems, then, *pace* Wright, that either functional propositions are out of place in biology or that some different account must be given of them, at least for natural functions. In the hope that a great deal of modern biology will not turn out to be nonsense, let us consider the latter possibility.

The rival account to Wright's, of natural functions at least, concerns the contribution made by an item, process, etc. to a *goal* or the *goals* of a system in which such items etc. occur. To say this immediately raises the problem emphasised by Wright, and thought by him insoluble on this 'systems-analysis' account, of how we are to distinguish between function and accident. If, for example, we consider any of the so-called 'behaviouristic theories' of goal-directed activity, where an account of teleological behaviour is given in terms of causal chains attaining a goal under a variety of environmental conditions, this problem seems insoluble. How can we, on this account, distinguish between the heartbeat's function, which is to circulate blood, and such non-functional 'accidental' effects as the production of noises. It might be argued that the fact that such systems-analysis accounts seem viable is largely due to the examples used to illustrate them where what are obviously functions or goals are smuggled into the analysis. We know already that the goal of the hunting wasp is its nest or the function of plant-hormone is to promote growth towards the light, but such goals and functions cannot simply be distilled out of the behaviouristic assumptions of systems- theories. To take a non-biological example, we know already that the function of the thermostat in a hot-water system is to control temperature – if we did not know this, then how possibly could we, on the systems-analysis account, choose as its function between regulating temperature, turning currents on and off, controlling the density of the water, maintaining the expansion of the containing vessel within close limits, etc.?

The problem highlighted by Wright is a real one. The plant that climbs towards the sun moves away from the Earth and hearts that circulate blood produce a complex of noises. What, then, distinguishes the goal or function from the accident? Wright is correct in believing that the distinction cannot be made simply by examining the containing system and the parts and processes within them, supposing that they could, without teleological presuppositions, be picked out. Ontologically, the causal chains which produce heart-sounds exist as boldly, so to speak, as those which end by circulating the blood – indeed, to a large degree they overlap. And the 'end-states' on which these chains converge – the sounds and the circulation – seem of equal worth. If, then, the distinction between function and accident can be made, the source of the distinction must in general, as Wright has argued, lie outwith the systems under consideration.

However, it is a mistake to look for this external source in an analysis of the meaning of biological functional statements. We might be prematurely disposed to accept an account like Wright's because of the connection it makes between functions and, despite some dissension, the currently respectable theory of natural selection. But the truth of the theory of natural selection is not the issue. The weakness of such an analysis is that it implies that a scientific theory, or, at least, the general form such a theory must take, can be got at simply by examining the meaning of teleological statements in biology. That we justifiably speak of the functions of liver, heart, etc. implies, on Wright's account, that the theory of consequence-selection, or some theory bearing important similarities to it, must be true. Now, although similarities in effects, in this case in the teleological structures of artifacts and organisms, may suggest similarities in the causes, there can be no logical guarantee that this must be so. It might have been, and in the future possibly will be, that the best scientific theory to account for biological structures bears no analogy at all to the idea of a designer of machines or customers selecting goods. The only way for Wright to escape this objection is to argue that things are the other way about, that we are justified in speaking teleologically of the structures of organisms just because we hold a theory of a certain kind concerning their origins. He is not necessarily committed to thinking that the cause postulated by such a theory must, as in Darwinism, resemble conscious consequence-selection; but at least he must hold that the supposed cause, whatever it is, is importantly analogous to some kind of cause involving intention and design. If we have a quite different theory then our right to teleological descriptions must be relinquished.

This view is surely fantastic. In the earlier part of his article Wright compares examples of conscious functions with examples of natural functions with the aim of convincing us of the logical similarity of the corresponding functional statements.

> Compare 'the function of that cover is to keep the distributor dry' with 'the function of the epiglottis is to keep food out of the wind-pipe'. It is even more difficult to detect a difference in what is being requested: 'What is the function of the human wind-pipe?' versus 'What is the function of a car's exhaust pipe?'
>
> (Wright 1976:216–17)

We are able to talk in this way of comparing the function of the wind-pipe with the function of the exhaust pipe because, first of all and independently of the question of the origin of the biological structure, the wind-pipe *is* just like an exhaust pipe. The fact that the comparison between organisms and machines can fruitfully be made originally provided a reason for believing that organisms are designed (although it was not long before sceptics, such as the eighteenth-century French materialists, were to challenge this) but this is independent of the brute fact that living things and their parts are somewhat like machines – and so it is, in this respect, as if organisms are designed. Wright's mistake is to think that an analogy, or 'parallel', may exist between designed and undesigned things only if a relevant analogy, or 'parallel', holds between the different causes of those things; but, clearly, the analogy may be pinned down at the other end of the causal relation, in the effects.

THE TELEOLOGICAL IMAGINATION

'Why do biologists search for functions? Because biological systems have them. Nothing could be more obvious' (Rosenberg 1985:43). This claim is, I think, correct but it does, once more, starkly raise the question of how these functions are discovered and distinguished from mere accidents. We should not overlook, first of all, that the functions of many parts of the body are, so to speak, given. This is true, in particular, of those organs which are under voluntary control, whose uses are known because we habitually and knowingly do use them in certain ways. That the eyes are for seeing is a fact that we know from the inside, as it were. Such functions were known long before the uprise of modern biology, as part of the stock of that general knowledge that stretches back to prehistoric times, and they set the task for biological science of finding out *how* these functions are achieved.

We should, I think, be wary of assuming that the thoughts of so-called primitive peoples are easily accessible to us modern 'sophisticates'; but we might guess that even with those functions instinctively known, as the phrase is, there will be connections, in the respective conceptual schemes, with external teleological principles or goals by which these functions are assessed. We can bring this out with reference to disease. Speaking of 'the world of the primitive mind', Arnold Sorsby claimed, lacking any understanding of the normal functioning of the body and all appreciation of the hammer-blows of environment in moulding and directing life, disease, as all other deleterious anomalies, could only be seen as evidence of malevolence on the part of an enemy.

(Sorsby 1941:19)

It is difficult to understand how 'primitive minds' could have any notion at all of 'deleterious anomalies' – whether or not they thought the causative agent was 'an ill-disposed enemy in their midst, a departed ancestor, an angered god, the rising moon, or the mounting storm' (Sorsby 1948:20) – unless they also did have an idea of the 'normal functioning of the body'. Again, the aim of primitive medicine, no matter what magical beliefs it enshrined, would have been the restoration of the proper functioning of diseased organs. To hint at the darker side of things, I might mention how warfare, primitive or not, presupposes knowledge of how the functioning parts of bodies contribute to the goals of survival.

Whatever we may think the correct account is of those ancient pieces of knowledge concerning natural functions, the much more recent comparison (especially since the renaissance) of organisms with machines does bring out the points that functions are picked out in relation to goals and that these goals are themselves picked out by reference to a background theory or general view. At the same time this background theory or view cannot be analysed out as part of the meaning of biological functional propositions.

Consider the heart. It is now obvious, although originally it took the genius of Harvey to discover the fact, that the heart is, or is very like, a pump. What do pumps do? They pump fluids. The function of the heart, then, is to pump a fluid of some kind, the obvious candidate being blood. The details of this account can then be filled out by further experimental investigations involving the structure and mechanical properties of the heart, by calculations concerning the volume of the blood, and so forth. For our purposes the details here are not important.[8] The important point is that a toe-hold on the way to giving functional accounts of some organs was given not by the general statement that organs are like machines but by the detailed comparison of them with actual machines or their parts.

But *why* was this comparison of organisms with machines made? It is here that the reference to a background of theoretical presuppositions must be brought in. We should notice, once more, the importance, from the time of Galileo on, of an effective science of mechanics which encouraged the mechanistic analysis of the things of the world including, as far as possible, living organisms. But also it was obvious to the thinkers of the time that living machines were designed by God and this belief, in itself, allowed the theoretical introduction of supposed goals, e.g. concerning the survival of organisms, towards which the machine-like parts of organisms were thought of as contributing. This suggests a reply to Andrew Woodfield's criticism of what he calls the 'projectionist' view of organic teleology – where one would say that it is *as if* a god had designed the heart – that 'equally, one could say, it is *as if* a god wanted the heart to make a noise and so designed it to beat' (Woodfield 1976:121). There is no 'equally' about it: the heart may be a bit like a noise-making machine but it is much more like a pump. Even if a god did make the heart as a noise-making machine it is still true that it is *as if* he made it as a pump and, moreover, it is much more *as if* he made it as a pump than *as if* he made it as a noise-making machine. This, of course, is connected with the further assumptions, however vaguely held, that the 'as if god' is a competent artisan, that he is rational, etc. – in fact, the same kind of assumptions concerning a supposed real god which Darwin was able to challenge by citing examples of incompetent biological designs and which are defended by creationists when they deny the existence of vestigial organs (Moore and Schultz 1974:434–6).

Similarly, then, it is with reference to the causal theory of natural selection that functions are discovered and verified – and the important distinction between functions and accident determined. Now, again, it is as an externally supplied theory, and not as part of the meaning of 'function', that the notion of natural selection helps biologists to determine the goals of functional items. This can be brought out by looking at J. Canfield's attempted definition of the concept of biological function in terms of usefulness: 'A function of I (in S) is to do C means I does C and that C is done is useful to S' (Canfield 1964:290). In fact, Canfield's definition attempts to incorporate the notion of Darwinian fitness because usefulness is itself analysed with reference to the relative probability of the organism (S) surviving or having descendants. Wright criticises Canfield's analysis as follows:

> Hanging a pacemaker on the sixth rib of a cardiovascularly inept lynx would be useful to that cat in precisely Canfield's sense of 'useful': it would make it more likely that the cat would survive and/or have descendants. Obviously the same can be said for the diagnostic value of an animal's heart sounds. So usefulness – even in this very restricted sense – does not make the right function/accident

distinctions: some things do useful things which are not their functions, or even one of their functions.

(Wright 1976:222)

We might try to reply, on Canfield's behalf, that Wright's examples are artificial. Canfield's analysis is meant to apply in certain contexts only: to natural situations. The sixth rib is not a pacemaker hook because the pacemaker is not a (natural) organ – it is *put* there by a lynx lover; and the heart is not a noise-making machine because heart sounds are not useful except in a highly artificial environment. Even if we consider cases where populations of animals are regularly treated in these ways so that evolution of some kind occurs – sixth ribs develop notches and hearts become thunderous – still it is not clear that we are now dealing with biological functions. It might be claimed that we have here examples of artificial, rather than natural, selection and that these organisms, like the worst examples of artificially bred dogs, survive only because the environment pampers them – that far from these organisms fitting their environments, the environments are made to fit them. It is this kind of thinking which gives at least some sense to the view of the social Darwinists that the welfare state favours the unfit at the expense of the fit.

If it is insisted that there is no essential difference between natural and artificial environments, as far as biological theory is concerned, then the answer now is that Wright's examples are beside the point. From the point of view of Darwinian theory – which is what Canfield's definition tries to capture – in the environments envisaged a fuction of the sixth rib *is* as a pacemaker hook and a function of the heart *is* noise-making. Similarly, looking like a sausage is a functional property of dachshunds. In these instances, and in these respects, the organisms are, in the Darwinian sense, adapted (or pre-adapted) to their environments. Wright's examples are beside the point because, in order to show that the characteristics under consideration are not functional, we have to refer them to a wholly irrelevant environmental context.

In fact, to make the above reply to Wright we have had to go outside Canfield's definition and appeal to the external theory of natural selection. This is shown not only by the fact that the decision whether or not to treat natural and artifical environments as the same is made with reference to that theory; it also comes out in such notions as that of pre-adaptation which refer to the fact (if the theory be true) that functional organs, bits of behaviour, etc. are heritable. We might, indeed, have made the argument against Canfield by pointing out that in natural environments all kinds of useful modifications will occur to organisms which, because they are not under genetic control, would not be regarded as functional by biologists. Once more, the full-blown theory of natural selection needs to be brought in.

BEYOND TAUTOLOGY

We can get some inkling of how it is that the theory of natural selection explains evolutionary change by appeal only to efficient causes – and yet, paradoxically, provides the goal to which organisms tend – by looking briefly at the common criticism that its central explanatory proposition is really nothing but a tautology. The claim is that, according to Darwinism, those organisms which survive (produce the most viable offspring) are the ones which are fitter than their evolutionary competitors. Yet, the criticism goes on, fitness and survival are circularly defined: the fitter organisms are defined as those that survive and those organisms that survive are defined as the fitter. As A.R. Manser has put it, 'there can be no independent criterion of fitness or adaptability: survival and adaptability or fitness are necessarily connected' (Manser 1965:26). It follows immediately from this claim that Darwinism has no explanatory power although some authors have tried to soften the blow by making out that the tautology involved is a magic one that somehow says something about the general categories into which we should place 'the independent variables involved in the evolutionary process' (Barker 1969:274). The short answer to this latter claim is 'a tautology is a tautology'.

There is no doubt that biologists often do define fitness in this way (Rosenberg 1985:127) without noticing the disastrous logical consequence of so doing. Matters are further confused by population biologists who use the symbol w to stand for what they call 'fitness' or even 'Darwinian fitness'. Here the concern is with the relative frequencies of genes which are passed on to subsequent generations. Thus two populations may be being compared with respect to 'fitness'. For one population we can represent its success in passing on its genes by the equation

$$w_1 = 1$$

The equation for the other population, which we can take here as being less successful, is given as

$$w_2 = 1 - s_1$$

where s is called the 'selection coefficient'.

It is unfortunate that w has been called 'fitness' because *all* that it represents is a relative frequency of offspring, and, as such, has a quite different meaning from 'fitness' as it appears in the Darwinian *explanatory scheme*. The sort of confusion that can result may be seen in the reply sometimes made to the criticism that selection could not possibly act on the very small inheritable changes that Darwinism postulates. This has been in terms of the mathematically demonstrable effect on future populations of very small relative fitnesses. Once more, the fitnesses referred to are only differential frequencies; and to assert that these would exist is merely to beg the question against those who argue, *on causal grounds*, that they could not.

In this case it is the critic who has the better understanding of Darwinian theory. The reply that needs to be made would involve showing that the 'insensible variations' postulated by Darwinism are not *causally* insensible, that they can *bring about* the small differences in the relative frequencies of offspring – only then can the Darwinian sit back and let the mathematics take over. This shows that the central tenet of Darwinism, 'the survival of the fittest', far from being a tautology, in fact is an hypothesis linking fitness causally with number of offspring. The fitter organisms are those which are better adapted or 'designed' to survive than their rivals in a given environment – that is why their 'design' tends to spread throughout the population (given the truth of the other propositions of the theory concerning competition for scarce resources etc.). And we can see now how it is that the Darwinian theory supplies the goal of organisms, success at breeding, relative to which the functions of organs etc. can be estimated. The goal of survival, in the Darwinian sense, is that end-state (ontologically no more important than any other) to which so many biological components contribute just because of the general mechanism underlying evolution.

THE QUEST FOR THE WHOLLY REAL

Teleology still lives but only barely, as a wraith sometimes called 'teleonomy'. There are no beckoning final causes calling chains of events into existence, nor does God, even if he exists as efficient cause, intrude into our reckoning of natural purposive systems. Descartes was right: whatever purposes God has in mind cannot enter into our accounts of finite mechanisms. This, it seems, is the lesson to be learned from the brilliant successes of, first of all, modern physics and then, since Darwin, biology.

Accounts of teleological systems, such as the one I have sketched, are often called 'reductionist' in one of the several senses of that word. Something goes out of one view of the world to be replaced by something disturbingly different — final causes are usurped by the natural efficient causes which were originally uneasily subservient to them. But that is only part of the modern picture. Physics and then chemistry and then, once more, biology have become, in their investigations of things, reductionist in another way. The ordinary efficient causes and their effects which, we think, we often enough encounter and grasp in our perceptions and dealings with the world, are taken as usefully illusory manifestations of the fields and elementary particles of reality. It behoves us, then, to look closely at this other bequest of science.

There is, however, another issue which must first be resolved. I have boldly, and some will think foolishly, spoken of 'reality' where the assumption is that scientists, philosophers and theologians try to find out what is the case. This is a whisper liable to go unheard in the clamour proclaiming that we have access only to 'perspectives' or that all non-falsified views are equally probable, which is to say equally improbable, or some such thing. Before, then, looking at the world as described by science we must take up the issue of whether or not the world *is* described by science.

Chapter 2
Biology and metaphysics

PRESUPPOSITIONS

In the depths, underlying the froth of the debate about Darwinism, lie profound metaphysical questions. We can see something of this by looking at an argument of P.T. Geach:

> Darwin's method in *The Origin of Species* is to put up a challenge of this form: You mention some ostensibly teleological feature of living things, and I will show how it could have arisen through casual variations and the elimination of ill-adapted varieties. And he seems to suppose that the accumulation of many such stories increases the probability of each story. The opposite is the truth. Any one such story is pretty improbable on the face of it; we often have no evidence whatever that such random variation and the perishing of unfit varieties took place as Darwin hypothesizes; and in view of the imperfections of the geological record, the irrecoverable perishing of soft tissues, and the like, we can in many instances be pretty certain that no better evidence is going to be available. The improbability of the whole theory is increased, not diminished, as one unlikely story succeeds another.
>
> (Geach 1977:75–6)

There is a great deal which is of interest in Geach's argument and a lot that could be said in reply to it. For the moment let us note that even if the evidence for Darwinism is in the poor condition ascribed to it by Geach – and one fallacy here is that Geach assumes that the recital of such 'just-so stories' constitutes the only possible evidence for the theory[1] – it could still be said that such imaginative reconstructions show that an explanation of the origin of species of a purely mechanistic sort is possible. It was precisely this possibility that was made fun of by thinkers such as Paley.

Here, then, a metaphysical option reveals itself. We can see things in a different light if we remind ourselves that a puzzling feature for scientists of the last century just was the fact that a purely naturalistic account in terms of efficient causes seemed highly successful for so much of the universe – including, in principle, the physiology of organisms. There was, then, something of a metaphysical predisposition to accept a materialist account of the world and in so far as this was rational it loaned some weight to an hypothesis that accounted for the origin of organisms in terms of a plausible-looking *mechanism* such as that of natural selection.

Metaphysical beliefs and speculations and arguments are not, and should not be, cut off from some supposed body of 'pure science' as the positivists would have us believe. In illustration let us return to Geach's worry about the theory of natural selection which he expresses by referring to 'a popular belief that Darwin has shown once for all that such teleological detail [of the living world] is all a delusive appearance'[2] (Geach 1977:76). Now Geach's concern here is, I think, very largely with matters of causality, of how it is that the teleology of living things, whether real or mere appearance, is brought about. But this issue can, itself, be interpreted in at least two different ways, each requiring what may broadly be regarded as a metaphysical analysis.

(i) The issue may be simply about what kind of efficient cause, spiritual or mechanistic, is responsible for 'teleological order'. As we shall, ourselves, later on be critically examining this question let us for now restrict ourselves to some metaphysical ground-clearing by sweeping out of the way what might seem to be an attractive compromise candidate – the theory of vitalism. This theory might seem to provide a reasonable 'middle way' between theism and Darwinism because the vital force it postulates is, on the one hand, analogous to the conscious, intending mind of the former view and, on the other hand, supposed to be fully immersed, as it were, in the material interactions of the latter hypothesis. But then we see that vitalism just will not explain what (at least at first sight) both theism and the theory of natural selection, in their different ways, do explain – the existence of biological teleology. Neither the 'intentions' of the vital impetus nor the way they are intimately glued within nature explain, except by *obiter dictum*, the functional order of the living world. And so Bergson's vital force, its choices sparking at every moment of history, lays down, by accident generously helped out by original impulses deep within it, here and there eyes and elsewhere reproductive organs (Bergson 1911:Ch.2). Life takes on the 'shape' of the vital impetus as iron filings take on the shape of a hand passing through them (Bergson 1911:99–106). It is difficult to see, with such a scheme, how any kind of functional account of organisms, analogous or not, could be correct – whether we could, for example, say that the eyes are for seeing any more than the impression of a hand in iron filings is for grasping.[3]

(ii) Geach also insists that teleological explanations are distinct from explanations in terms of efficient causes in the sense that quite different orders of causality are involved so that 'the idea that scientific progress in finding out efficient causes somehow discredits teleological descriptions, or progressively reduces the area of their application, seems to be logically unfounded' (Geach 1977:72). The very notion of quite separate orders of causality, which do not impinge on each other, is suspect but, as Geach does not elaborate on the idea, I shall take it up as it appears in a recent ingenious defence of the Aristotelian concept of final causes in order to show something of the problems that arise with it. Thus T.L. Short has argued that teleological explanation in terms of final causes is required 'to explain what mechanical causation by itself cannot explain, namely the emergence of order from disorder or of uniformity from variety' (Short 1983:311). These final causes, which 'are abstract types that so influence processes of mechanical causation that they tend to bring about their own actualization' (311) are needed in the explanation, in terms of statistical mechanics, of the tendency of isolated systems to reach a uniform temperature ('uniformity from variety'), and the explanation, in terms of natural selection, of the tendency of populations of organisms to evolve. We might wonder just *how* these final causes, taken as abstract types, could be causally potent: surely, we might say, only concrete existents (atoms or galaxies or wombats or whatever) can enter into causal relations. Short thinks not, as he shows in a passage where he also tells us just what *are* the final causes in the two cases under consideration.

> The examples of statistical mechanics and the theory of natural selection make it clear how final causes produce finious processes ['finious' is a term invented by C.S. Peirce to refer to end-directed processes]. The type of result toward which the process tends is built into a principle of selection which variations that are retained satisfy.... In the one case it is simply a matter of extremely high probability that any combinations of molecular motions that actually do occur will satisfy the type, 'no decrease in entropy'. In the other case, it is a matter of likelihood that variants that do not satisfy the type 'relatively better suited for reproductive success' will

be prevented from reproducing by one or another mechnical event or condition.

(Short 1983:314)

With the help of what Short later says in answer to possible objections we can glean two things from this passage. First, the abstract types that are the final causes just are certain principles of selection. This seems to be what is meant when he says that 'The type of result . . . is built into a principle of selection, etc.'; and this interpretation is confirmed by what he later says about evolutionary explanations where he claims, 'A principle of selection is the cause given for why variations in inheritable characteristics tend to result in species adapted for survival' (Short 1983:314).

The second point is that what these final causes, as principles of selection, bring about are certain *general tendencies*. What is explained by statistical mechanics is the general tendency towards no decrease in entropy and what the theory of natural selection explains is the tendency towards the survival of the better adapted. The explanations are held to be non-mechanistic just because they are of general tendencies which are accounted for without reference to the particular mechanistic events or processes to be found within a particular exemplification of the relevant tendency. With reference to the theory of natural selection (and the point is similar for statistical mechanics) Short puts the matter as follows:

> But since we predict and explain the general tendency without knowledge of its particulars, and since we know that the tendency would very likely be the same even if the particulars were different (even if other species had evolved instead, they would probably be pretty well adapted for survival too), it follows that the mechanistic explanation of these particular developments is *not* the explanation of the general tendency.

(Short 1983:314)

It is just here that we must keep our wits about us. I have already suggested that we might raise questions about the possibility of abstract types, whether these are taken as 'principles' or whatever, being causally efficacious. Short's response is to make fun of such questions. We sceptics are narrow-mindedly mechanistic, that is, we think 'an abstract type could not be a cause unless it got out there and pushed something around – unless, that is, it occupied a point in space and time and exerted a force or was a force exerted from that point' (Short 1983:314). Quite so. I, at least, do believe something like this.

But, says Short, this merely begs the question because 'if there is a final causation at all, it cannot be of the same nature as mechanical causation' (314).

Short has a quick way with conceptual thickets but let us ignore that and see how he thinks the issue can be put in a non-question-begging way: 'is any phenomenon explained by reference to something that is not a mechanical cause?' (314). The answer, he thinks, is 'Yes' and it is here that he makes reference to the examples where 'we predict and explain the general tendency without knowledge of its particulars' and where 'we know that the tendency would very likely be the same even if the particulars were different' (314).

Now in the quotation I gave three paragraphs back Short does not demonstrate that we must believe in final causes – all he shows is that 'the mechanistic explanation of these particular developments is *not* the explanation of the general tendency'. It does not follow that because particular mechanistic causes are not mentioned in explaining the general tendencies of closed systems and evolution therefore some other type of cause must be operating. A rival possibility – I would say *the* rival possibility which only has to be mentioned to become the probability – is that the *details* of mechanistic causes do not have to be mentioned just because the details are not required in explaining the generalised end-states towards which some systems tend. For example, given an isolated inhomogenous mass of gas molecules, all we need to know, *in a general way*, is that they interact according to mechanical principles and then given that, plus statistical reasoning, we can deduce that the gas will become homogenous.

I shall now demonstrate that final causes *cannot* be invoked in the processes mentioned by Short. I shall first make the point that, no matter how different final causes are supposed to be from mechanical causes, if they are active then they must have effects and to have effects in the world must make a difference to the world. To say this, I take it, is not to be involved in mechanistic bigotry. But now when we look at the details of the scientific account of the evolution of closed systems and of populations of organisms there is just no room, as it were, for these extra effects.

Consider an enclosed gas whose molecules are dispersed throughout its volume in a non-random way – e.g. the molecules at one end of a box have, on average, a higher velocity than those at the other end. What will happen if no energy is allowed to enter from outside? If we assume a Laplacean deterministic model then the scientific account asserts, roughly, that the molecules will disperse throughout the volume in such a way that eventually the average velocities of any large selections of molecules, taken anywhere within the box, will be much the same. Fast molecules, through collisions, speed up slow ones and slow molecules similarly slow down fast ones. It is for this kind of reason that eventually, if the population of molecules is large, thermal equilibrium is reached.

Consider other enclosed volumes of gas, as many as you wish, whose (large) populations of molecules take up quite different non-random distributions. Precisely the same thing will happen in each of them (with very rare statistical exceptions). So all (or nearly all) of them will reach equilibrium for the same reasons involving mechanical interactions etc. In each case the explanation for the final equilibrium state is a full one and does not mention any causes other than mechanical ones. So if the *only* causes acting in *each* isolated system that attains equilibrium are mechanical causes then the only causes acting in *all* the isolated systems must be mechanical causes. A general final cause does not get a look in and, in fact, if it did would, like Maxwell's demon, be expected to disturb the various states of equilibrium achieved in each system.

DRAWING TEETH AND BLUNTING CLAWS

Modern Darwinism does not require us to believe that nature is literally 'red in tooth and claw' but, nevertheless, it may be seen as having very nasty implications indeed. John Galloway has expressed the feeling here:

> The trouble with evolution is that it is such a bleak creed – nowhere so apparent as in Jacques Monod's *Chance and Necessity*. The bleakness is sometimes disguised by the humanity and good humour of its proponents, and their enthusiasm for being able to offer us a theory of life, including ourselves, at once illuminating and apparently philosophically plausible. But, for anyone who is thoughtful about existence, evolution is the skull below nature's often beautiful face.
> (Galloway 1988:67–8)

This skull, grinning and smirking beneath both nature and our dreams of her, has been the cause of much alarm. Many thinkers, sensitive to the real or imagined implications of the theory of natural selection, have tried to soften its impact in various ways. Let us take up, once more, the question of the metaphysical import of the theory particularly as it bears on the existential claims of religion. Leaving aside for now those arguments which try to demonstrate the falsity or the vicious logical circularity of Darwinism, most attempts at 'reconciliation' involve outright relativism about science or religion or both; or if realism is embraced a covert relativism still in the form of 'every man to his own last' often creeps in. In both cases attention is drawn from the substantive issue of the *truth* of propositions and confusingly directed to the 'methodological' question of *how* it is people arrive at their beliefs. It is, one might say, methodology divorced from reality and refusing to acknowledge the awkward offspring of their original union.

These attempts at compromise can be seen in some of the responses to the recent loud inanities of the self-styled 'scientific creationists'. Thus George M. Marsden has traced the opposition creationists express to evolution in part to their espousal of an extreme Baconian inductivism which leads them to distrust theories that venture too far beyond experience (Marsden 1984). Marsden, in fact, shows a tolerance for creationist thought which many others, including myself, lack. He achieves this by, first, confining his discussion largely to the analysis of fundamentalist methodological presuppositions, ignoring the more particular anti-evolutionary arguments produced by prominent creationists. If the latter arguments are examined they are seen often to be desperately, deliberately and therefore despicably confused. Second, Marsden espouses a comfortable Kuhnian relativism so that he sits cheerfully above the dust writing of 'paradigm conflicts' between theories whereby 'Communication is nearly impossible and each party thinks that members of the other are virtually crazy or irremediably perverse' (Marsden 1984:109). In this case, the members of one party, the creationists, *are* virtually crazy or irremediably perverse.

If we do convince ourselves that some creationists are not so much crazy (and therefore deserving of our charity) as perverse, of what perversion do we accuse them? Their basic fault, surely, is to sin against the truth. It is instructive here to compare Marsden's easy-going relativism with how Kenneth Miller sees things when describing, in the same volume, a debate he had with Henry Morris. In reply to the argument that radiometric dating techniques indicate a great age for the Earth Morris said, 'We now know that decay rates do vary.' Miller comments:

> How much do these rates actually vary? Enough to be consistent with a much younger age for the earth? Not at all. The maximum reported variability (at very great extremes of temperature and

pressure) is less than 4 per cent. Stacked up against the 50 million per cent discrepancy which all of this demands, this objection looks a little pale, to say the least!

(Miller 1984:37–8)

'Here', as Miller further remarks, 'you can see one of the reasons why the scientists who are willing to confront creationists publicly often have a problem controlling their tempers' (38). I surmise that Miller's own surge of adrenalin, if such there was, was caused by what he saw as Morris's wilful and culpable attempt at obfuscation.

The issue of truth once more raises the spectre of metaphysics. If we eschew the currently fashionable relativism or scepticism about science then we must hold that science is about what is the case. And if we think the same of religion then we have no logical guarantee that propositions from these two areas cannot be brought into relation. In a backhanded sort of a way we can praise the creationists for having made this clear. Indeed, when it comes to the matter of education they have sometimes been more clear-headed than their opponents.

Thus, in 1972 the National Academy of Sciences in America passed a resolution stating that 'Religion and science are ... separate and mutually exclusive realms of human thought' (Wade 1972:728) as if these matters are to be decided by vote. It is arguable that the separatist view of science and religion expressed in the above responses reflects, just as much as do the creationist's manoeuvres, the sharp distinction between church and state made by the American constitution. But admirable as that dogma is in lessening dissension among potentially warring factions, its value is purely pragmatic and, as with the sentiments expressed above, provides no argument for the logical or metaphysical doctrine of the complete separateness of science and religion. However, whatever the underlying motives or anxieties promoting this position, it is possible to find arguments for it. It is here that what may broadly be called 'methodological issues', concerning how propositions are arrived at or how firmly they are held and so forth, are often confusingly mixed in with the different issues of the truth or falsity of, and the logical relations between, propositions. For example, Robert Root-Bernstein has put the matter as follows:

> The evolution–creation controversy is not what it first appears to be. Creationism is not a scientific alternative to evolution, no matter how often the creationists insist upon placing 'scientific' in front of 'creationism'. Creationism is a religious belief. The present

controversy is not, therefore, born of scientific problems; it is born of the misrepresentation of a religion as a science. In consequence, the real issue to be discussed is not whether creationism is a valid scientific alternative to evolution, but what relationship should exist between scientific ideas and religious beliefs.

(Root-Bernstein 1984:82)

Well, what relationships should exist between science and religion? Root-Bernstein believes the answer to this question is 'None' inasmuch as science and religion constitute (or should constitute: I am not sure how he wants to be taken) quite separate 'domains'. However, the passage quoted above shows quite the opposite. 'Creationism is not a *scientific* alternative to evolution,' he says; in fact, 'Creationism is a *religious* belief' (my emphasis in both cases). To show that creationism, as a religious belief, is not a scientific alternative to the scientific belief in evolution is not, without further argument, to show that it is not a *logical* alternative to evolutionism. Confusion arises here because of the very general use of the terms 'religion' and 'science', so let us try to clarify matters by looking at a couple of propositions, the one accepted by creationists and the other by evolutionists. Compare 'Life began a few thousand years ago' with 'Life began over three thousand million years ago'. If the first proposition is true the second is false and vice versa. But the first proposition is religious and the second is scientific so here we do have a clash between science and religion.

This conclusion is not at all affected by Root-Bernstein's claim that the controversy between evolutionism and creationism 'is born of the misrepresentation of a religion as a science'. After all, it is *religion* which is being misrepresented. It is true, of course, that the 'scientific' arguments presented by the creationists are so much moonshine and that their real reasons for their belief are quite different, but this brings out the point that there are different 'methodologies' involved in the ways creationists and scientific evolutionists arrive at, and hold on to, their rival propositions. We *call* the creationists' beliefs 'religious' because they appeal to sacred scriptures to back up their views of the origin of life, because of the close connection they perceive between beliefs in origins and moral matters, because their minds are unshakeably made up on such issues – because, in fact, of a large number of such characteristics concerning how they hold their beliefs. All this we can contrast with how scientists go about their work. But now, although the scientific and religious domains thus represented can be said to differ in this matter of how propositions are arrived at, and how they are held onto, this implies nothing whatsoever as to the relations of compatibility etc. existing between propositions in different 'domains'.

Matters are liable to be confused because there is not one, and only one, simple criterion whereby we distinguish religion from science. We may regard a belief as religious for any one reason or for several and the same is the case for calling a belief scientific. Moreover, the criteria may overlap so that for certain purposes a proposition entertained by someone may correctly be said to be religious while for other purposes the same proposition entertained by one and the same person may equally correctly be labelled scientific. The reason we are tempted to go along with pleas for separation is that although such propositions as 'Wombats have existed for less than ten thousand years' and 'There once existed fire-breathing dinosaurs' are religious by what I have loosely called methodological criteria, by the criterion of the kind of thing they assert about the spatio-temporal world they are scientific. We may be further moved in this direction because the creationists' assertions are examples of silly science so that we are only too pleased to see them expunged from the science syllabus. However, if my argument here is correct we do not have available to us the convenient move of shunting these false propositions into some quite different logical domain just because, noticing the way their proponents arrive at them, we decide to call them 'religious'.[4]

If we take a resolutely realist view of science and religion, then, in discussing the logical relations between them, we should be particularly concerned with what the propositions in these 'domains' assert. In fact, it can be as misleading, in such a context, to label the propositions 'religious' or 'scientific' as it is to call them 'sexist' or 'bourgeois'. In either instance attention is drawn from the important issues of whether they are true or false, meaningful or meaningless, and we are led simply into taking sides. In his Gifford Lectures for 1912 and 1913 A. Seth Pringle-Pattison elegantly put the position:

> Unless the objects of religious faith are real, theology is entirely in the air; and if they are real it is impossible to treat the world of religious belief and the world of fact, as science and philosophy handle it, as if they were two non-communicating spheres. Reality is one, and, after all, the human mind is also one, and not a bundle of unconnected and conflicting faculties.
>
> (Pringle-Pattison 1920:58)

This view may still be resisted even by some of those who agree with the realist interpretation of both science and religion; and it may be objected, with some justice, that the case for the existence of logical connections between these two spheres is too easily made by picking on the clash between fundamentalist Christianity and science. If we were to choose different exemplars of religious belief, more profound ones, perhaps, then the correct attitude would be to regard religion and science as being concerned with different *aspects* of reality. Michael Ruse has made a nod at least in this direction by quoting John Paul II. 'The Bible tells us where we are going to. Not where we came from' (Ruse 1986b:479).

It must be admitted straightaway that if two propositions are about different 'aspects' of the world then there may be no immediate logical connection between them. If Jack asserts that God made the universe 10^{10} years ago and Jill claims that replicating clays were the precursors of modern life there is, as yet, no call to logical conflict. But nor is there if Jill says that the burning of coal in her fireplace is due to oxidation while Jack says that the very similar burning of coal in his (different) hearth is the result of the transfer of phlogiston. I am not here making a tricky point about incommensurability of theories or whatever. It is simply that, as they stand, these two propositions are sublimely indifferent to each other and they could both be false or they could both be true or one could be true and one false.

In fact, although we might, if we have absorbed Popper's special brand of scepticism, entertain the first possibility, we would certainly rule out the second and would claim that at most only one of the propositions could be true. Why is this? The answer to this question is complicated by the fact that, if we know a little history of science, the chances are we know the way this particular debate was decided so let us look back to the time when it was a live issue. When Lavoisier and Priestley gave their different accounts of the combustion of stuffs in their different laboratories they were in conflict and this was so because their thoughts ranged far beyond their individual packets of burning materials. Their experiments and observations were as particular as the different mobs that persecuted them in Paris and Birmingham; but their intellectual interests were global. In short, their respective theories about the mechanism of combustion were meshed with views about the uniformity of nature. If conflagration in Paris is by oxidation – to pick a winner after the race is over – then so it is in Birmingham and anywhere else in the whole wide universe.

Two unrelated propositions may be brought into connection by a third. It is this elementary logical fact, which in these times sadly needs emphatic reassertion, that talk of 'aspects' tries to avoid. Suppose we come right out and speak of a supernatural aspect and a natural aspect, how is this guarantee against an impertinent mind seeking to link the two unless, indeed, the supernatural is also said to be the wholly other and therefore the wholly unknowable and unutterable? And, of course, Darwin's theory of evolution by natural selection was seen by the more intelligent and sensitive thinkers of the time, including Darwin himself, to raise questions concerning the relation of God to the world. No longer able to believe in the special divine creation of the separate species of organisms, recourse was made by some to the notion of the divinely created laws of nature which brought about the evolution of living things. Such a view of a grand, lawful order of things was seen as more suited to the majesty of God than the idea that he continually grubs around in the world He made. As Darwin said in the concluding paragraph of *The Origin of Species*, 'There is grandeur in this view of life.' Grandeur there may be, but once this position is taken further questions press in upon us. It is but a short step from speaking of 'laws of nature', which suggests still the notion of divine commands, to referring to 'natural laws' which are taken as wholly immanent in nature. This short step is, as Bishop Berkeley would have insisted, along the road to deism beyond which lies the abyss of naturalistic atheism.

FOR REALITY

I take it as given that theistic religion has a heavy metaphysical commitment, although even this has been denied. But what of science? Is it really so obvious that it tells us anything about the world rather than, say, merely allowing us to manipulate it? And so we find Barrow and Tipler arousing our interest by presenting us with a large volume on the 'anthropic principle', in which the deepest questions of cosmology and biology and the origin of things are discussed, only to drown our metaphysical longings in cold water:

> the authors are cosmologists, not philosophers. This has one very important consequence which the average reader should bear in mind. Whereas philosophers and theologians appear to possess an emotional attachment to their theories and ideas which requires them to believe them, scientists tend to regard their ideas differently. They are interested in formulating many logically consistent possibilities, leaving any judgement regarding their truth to observation. Scientists feel no qualms about suggesting different but mutually exclusive explanations for the same phenomenon. The authors are no exception to this rule and it would be unwise of the

reader to draw any wider conclusions about the authors' views from what they may read here.

(Barrow and Tipler 1986:15)

Yet, despite the anti-metaphysical strictures of logical positivism – which seems, still, to be the official philosophy of many practising scientists – and, despite the vast army of latter-day relativists and sceptics sneering in concert at the very notion of truth,[5] at least some of the propositions of science appear to tell us, or try to tell us, what is the case. Against a determined sceptic the case for scientific realism can never be made out. However, for those less stringent in their intellectual standards – who will allow, for example, that there are people other than themselves or that the universe exists at least as far out as the orbit of Pluto – some moves in this direction can be made.

It is, indeed, strangely paradoxical that as scientists have brought to light all kinds of previously hidden individual existences, from quarks to ancient fossils, the philosophy of science has often ignored this metaphysically exciting fact and has concentrated its attention on the logical character of *laws*. When this approach was combined with the positivists' anti-metaphysical metaphysics of purely private sense-data the tendency was to see these laws not as 'laws of nature' but, *à la* Berkeley, as mere recipes for predicting, or bringing about, a hoped-for continuing regular coherence of sensations. In any case, the emphasis on laws at the expense of particular occurrences, whether or not taken as sense-data, led to playing down the existential import of propositions concerning the latter and concentrating almost exclusively on their role as test-statements for universal propositions. In this way philosophy of science was able largely to ignore what science was telling us about the world and concentrate on such 'logical' issues as induction and the problem of how a necessarily finite number of observation-statements can be said to confirm a universal proposition. It was on such issues that the philosophy of the 'philosopher of the century', Sir Karl Popper, took wing. Induction, he said, is impossible and so is the confirmation of theories. The mark of a scientific theory, as distinct from a piece of metaphysics, is that it is falsifiable. This breakaway move, supposedly superior to strict positivism in its humbling implication that we really cannot know anything at all, like the orthodoxy from which it sprang kept the here or there, now or then actual facts of the universe in their place as the source, merely, of test-statements.

The nonsensical implications of this philosophy have, under the guise of open-mindedness, been grasped enthusiastically by Popper and his followers. Here, for example, is G.D. Wassermann, in this respect a Popperian purist, prepared to belabour evolutionary biologists with his methodological presuppositions. Those theorists who try to explain particular evolutionary events, e.g. the evolution of the lungfish, do not, in the strongest version of his argument, even succeed in doing poor science: their researches are shamefully metaphysical even though they are reported in supposedly reputable scientific journals and not, for example, in the *Review of Metaphysics*.

It has to be emphasised that Wassermann's objections to the propositions of historical biology have to do with the fact that they are existentially quantified – they are about particulars and they assert existence. In fact one can trace a progression in his views. His 1974 position is that *pure* science consists of theories about general classes of things although there are no logical objections raised against the investigation of particulars. 'As a rule', he says, 'scientists are not concerned with the unique and idiosyncratic' (Wassermann 1974:31); and shortly afterwards he makes the connection with pure science when he claims that 'pure psychologists are not interested in studying particular habits of individual people for their own sake' (31).

Wassermann is here simply mistaken. The contrast with pure science, which I take it is concerned with enquiry for its own sake, is not the investigation of particulars but *applied* science. Purity of scientific intent lies not in the generality or particularity of the facts examined but in the *direction* of the investigator's interests and it is possible for both a pure and a technological interest to be taken towards the same particulars (and, I would add, laws). Thus both Woese (1981) and Brierley (1982) are interested in the archaeobacteria – the former because of the light they throw on evolutionary relationships and the latter, as befits the president of Advanced Mineral Technology Inc., because she thinks that some of them are potentially among the 'small servants of man' that will help in the mining of minerals such as copper.

There is, however, the further point that, even though pure, the scientific investigation of particulars is trivial where the underlying assumption is the Popperian one that the fundamental activity of science is the framing and testing of general hypotheses. For Wassermann most reported examples of natural selection are not 'significant' because they 'represent an ensemble of isolated case histories, which do not explain how selection functions or has functioned at the genetic level[6] (Wassermann 1978:236). In particular, they are insignificant because they throw no light on what he calls 'Lewontin's fundamental question: "What proportion of observed genetic variation is maintained by natural selection?"' (Wassermann 1978:236). Even in those investigations of balancing selection which might throw light on the fundamental question – such as that of Harrison (1977) on the parallel variation of enzymes in sibling species of cricket – it is enough to show statistically that selection has occurred and there is no need to discover just what are the selective factors.

Now even Popper admits, although as an afterthought, that scientists – real scientists, that is – take time off from the attempted framing and falsification of general theories in order to apply these theories in the understanding of particulars (Popper 1957:vol.2,261–3). However, even here, he claims that, with sciences such as physics and biology, 'we are predominantly interested in the universal laws or hypotheses' (263) and we may note that in his reply to Kneale (1974), who dared challenge this view, Popper once more diverts the question into one of the testing of universal propositions (Popper 1974a:987–9).

The reply to both Wassermann and Popper surely is that there is a large number of occurrences which, in their own right and not merely as tests for general theories, are crying out for investigation and explanation. Consider the example of the evolutionary origin of sex. One might be interested in it merely as a test case for Darwinism but it surely, in its own right, poses a mass of interesting questions. What were the evolutionary steps leading to full-blown sexual reproduction? What was the original selective advantage of sex, bearing in mind that so-called 'sexual reproduction' actually produces one individual from two (Smith 1978). These questions, although presupposing general propositions concerning the role of natural selection etc., just *are* addressed to that 'unique and idiosyncratic' event, the origin of sex. Indeed, contrary to Wassermann's view, in large measure it is its uniqueness and idiosyncrasy which attracts the interest.

Once we are free of the prejudice that the investigation of particulars is necessarily exploitative, or concerned only with testing general hypotheses, then numerous examples of pure scientific enquiry into individual events, processes, etc. come to mind. Thus scientists, with motives as pure as the driven snow, have taken an interest in the solar system (Copernicus 1959), *the* whole universe (Weinberg 1977), *the* origin of life (Oparin 1953), *the* evolution of the eucaryote cell (Margulis 1971), *the* cockney language (Barltrop and Wolveridge 1980) and so on. In order to drive the point home consider the following example of pure enquiry, taken from 'hard' science, into a particular 'historical' event. There is a theory that a particular thing, the sun, was caused to exist by a particular event, a supernova

(Schramm and Clayton 1978). According to this view a large star exploded about 4.6 billion years ago and the resulting shock-wave caused a nearby cloud of gas to contract to form the solar system. The theory was first suggested by the discovery of anomalous ratios of certain isotopes in a single meteorite which landed in Mexico, although these ratios have since been discovered in other meteorites of the general type known as carbonaceous chondrites. Already, in saying that the meteorite contains isotopes of such and such a kind, a whole mass of physical and chemical laws is being brought to bear on the one object; and when one goes further and says that the isotope ratio is anomalous, further historical etc. propositions are assumed concerning, for example, the chemical composition of the original protosolar cloud. All this is then tied in with theories about the birth and death of stars, the synthesis of elements, the structure of the galaxy and so on. But the important point is that the interest is in that particular historical event, the birth of the solar system.

I take it that the theory described above is not trivial – it seems interesting enough. However, it is just here that we come up against Wassermann's full-blown charge that, interesting or not, the theory is not a piece of science just because the proposition expressing it is existentially quantified. To illustrate his charge Wassermann uses the more homely example of Smith catching influenza:

> some metaphysical thinkers feel tempted to 'explain' Smith's infection by saying: there must have been some one from whom Smith caught the disease. But this is an existentially quantified and, hence, unfalsifiable metaphysical statement, which does not explain anything. If instead we ask 'What is the mechanism of influenza infection?' then our answer may refer to a universally quantified scientifically testable theory involving the structure and mode of action of influenza viruses, their modes of propagation through the population and their pathogenic effects.
>
> (Wassermann 1978:228)

Similarly, then, the objection to accounts of particular evolutionary events is that these involve existentially quantified statements which *hence* are unfalsifiable (and thus metaphysical). The only scientific evolutionary theories are, once more, those about general population genetic *mechanisms*. However, the matter is somewhat complicated by the fact that Wassermann also often objects to theories about evolutionary occurrences that they 'invoke unfalsifiable *ad hoc* hypotheses' (Wassermann 1978:228). We might be tempted to think that

Wassermann here has a further argument against theories about particulars because, since Popper, we have become accustomed to think of *ad hoc* hypotheses as propositions irresponsibly put forward to avoid falsification at all costs. This is perhaps the meaning Wassermann has in mind when he describes as *ad hoc* Kimura's attempt to explain, in terms of population bottlenecks, the fact that the amount of heterozygosity in organisms is nowhere near the figure the neutral theory predicts (Wassermann 1981:426). However, this is not his normal usage. Apart from referring to such things as mathematical approximations and simplifying hypotheses as *ad hoc* (Wassermann 1974:28), *ad hoc* propositions are just those that refer to the special conditions in which particular processes of natural selection etc. occur. Far from rendering theories unfalsifiable, *ad hoc* hypotheses in this sense are a necessary condition for their falsifiability. Part of the same absurdity of Wassermann's methodological principle is that it leads directly to the conclusion that *all* scientific theories are empirically untestable.

Apart from reasons of his own for a particularly florid scepticism – in which he denies that it is reasonable to assert the existence of anything at all (Wassermann 1974:9–13) – Wassermann's talk of 'falsifiability' indicates that his philosophy of science springs from that of Popper. Now Popper, it may be said, has clearly seen that science cannot do without propositions about particulars as was shown by his shock at Kneale's 'misinterpretation' of him on this issue. Science includes existentially quantified statements as test-statements, as potential falsifiers of universal propositions. However, if we pursue the matter further – and leaving aside the problem of how we can come to know the truth even of test-statements (Deutscher 1968) – then it is possible to show that, with reference to the investigation of particulars, there is something seriously wrong with Popper's philosophy of science. This is because the doctrine of falsifiability is fundamentally a sceptical one and cannot, in any real sense, explain particulars.

Popper, of course, accepts that his doctrine of falsifiability entails that the universal propositions of science cannot be shown to be true or likely: they can be falsified but not confirmed. We find this sceptical position, in its pristine form, stated clearly in *The Logic of Scientific Discovery*.

> we must not look upon science as a 'body of knowledge', but rather as a system of hypotheses; that is to say, as a system of guesses or anticipations which in principle cannot be justified, but with which we work as long as they stand up to tests, and of which we are never

justified in saying that we know that they are 'true' or 'more or less certain' or even 'probable'.

(Popper 1959:317)

It follows immediately that if we have no idea whether or not the theories we use to 'explain' particular events – e.g. the evolution of the eucaryote (nucleated) cell – are true or probable, then the only possible sense of 'explain' is a conventionalist one. There can be no hope of explaining events in the realist sense of, for example, showing why they are as they are, or even that they have occurred at all and the only thing left to do, unless one just gives up science, is to arrange one's universal and particular propositions in a certain kind of order. It is no wonder that, in their dispute with evolutionists, 'creationists' have found a friend in Popper: they simply arrange their biological propositions in a different order but with a little help from God and the Bible.

This issue confronts Popper in its starkest form in physics because it is clear that in physics there occur strictly existential statements, i.e. existential statements with no reference to time or place. Thus, he admits 'that there are theories even in physics which have the form of strictly existential statements', e.g. the theory, based on a 'gap' in the periodic table, that an element of a certain atomic number exists (Popper 1959:69). This example, if taken at its face value, falsifies falsification because (i) it shows, contrary to the main drift of Popper's philosophy, that not all the fundamental theories of science are about laws, (ii) strictly existential statements, on Popper's admission, are not falsifiable, and (iii) strictly existential statements are verifiable. Popper's treatment of this problem is astonishing.

We may note, first, that it was this very issue of strictly existential statements in science that was raised by Kneale (1974) and that Popper deals with it by pretending it was about the problem of test-statements. However, Popper's 'solution' is to make strictly existential statements pop in and out of metaphysical space in a most alarming way. The thesis becomes: Strictly existential statements are metaphysical unless accompanied by other statements when they may 'add to the empirical content of the whole content' (Popper 1959:69). Thus the element hafnium 'was not discovered merely on the basis of an isolated, purely existential statement' but 'all attempts to find it were in vain until Bohr succeeded in predicting several of its properties by deducing them from his theory' (69). However, we are no further forward because, according to Popper, the propositions from which the several properties of hafnium were deduced are themselves strictly universal. This means that the now complex proposition about hafnium remains strictly existential and there is no change in the logical situation. The reference to the strictly universal propositions of Bohr's theory is a smokescreen.

As I have already remarked, this example is embarrassing for Popper's thesis because strictly existential statements are *verifiable* – they are metaphysical sore thumbs jutting out into the real world. In fact, the reference to the strictly universal propositions of Bohr's theory diverts our attention from what these propositions led to – the *discovery* of hafnium – and directs it to the issue merely of their logical form. The existential proposition now being hidden under a blanket of theories, we may be easily persuaded that the only real issue still is testability, i.e. falsifiability. But, of course, Bohr's theory, in telling scientists what properties hafnium possesses (besides having atomic number 72) increased the chances of their *finding* it. It helps if you know what you are looking for. It helps even more if you know, even roughly, *where* to look, which accounts for the importance of what Popper calls singular existential statements. These two things may be closely connected; e.g. theory might predict that a particular element is built up from simpler elements at a temperature of several million degrees – in which case it might be wiser to search for it in the interior of stars rather than in the Antarctic.

Scientists *discover* elements and by doing so *confirm* strictly existential statements. This point about the confirmation of existential propositions, and not only strictly existential ones, can be made by reference to the theory that the chloroplasts of higher plants are really cyanobacteria (blue-green algae) descended from an original individual (or perhaps from a few individuals) which entered into an endosymbiotic union with a eucaryote cell. Not only is this theory almost certainly true but one can see how, historically, the theory *gained* in plausibility. There were, first, very general considerations in its favour: chloroplasts look like cyanobacteria and endosymbiosis is known to occur in certain protozoa, e.g. in *Myxotricha paradoxa*, itself a symbiont in the gut of termites. It was then discovered that chloroplasts are capable of a limited existence outside the plant cell and, intriguingly, that they possess their own DNA (Avers 1974). By this time the theory already had a certain plausibility but the clinching argument came when the 'code' of chloroplast RNA was directly compared with that of other organisms and found to correlate very strongly with cyanobacteria RNA. In fact, Woese (1981) has no hesitation in classifying *Euglena* chloroplasts as cyanobacteria.

Now one might still retreat into absolute scepticism as do, in fact, both Popper and Wassermann: we cannot know that there is a glass in front of us because glasses have dispositional properties (Popper 1959:94–5) or because we cannot rule out the possibility of suffering from a kind of metaphysical Korsakoff's syndrome (Wassermann 1974:11–12). In fact, the examples I have just discussed are meant to force the issue. Is it or is it not the case that the theory of the symbiotic origin of chloroplasts is true; and is it or is it not the case that this theory gained in plausibility as the evidence came in? Scepticism aside – and ignoring homilies about it being better to travel than arrive – the fact that scientists do achieve what Popper and Wassermann think is impossible raises important issues.

Very briefly, we may observe, first, that it indicates that science can tell us something about 'the furniture of the earth' even though Popper thinks that the propositions which do this exist in the mansions of heaven. Second, there is the fact that true, and *known* to be true, propositions are often deduced from theories. This, in turn, shows that scientific theories do not consist only of strictly universal propositions: some scientific theories must assert existence. To speak 'metaphysically', as Popper and Wassermann would have it, we might say that together the universal and existential propositions of science tell us something about the structure of the world (Harre 1970). This brings us directly to the question of the truth of scientific theories. Why is it that scientists trust a previously successful theory when, for example, it predicts the existence of a new element? Why do scientists look for it, or try to make it, and why is it rational to do so? We might, I suppose, appeal to a weird inductive argument – just because the theory has worked in other situations, it will work in this one – but Popper certainly would reject this. The alternative is that the theory works in this new circumstance, and it is rational for scientists to believe it will work, because it is true (or, at least, very much on the right lines) – otherwise the success of the theory is merely a huge coincidence or a successful magical incantation.

Now fortified, we may return to Wassermann's criticisms of what I have called 'historical biology'. Let us look, in particular, at his *bête noir*, those theories which attempt to explain individual occurrences of the evolution of special characteristics of organisms by relating them to definite environmental features. In fact, Wassermann's case is made to appear much stronger than it really is by an example he gives in a quotation from Lewontin:

In particular a species of bird with a small bill may evolve a large bill size, because some aspect of the environment has changed so that large-billed birds now have more offspring. Or the species may split into two new contemporaneous species with different bill sizes, because geographically separated populations of the original species lived in different environments in one of which large-billed birds are more fecund, while in the other small-billed birds left more offspring. Such a theory can never be falsified for it asserts that some environmental difference created the condition for natural selection of a new character. It is existentially quantified so that failure to find the environmental factor proves nothing, except that one has not looked hard enough.

(Lewontin 1972:181)

Here we have the now familiar doctrine that existentially quantified propositions cannot be falsified. As a matter of fact, I think they can: they can, for example, be falsified by true universal propositions which imply their falsity. But if our interest is in the truth of theories about particulars then all that Lewontin's example shows is that it is often difficult to arrive at it because of a lack of relevant information. As Charlesworth (1982:135) puts it, 'we are usually so ignorant of the genetic structure of fossil populations and of the relations between environment, fitness and morphology that we cannot provide explanations for any particular historical pattern of evolution'. However, even Lewontin's hypothetical example does not rule out the possibility of further discoveries – perhaps involving hypotheses about the functions of beaks derived from engineering principles – which in turn lead to possibly confirmable theories concerning the environments to which the birds adapt.

In any case, there are examples and examples. Consider the actual case of the evolution of the different species of widow birds. These are African parasitic birds of the subfamily Viduinae which lay their eggs in the nests of various estrilid finches. Among the remarkable adaptations of the widow bird is the fact that its young closely mimic the young of the appropriate host in such details as mouth markings, gestures, calls, etc. The adult male even incorporates bits of the appropriate finch song in its sexual call thus ensuring that it attracts and mates with females of its own species. It has been established that closely related species of widow bird parasitise similarly related species of finch and this gives the clue to their evolution:

Such species-to-species relations can be understood only if one assumes that a long time ago the widow birds began to arise from a single viduine prototype species that had started to parasitize a single species of estrilid finches. When this ancient estrilid species began to evolve into several species, the widow birds were forced to follow suit, because only by doing so could they evolve mouth markings sufficiently like those of the evolving new species of potential hosts. Of course, each widow-bird population that failed to achieve such an adaptive process was destined to become extinct, since its mismarked offspring would starve to death in the nests of hostile hosts. In this way the evolution of the adaptively successful widow-bird species both parallels and reflects the evolution of their chosen hosts among the numerous species of estrilid finches.[7]

(Nicolai 1974:98)

As with the theory of the origin of the sun, scientists are able to produce a plausible account of this particular complex event, the evolution of widow birds, by making use of a set of general and particular propositions.

Chapter 3
The stuff we are made of

BEHIND APPEARANCES

Modern biology has had much to say about the fundamental constitution of living things, including humans, and a good deal of it has been strongly reductionistic. If we leave aside the attempts of the logical empiricists to find logical relations of the appropriate sort between *propositions* – e.g. between the propositions of classical Mendelian genetics and those of modern biochemical genetics – then it seems that roughly two kinds of ontological reductionism have occupied thinkers in this area. On the one hand there are what we may generically refer to as naked ape types of theory and, on the other, there is the view of biochemists, such as Jacques Monod (1974), that organisms (including humans) are nothing more than collections of molecules in certain complex relationships. Here the difference between the two kinds of theory appears as a difference in the level of explanation, taking this as relative to ordinary, everyday descriptions of the world. Naked ape types of theory, including behaviouristic, socio-biological, etc. theories, remain close to everyday descriptions – it is just that one commonly noticed piece of behaviour is explained away as really being some other commonly noticed piece of behaviour as when it may be said that love is but lust with a fancy name. With the molecular biologists the world they describe seems quite different from the one that, in our non-speculative moments, we seem to inhabit. Colours, sounds, familiar objects all vanish.

If, for the time being, we accept this rough distinction between the two kinds of reductionist explanation, then we may notice that theories of the naked ape type – which try to pick on a few things to explain everything (both the few and the many things coming, in the first instance, from the level of the macroscopic) – are open to the sort of objection Robert Boyle used against the 'chymists' of his time. In the

Sceptical Chemist Boyle argued against the then current theories of the 'elements' or 'principles' of matter (whether these be taken as earth, air, fire and water or, as in a rival scheme, salt, sulphur and mercury) that he could see no reason why these should be picked out of a myriad others, e.g. oils, as *the* elements. Similarly, why should certain bits of behaviour, e.g. sexual behaviour, be picked out as *the* important bits when it is clear that there are many kinds of behaviour? By their very nature such theories are liable to leave important things unexplained. Boyle argued that the excessive narrowness of the chemical theories of his time, and their consequent lack of explanatory power, was heavily disguised by obfuscation of various sorts so that, for example, the chemists' elements took on all kinds of occult qualities. We might expect, in our time, to detect similar techniques at work in behaviouristic theories, sociobiology, etc. where the existence of what does plainly exist, e.g. consciousness, altruism and so on, is either denied or in some way redefined so as not to constitute a threat to the theory. Often enough the redefinition of ordinary terms may serve to disguise various indecencies committed in the name of science, as when behaviourists use the term 'punishment' in a technical sense to designate actions which, in ordinary language, would properly be described as assault. In particular, we should be on the lookout for the supposed basic elements of human nature taking on magical qualities so that, for example, the 'hunting instinct', supposedly exclusively possessed by men, becomes transmuted into the *naturally* male-dominated *pursuit* of knowledge; and where, with as much right to the carefree use of metaphor, feminists might claim that the *birth* and *nurture* of theories is an expression of the 'mothering instinct'. Such thinking, as many authors have pointed out, very often has a plainly ideological function.

In so far as a sharp distinction can be made between the different levels of theory such criticisms of naked ape type theories are just. However, the comparison with the theory of the elements suggests that a sharp distinction cannot be made between different levels of theory in this way if these are taken in relation to everyday descriptions. What, on one view, might be seen as the attribution of merely occult qualities to the elements, in order to save appearances, may, on a different view, be more kindly regarded as an attempt to look behind the complex, changing world for ultimate principles of explanation. On this account, the chemists of Boyle's time are squarely in the western intellectual tradition of trying to find what it is that lies beyond the world of appearances and, in some sense, explains that world. It is merely that, unlike the atomists, say, they picked on the wrong kinds of things or qualities for their explanations. Similarly, hypotheses of hunting instincts etc. which, from one point of view, seem to be magically transmuted into activities usually seen as quite distinct from hunting etc. behaviour, may also be seen as attempts to penetrate behind appearances.

The latter interpretation can be illustrated by reference to pre-Socratic thought where the attempt was first made to find the basic stuff or stuffs of the world. Thales suggested it was water, perhaps, as Aristotle suggests in the *Metaphysics*, 'from observing that the nutriment of everything is moist, and that even heat is generated from moisture upon which it depends for its continued existence (Aristotle 1961:58). We might guess, from this suggestion of Aristotle, that the important transition in Thales's thought is from the more primitive question, 'Where do the things of the world come from?' which was hitherto answered by means of stories about the gods, to the question, 'What are the basic elements, or what is the basic stuff, of things?' If one asks the latter question then a satisfactory answer to it must involve choosing a candidate that, first, can be shown to be ubiquitous, to be in all things, and, second, has the right properties to explain the apparent diversity of things. That water satisfied the first condition might have been suggested by what Aristotle (1961:58) gives as Thales's second reason for picking on it, 'that the seeds of everything have a moist character, and that water is the first principle in the character of all moist things'. Perhaps Thales thought the second condition was satisfied partly because he thought that one could observe, as a matter of fact, creatures emerging from watery substances such as the sea or semen; but partly, also, because he knew that water existed as various *phases* (liquid, solid and gas) and so, to that extent, could explain the apparent diversity of things in the world.

If this account of what Thales was about is anywhere near the truth then we can see that, like the seventeenth-century chemists or the twentieth-century naked ape theorists, he is picking on some one kind of thing to explain the characteristics of a multitude of things; and that, by doing this, he founds that intellectual adventure which endeavours to discover what lies behind the many perceived things. To pick on water as the basic stuff of the world is, of course, to lay oneself open to the criticism, used by Thales's successors, that it simply will not explain the great diversity of objects. However, we can see with Thales two characteristic features of reductionist theories. The first is that the entities referred to by the reducing theory are picked as having certain general characteristics, e.g. the capacity of water to form the three phases of solid, liquid and gas, by which the entities referred to by the reduced theory or description are accounted for. The second and correlative feature is that some characteristics only of the world that is said to be reduced are directly explained – thus Thales's theory may be said to explain, in a general way, why the world is made up of solids, liquids and gases but not the particular properties of, say, rocks, alcohol and mist. These two features stand in a potentially dialectical relationship. That, for example, there are features of the perceived world that the original hypothesis of water as the basic stuff does not explain might have led to modifications of the latter, so that water hypothesised as the basic stuff comes less and less to resemble water as we find it in rivers and seas; and, indeed, might have eventually been used to explain the properties of ordinary water along with those of other, everyday objects. As the reducing theories gain in explanatory power, the entities they postulate become further and further detached from the common objects they explain. The other side of the dialectical coin is that, as these reducing theories develop in this way, they may come to affect our view of what it is about the perceived world that needs explaining.[1]

Historically, because of its modest explanatory power, the water hypothesis was not modified in this way but was replaced by other equally mundane candidates. But as long as the basic principles or elements were taken as ordinary things of the world their appearance in explanatory theories was, like the crudities of the modern naked ape theorists, bound to be connected with viciously *ad hoc* arguments if these 'explanations' were even to appear to work.[2] What was required if this approach was to prove fruitful was the postulation of elements that, although bearing some analogy to the things of the world (and from where else could such an idea initially be got?), remained at some distance from it; and also that the properties attributed to these elements be such that they explain, in some profound way, the characteristics of the world as we perceive it. If such a theory is possible we need not expect it to be entirely correct straight off; but what we might anticipate is that the dialectical relation between it and the level of everyday observation, to which we earlier referred, will be fruitfully established. Such was the atomic theory of Democritus and Leucippus.

This is not the place to go into the question of the original intellectual source of atomism or of its revival in the Renaissance. However, its explanatory power, compared with earlier theories of the fundamental constituents of the world, is evident. Atoms could be said to lie behind the perceived world in the apparently straightforward sense that they were too small to be seen; while, at least at first, they were held to have understandable properties, such as motion, shape, solidity, etc., which were taken from this same perceived world. These supposed properties of atoms could explain many important features of the world, first in a qualitative way – as when Lucretius explains why water seeps through rock – and then in a precise mathematical way in explanation of such things as the gas laws. Once established the atomic theory sets going the dialectical process with the result that atoms lose many of their easily understood properties, such as hardness (so that no longer are both the hardness of rock and the malleability of clay, for example, explained in terms of lots of little hard things disposed in certain ways), and take on new and stranger ones. In this way atomic theory comes to explain more and more things in terms of properties which, although very strange indeed, are saved from the charges of vagueness and magic by their precise mathematical formulation and empirical testability.

ATOMS AND THEIR QUALITIES

The strangeness of atomic theory may lead to doubts about just what it is that it asserts about the world and is, I suppose, one reason for J.B.S. Haldane's comment, 'My own suspicion is that the universe is not only queerer than we suppose but queerer than we *can* suppose.'[3] This aside, it is clear that atomic theory has been enormously successful in accounting for some of the more remarkable features of living things. For example, Kant's belief that organic form could never receive an explanation in terms of 'mechanical causation' has received an answer in the details of nucleic acid and protein chemistry. However, atomic theory seems to suffer still from the defect of the earlier reductionist theories – of water or whatever as the explanation of everything – that it, in fact, explains only some things. Even worse, atomic theory appears to legislate out of existence what seems plainly to exist. From its inception it has been embarrassed by the so-called secondary qualities – colour, sound, etc. – which its proponents have tried variously to dispose of by describing them as conventions, mere names and so on and pre-eminently by locking them away in that convenient, non-material box, the mind. The world, in itself, is a colourless, soundless, smell-less affair which none the less manages to titillate the senses so that they take on the garb of the more flashy secondary qualities.

The intellectual tension caused by splitting and pulling apart the primary from the secondary qualities can be seen in the work of that honest underlabourer for science, John Locke. We can see the problem arising if we ask the question: What distinguishes atoms from the empty space they are supposed to occupy? Locke, closely following Robert Boyle, maintains that atoms possess primary qualities only. What are these qualities? Locke's list varies somewhat but we can take the following as typical: 'These I call *original* or *primary qualities* of body, which I think we may observe to produce simple ideas in us, viz. solidity, extension, figure, motion or rest, and number' (Locke 1964:112).

Now if we look closely at this list then it seems evident that solidity is the only one of the primary qualities capable of doing the job of differentiating atoms from space. But what *is* solidity? He distinguishes it from hardness by saying 'that solidity consist in repletion, and so an utter exclusion of other bodies out of the space it possesses' (Locke 1964:105); but, of course, to be replete is to be stuffed with, or full of, something or other and we still do not know what this something or other *is*. The trouble now is (if we stay within Locke's scheme of primary and secondary qualities and within his empiricism) that the only kind of qualities with which we are directly acquainted and which are space-filling just are the secondary qualities. Colours and warmths, for example, occupy definite positions and take up shapes in space. In fact, Locke tries to save his empiricism by illicitly making the notion of solidity straddle the divide, on the one hand, between primary and secondary qualities and, on the other, between a directly perceivable quality and one that is not perceivable but which *explains* the space-filling and causal properties of bodies.

We can see this tension right at the beginning of his extended discussion of the 'simple idea' (that is, the simple sensation) of solidity: 'The idea of *solidity* we receive by our touch; and it arises from the resistance which we find in body to the entrance of any other body into the place it possesses till it has left it' (Locke 1964:103).

Already we can see him mixing up talk of the sensation of touch (what we might call a solidity-sensation) with what *causes* that sensation (resistance). (And, of course, if we are realists we should not accept that we get the notion of one body resisting another only from touch: we can, for example, just as well *see* bodies resisting each other.) And at the end of the same section he makes the move of claiming that the purported explanatory notion of solidity is the very same as, or is very similar to, the simple *idea* of solidity which we get through touch:

And though our senses take no notice of it but in masses of matter, of a bulk sufficient to cause a sensation in us, yet the mind, having once got this idea from such grosser sensible bodies, traces it further, and considers it, as well as figure, in the minutest particle of matter that can exist, and finds it inseparably inherent in body, wherever or however modified.

(Locke 1964:103)

But the simple idea of solidity cannot be the same as the explanatory notion. The *idea* is just that, one of several, independent ideas or sensations whereas the *notion* of solidity is meant to explain several things about matter. And so he tells us:

By this idea of solidity is the extension of body distinguished from the extension of space, the extension of body being nothing but the cohesion or continuity of solid, separable, movable parts; and the extension of space the continuity of unsolid, inseparable, and immovable parts. Upon the solidity of bodies also depend their mutual impulse, resistance and protrusions.

(Locke 1964:106)

This 'quality' of solidity obviously is not gained directly from experience and the pressing questions arise of what it possibly can be and how we can get to know what it is.

LEVELS OF DISCOURSE AND LEVELS OF REALITY

Atomic theory, or its near relation, molecular biology, now claims to be able to give, in principle, a complete reductive account of sentient organisms. We are, in the first analysis, not much more than complex bundles of nucleic acid and protein and, in the last analysis, mere structured heaps of quarks and leptons. Many people have, naturally enough, disliked the idea that there is no place in the world for colours, scents and so forth and have liked even less the thought that nowhere, not even in their own heads, is there a mind to be found.

A move, popular among a number of biologists and philosophers who have reflected on these issues, has been to introduce the notion of *levels*. In this way they hope to retain realism about science while, at the same time, escaping reductionism and its implication. Thus, it might be said, although it is true that at one level, organisms are composed of quarks and leptons, it is also true that, at a different level, they are made of cells and, at a different level still, they may be conscious beings. Very often such claims are combined with a notion of 'emergent evolution' in which it is held that quite new properties, such as consciousness, come into existence with, say, the increasing complexity of things. In any case, it is important to notice that these different levels – in which what gets squeezed out at a lower level may be restored at a higher – are taken as having independent, real existences. There is no question of the reduction, even in principle, of upper levels to lower.

It should at once be remarked that the ontological reductionist is not refuted by the fact that biologists, in their explanations, often mix descriptions and theories from different levels. It does not follow from the fact that the mixing of levels of *discourse* is frequent, and often necessary, that there must, therefore, be different *ontological* levels. James J. Gibson has tried to refute those reductionists who, 'impressed by the success of atomic physics, have concluded that the terrestrial world of surfaces, objects, places, and events is a fiction' (Gibson 1968:21–2). His answer to this is:

> The world can be analyzed at many levels, from atomic through terrestrial to cosmic. There is physical structure on the scale of millimicrons at one extreme and on the scale of light years at another. But surely the appropriate scale for animals is the intermediate one of millimetres to kilometres, and it is appropriate because the world and the animal are then comparable.
>
> (Gibson 1968:22)

The reductionist's reply to this will surely be that mention of the supposed features of macroscopic objects, in explaining animal behaviour, is simply a methodological convenience – or even a methodological necessity. For example, in the explanation of visual perception statements about the patterns of light and shade on objects may be mixed in with statements, at a different level, concerning the cells of the retina and the brain and yet others, at still another level, about photons. But one may take advantage of this methodological mix without being committed to the real existence of all the supposed levels.

Similarly, there is more to the reductionist's case than justifies its dismissal, as Max Deutscher has recently undertaken, as a piece of obsessional thinking. Deutscher claims that the answer to the 'feeling' of reductive materialism 'lies in reminding ourselves of the plurality of facts and conceptual forms, and in regaining a free capacity to shift our perspectives' (Deutscher 1983:81). As barely stated this objection merely begs the question because, whatever may be the case concerning the plurality of conceptual forms or perspectives, the reductive materialist's argument just is that, in the sense required, there is *no* plurality of facts. As Stephen W. Hawking (1988:60) has put it: 'Since the structure of molecules and their reactions underlie all of chemistry and biology, quantum mechanics allows us in principle to predict nearly everything we see around us, within the limits set by the uncertainty principle.'[4]

It would, says Deutscher, be as difficult 'to bring a volcano as to bring consciousness into a picture which allows no character or description except that contained within basic physics' (Deutscher 1983:81–2). No doubt; but this incapacity, by itself, does not show there is anything more to a volcano than a collection of fundamental particles. It does not force the conclusion that

> It is foolish to deny that volcanoes are composed of the elementary particles, and equally foolish to suppose that a story in terms of elementary particles presents *the* reality of things, whereas a story in the large scale about volcanoes and lava flows presents only a superficial appearance of the world.
>
> (Deutscher 1983:82)

Part of the problem here is that Deutscher does not spell out his 'story in the large scale'; and a reductive materialist would surely claim that the *full* story in the large scale, if only it were possible to tell it, would be in terms of the fundamental particles which together make up the volcano. As a matter of fact, scientists do try to give as fully a reductive account as possible of matter 'in the large' and in some cases, as with the quantum mechanical explanation and prediction of the properties of crystals and fluids, they have achieved remarkable success.

This last point deserves further emphasis because it also has force against Popper's claim that there have been very few successes for the proposed reductionist programme (Popper 1974b). The reductionist can, of course, here simply fall back on the fact of the great complexity of many things in the world. This is a hindrance to a full reductionist account being given of organisms, for example. But the reductionist can go further than this and point to the many successful achievements of the quantum mechanical theorists in recent years. These theorists have been able to explain and predict the properties of many materials, for example, because they have found ways of making simplifying assumptions concerning their constituent atoms. These simplifying assumptions, themselves, depend on the presupposition that a full account of materials does depend on quantum-mechanical principles. Thus the wave functions of the all-important valence-electrons of an atom can be calculated to a good approximation by treating the nucleus and the inner electron shells as together constituting a 'pseudoatom' and this is an important step on the way to predicting important properties of crystals such as gallenium sulphide. As Cohen *et al.*, from whom I take this account, put it:

> Today the quantum mechanics of materials has become both conceptually and practically a simpler study than the study of the electronic structure of atoms having more than one possible valence-electron configuration. Through worldwide collaboration on pseudoatoms, alchemy, the original black art of materials science, is now well on its way to becoming one of the better developed parts of human knowledge.
>
> (Cohen *et al.* 1982:79)

Similar remarks could also be made about the theoretical and practical investigations of fluids.

Unfortunately, the point is obscured by some authors who present us with a mishmash of levels of description and levels of actuality. Thus Steven Rose, partly to allay our fears about the implications of reductionism for the dignity of human beings, tells us 'that there are many levels at which one can describe the behaviour of the brain' (Rose 1976:28); but he vacillates between talking about levels of description, which are in different 'universes of discourse', and discussing whether or not there can be causal relations 'between the point-set on one level and that on another' (29). The way he answers the latter question, by suggesting that we should be cautious in attributing causal rather than mere correlative relationships, suggests that he is now speaking of ontological levels so that, for example, the state of being in love occurs on one level and is correlated with molecular changes on another (36). On the other hand, it seems that for Kathleen Wilkes there could be no question of a confusion of levels of language and ontological levels because ontological questions just *are* questions about language. In the midst of her spirited defence of physicalism about the mind–body problem she suddenly admits 'that the ontology, terms and explanations of common sense have nothing to do with physicalism' (Wilkes 1978:46). This, she says, 'may leave one with a residual unease' (46). The result of her own unease is a loss of nerve and she diverts the ontological question of whether, if physicalism is true, common sense may also be so, into one of 'forms of discourse', each with its own 'integrity'. We can then, she assures us, find 'some comfort in the reflection that although we may be no closer to discovering the nature of reality, we have at least shown ourselves better aware of the complexities of the term 'reality'' (48). At the end of all this one wonders what she possibly can mean by her statement, 'the kind of psychology in which we are interested is the kind that takes for granted the assumption that physicalism is true' (45).

ONTOLOGICAL LEVELS

When we come to examine the notions of those thinkers who clearly espouse the doctrine of different levels there are further problems. There are variations in what are supposed to exist at different levels – qualities, laws, 'principles', things all have their advocates – and it may even be the case that, in a given hierarchical schema, different kinds of 'entities' occupy the various levels, e.g., things at one level and 'principles' at another. If we leave this problem aside there are still often difficulties in the interpretation of the concrete examples that various thinkers give. Thus consider the hierarchical list of levels proposed by Popper:

(12)　Level of ecosystems
(11)　Level of populations of metazoa and plants
(10)　Level of metazoa and multicellular plants
(9)　Level of tissues and organs (and of sponges?)
(8)　Level of populations of unicellular organisms
(7)　Level of cells and of unicellular organisms
(6)　Level of organelle (and perhaps of viruses)
(5)　Liquids and solids (crystals)
(4)　Molecules
(3)　Atoms
(2)　Elementary particles
(1)　Sub-elementary particles
(0)　Unknown-sub-sub-elementary particles?
(Popper and Eccles 1977:17)

There are some problems of detail concerning this table which Popper himself notices but they need not detain us. Instead, let us note that these different levels have, in some sense, quite independent existences for Popper as is shown by the fact that there are supposed to be causal interactions between them ('upward' and 'downward' causation). Indeed, for Popper reductionism is distinguished from non-reductionism in that the former view holds that causation is in one direction only – from lower to upper levels – while the non-reductionist believes that causation is possible in both directions:

> what Table 2 suggests may be characterized as the principle of 'upward causation'. This is the principle that causation can be traced in our Table 2 from a lower level to a higher level but not *vice versa*: that what happens on a higher level can be explained in terms of the next lower level, and ultimately in terms of elementary particles and the relevant physical laws. It appears at first that the higher levels cannot act on the lower ones.
> (Popper and Eccles 1977:19)

Popper holds that the reductionist, poor simple-minded fellow, is taken in by appearances and that there is really also downward causation from upward to lower levels. We should say, first, that to describe the reductionist position in this way is preposterous. For the reductionist there is no question of there being either upward or downward causation for the simple reason that he does not believe in the existence of different levels at all. What exists, and the only things that exist, are sub-atomic particles or, perhaps, sub-sub-atomic particles.

Second, I am entirely bemused by the examples Popper gives us in support of his thesis of downward causation even though he claims 'these examples make the existence of downward causation obvious' (26). One example is the following:

> Downward causation is of course important in all tools and machines which are designed for some purpose. When we use a wedge, for example, we do not arrange for the action of its elementary particles, but we use a structure, relying on it to guide the actions of its constituent elementary particles to act in concert so as to achieve the desired results.
> (Popper and Eccles 1977:19)

Similarly, he says,

> Stars are undesigned, but one may look at them as undesigned 'machines' for putting the atoms and elementary particles in their central region under terrific gravitational pressure, with the (undesigned) result that some atomic nuclei fuse and form the nuclei of heavier elements; an excellent example of downward causation, of the action of the whole structure upon the constituent particles.
> (Popper and Eccles 1977:20)

It is as if, with wedges and stars, the 'whole structure' of these things floats free from the fundamental constituents and, from its superior height, acts down upon them. I, for one, cannot make sense of this supposition.

We can see a related confusion in the work of those thinkers who wish to defend the notion of an infinite number of levels of physical being. David Bohm, for example, has urged that the history of atomic physics suggests that just as beneath the level of macroscopic objects there lies the level of atoms and molecules and beyond that again the level of 'fundamental particles', so, at least in principle, the physicist might go on and on discovering, without end, level after level (Bohm 1961). Now I think that in some sense the universe may be infinitely complex, and that, because of this, scientists may find eternal employment in unravelling the complexity; and it may also be that, despite their efforts, scientists will never get down to ontological bedrock; but it does not follow from this, nor indeed does the view make much sense, that there could exist an infinite number of ontological levels or strata. Indeed, I do not think there could exist more than one such level.

Once more the spatial metaphor of 'levels' in discussions of ontology is highly misleading. It is not the case, for example, that there is one set of entities, the protons, and *also* existing 'beneath' it, in some strange ontological space, a swarming sea of quarks which somehow supports its protonic flotsam and jetsam. The scientist, in finding out that protons are *really* triads of quarks in close interaction is discovering that there are no such separate things as protons – or, what comes to the same thing, that protons, in being made up of triads of mutually bound quarks, just *are* those threesomes in bondage. To believe otherwise would, if the belief were rigorously followed through, involve awkward questions about the causal interactions between the protons and their 'constituent' quarks, remembering that the existence of the latter was, in the first place, postulated in order *fully* to explain the behaviour of those clumpings in space–time that were originally called 'protons'. Even if it were found that the quark theory did not provide a full explanation, that, for example, it were necessary to postulate some kind of 'membranes' to contain the separate triads of quarks, it would still be the case that the quarks and the 'membranes' all exist in causal interaction at the one level. The attempt, then, to postulate an infinite series of levels of physical existence would be to believe in an infinite series of 'seemings to be' perched upon nothing at all.

POLANYI'S NOTION OF LEVELS

The reductionist's ability plausibly to deflect apparent counter-examples into the basket of merely methodological issues must strengthen his ontological claims. In fact, it is possible to show that in one recent influential positive defence of the idea of levels, that of Michael Polanyi (1976), the argument depends for its apparent strength on an illicit mixing of ontological, and what may be loosely called methodological, claims. Because of this and other confusions the argument is difficult to state concisely. For convenience, I will first use Marjorie Grene's very clear formulation.

> Since they [reductionists] declare the processes of growth and heredity have been shown to be determined by a sequence of DNA molecules, biology has already been reduced, on principle, to biochemistry; the completion of the job is routine. Granted, however, that DNA has precisely the power they claim for it, its operation demonstrates, on the contrary, that biology is *not* reducible to biochemistry (and ultimately to physics). What makes DNA do its work is not its chemistry but the order of bases along the DNA chain. It is this order which functions as a code to be read out by the developing organism. The laws of physics and chemistry hold, as reductivists rightly insist, universally; they are entirely unaffected by the particular linear sequence that characterizes the triplet code. Any order is possible physico-chemically; therefore physics and chemistry cannot specify *which* order will in fact succeed in functioning as a code.
>
> (Grene 1974:56)

This argument, which Grene thinks 'appears incontrovertible' (56), would, if valid, beard the reductionist lion in his den. In fact, the argument very clearly is fallacious. If we look closely at the last sentence quoted above we perceive an equivocation. When Grene says, of the bits that make up the DNA molecule, that any order is possible physico-chemically she is thinking, as in the preceding sentence she states, of the *laws* of physics and chemistry; and scientific laws, by their nature merely allow *possibilities* – they do not, by themselves and in the absence of a statement of initial conditions, state what *must* happen. When she concludes that 'physics and chemistry cannot specify *which* order will in fact succeed in functioning as a code' then, if her argument is to bear on the reductionist claim, she must now be thinking of the actual entities, including forces etc., that chemistry and physics describe. The conclusion must be that the structure of a particular

DNA molecule is not due to the way its constituents as originally independent entities bumped up against, and reacted with, each other and this is borne out by the way Polanyi puts it: 'As the arrangement of a printed page is extraneous to the chemistry of the printed page, so is the base sequence in a DNA molecule extraneous to the chemical forces at work in the DNA molecule' (Polanyi 1976:132). Because of this equivocation, the conclusion does not follow. Once we do not feel forced to swallow the conclusion, because of the apparent reasonableness of the argument that led to it, we may feel free to examine it in its own right. When we do this we surely must see just how outrageous Polanyi's view is. The correct view would seem to be that it is just because the constituents of DNA are what they are, and because of the forces between them, that the laws of physics and chemistry 'are entirely unaffected by the particular linear sequence that characterizes the triplet code', i.e. that these laws 'allow' any *linear* sequence while ruling out other configurations.[5]

The virtue of Grene's formulation of Polanyi's argument is that it allows us very quickly to see what is wrong with it. However, as Polanyi puts it, the argument comes embedded in a longer discussion, where there is a confusing mixture of ontological and 'methodological' issues, and itself then takes over this same confusion. It is precisely this that makes the argument seem so plausible. There is a hint of what is happening in Grene's account when she says, 'What makes DNA do its work is not its chemistry but the order of bases along the DNA chain. It is this order which functions as a code to be read out by the developing organism.' One's immediate response to this is that there is no distinction between the chemistry of the DNA molecule and the order of the bases any more than one distinguishes between the chemistry of acetic acid and the disposition of its component atoms. One might say the structure of the molecule *is* part of its chemistry. The fatally confused step is when Grene goes on to say that the order of bases 'functions as a code' as if acting as a code involved something over and above acting chemically. In fact, her talk of the code being 'read out by the developing organism' should not be taken as a mere rhetorical flourish, as one might imagine it being used by a hard-line reductionist like Francis Crick, but is precisely where the whole confusion lies. This comes out in Polanyi's exposition where he talks at first of the DNA code ('a linear sequence of items' (Polanyi 1976:131)) which has 'information content' that, as he makes clear, is given by 'the numerical improbability of the arrangement' (132); but then immediately goes on to change his mind as to what 'information content' really is.

A printed page may be a mere jumble of words, and it has then no information content. So the improbability count gives the *possible*, rather than the *actual*, information content attributed to a DNA molecule; the sequence of the bases is deemed meaningful only because we assume with Watson and Crick that the arrangement generates the structure of the offspring by endowing it with its own information content.

(Polanyi 1976:132)

Polanyi has gone from speaking of 'information content' in a technical sense, as used in information theory, to a quite different use more akin to 'meaning' as when we speak of the meaning of a piece of prose. It is, of course, the first sense which is used in biological *science* and will be insisted upon by the reductionist as posing no threat to his reductionism.

This blatant mystery-mongering has its purpose. For Polanyi wishes to regard the DNA molecule as a mixture of blueprint and engineer which somehow *constructs* the living organism. 'Can the control of morphogenesis by DNA be likened to the designing and shaping of a machine by the engineer?' he asks (132), and answers in the affirmative. The point of this comparison is that he has earlier likened organisms to machines and has tried to show that even with ordinary machines, such as clocks, a reductive account of them cannot be given. This is because a machine 'works under the control of two distinct principles. The higher one is the principle of the machine's design, and this harnesses the lower one, which consists in the physical–chemical processes on which the machine relies' (128). We might be tempted to regard the higher principle, that of the machine's design, which he describes as a 'boundary condition', as merely referring to the design of the machine as it is embodied in the machine, i.e. as the machine's structure; and then talk of the lower principles, i.e. the physical-chemical processes, as being 'harnessed' by the higher is at most a misleading metaphor. In one mood he does speak in this way as when he says,

> This harness is not unbreakable; the structure of the machine, and thus its working, can break down. But this will not affect the forces of inanimate nature on which the operation of the machine relied; it merely releases them from the restriction the machine imposed on them before it broke down.

(Polanyi 1976:128)

If we are thinking, in this way, of the machine, in itself, then its structure does not harness its matter as a rider harnesses a horse – this sort of language can only be a florid way of saying that the structural arrangement of the material has to be given as an initial condition before, from it and the laws of mechanics etc., we can say what shall happen. There is no question here of higher and lower 'principles' and, therefore, no threat to the reductionist's position.

This is disguised by the fact that Polanyi does not consistently refer to the machine and its structure, in itself, but also brings in the idea of the *constructor* of the machine. It is not now merely a question of the machine's structure harnessing the laws of nature – an innocuous idea if interpreted correctly – but the quite different concept of an *engineer* harnessing them.

> The structure of machines and the working of their structure are thus shaped by man, even while their material and the forces that operate them obey the laws of inanimate nature. In constructing a machine and supplying it with power, we harness the laws of nature at work in its material and in its driving force and make them serve our purpose.
>
> (Polanyi 1976:128)

This way of putting the matter is not a mere verbal slip but is essential for whatever show of plausibility the argument has. Of course, in a sense, the engineer harnesses the laws of nature by bringing bits of matter into certain relations. But in saying this we are no longer thinking of higher and lower principles 'in' or 'of' the machine which is the conclusion Polanyi desires. If we are to speak, still, of two principles then it should be clear that there is now only one principle for the matter which makes up the machine and that the other resides with the engineer, which is only a complicated way of saying that there are two things in a certain relation to each other. Once seen in this light there seems no reason why a reductive account should not be given of the complex system: engineer plus machine.

In a loose way we can say that there is a confusion of ontological with methodological questions in that bringing in the engineer brings in a consideration of *interests*. The engineer, we might say, has a particular *interest* in the structure of a machine, either in bringing it about or in merely studying it. Similarly, a chemist may be interested in the atoms of which it is made. In fact, Polanyi, when speaking of a distinction he makes between machine type boundaries and test-tube type boundaries, seems to distinguish between the two according to whether our interest is in the boundary or the matter that is bounded (129); and that it is a purely methodological distinction is further suggested by his remark that 'By shifting our attention, we may sometimes change a boundary from one type to another' (129). Also, in his *Personal Knowledge*, in what may plausibly be seen as a fore-runner of the argument here criticised, Polanyi distinguishes between the physics and chemistry of machines and their 'operational principles', the latter being *'rules of rightness*, which account only for the successful working of machines but leave their failures entirely unexplained' (Polanyi 1962:328). Here, again, I think we can easily detect questions of interest being confused with questions concerning the fundamental nature of things but I shall not pursue the issue further.

THE CONTRADICTION IN THE NOTION OF LEVELS

To assert the existence of different levels of 'principles' etc., unless this is taken as an obscure way of referring to different things interacting in a common environment, is to invite a criticism of the kind used to effect by the late Professor John Anderson (1962) and dubbed the 'two worlds argument' by John Passmore (1962). This is that once two ontological levels, two distinct kinds of being, are distinguished then there is no way that they can, without contradiction, be brought together again in mutual interactions. The power of Anderson's argument is evident as it is employed against such metaphysical ideas as the ontological distinction between the platonic forms and the world of becoming or between God as the wholly other and the finite world he creates. However, it can also be used where the proposed ontological 'split' is not, at least at first sight, as wide as this – including Polanyi's hierarchies if we take these to be ontological. For now it seems that in machines, for example, with the operation of higher order principles, the matter of which the machines are composed must act out of character. This is so because, in not taking these higher order principles as merely what occurs when bits of matter come into a certain relation with other things in the universe, e.g. engineers, they must be regarded as of the nature of those bits of matter. By then saying that the lower order principles are 'open' to the higher, i.e. that they go on irrespective of the existence of the higher even although the latter also affect the action of the former, he is asserting that the matter of machines has both the character X and not-X. The argument has been put by P.H. Partridge for the general notion of emergent evolution. After arguing that the concept of causality as creative emergent evolution must take its sense from a supposed contrast with a preformationist idea of causality, where the effect somehow lies within the cause, he continues:

> The theory of preformationism simply means that the effect is deducible from the cause alone, or is necessitated by the cause, it being the nature of a particular cause to produce such an effect. If, then, it is the nature of A to produce the one effect B, when A 'transcends itself' by producing C, it is not acting according to its nature, but according to some other nature that is not its. Hence, the assumption that a thing both necessitates and creates implies that it is both itself and not itself, and this difficulty can be met not by a revision of logic, but, if we are unwilling to give up the notion of emergence as a special and peculiar occurrence, by the invention of some higher, mythological power asserting itself through the cause.
> (Partridge 1934:161)

If it is denied that the concept of emergent evolution involves the underlying assumption of these two different kinds of causality then the idea must be of one kind, which is creative in the sense that the effect is different from the cause, but with which one can nevertheless distinguish causes which have the most remarkable effects: effects which, as Samuel Alexander suggests, must be accepted with 'natural piety' (Alexander 1920:vol.2, 47). There is here clearly a problem of how we distinguish between emergent and non-emergent effects although Alexander's own belief in the emergence of material things from naked space–time – as though space–time were a kind of unsuccessful porridge – may suggest there are some paradigms of the former. The point here seems to be that if such astonishing effects do burst forth in the cosmos then the rational course is not to accept them with 'natural piety' but to try to understand them and this involves finding out what their real causes are.

An illustration of this point is afforded by a defence of the idea of emergence by the British Communist, John Lewis. Consider his account of the evolution of the DNA molecule:

> What has to be noted is that (a) the process is wholly explicable in a succession of physical states operating under physical laws which (b) bring about the complete novelty of the DNA molecule possessing new properties and operating under its own laws.
> (Lewis 1974:50)

Certainly the DNA molecule is unique (which is the term Lewis usually uses and which I take to be synonymous with 'completely novel') but only in the sense that it is a unique spatial arrangement of its constituent atoms which, given what they are, will, in the relevant circumstances, fall out in the order they do. In this sense, the water molecule is also unique and, indeed, any molecule we care to think of. Of course, *in a sense*, the DNA molecule possesses new properties but only in the sense that any molecule possesses new properties, that is, those properties fitting for the kind of thing it is; but this sense does not exclude the fact that these new properties are fully explained in terms of the constituent atoms including the spatial etc. relations between them. In fact, the chemistry of one virus, ϕX174, has been worked out completely, and the sequence of 5,375 nucleotides along its DNA, and what it 'codes' for, is fully known. The DNA of ϕX174 did spring some surprises, connected with the details of the coding, but these were ordinary chemical surprises. It did not, for example, suddenly start whistling 'Waltzing Matilda' (Fiddes 1977).

Suppose we do accept the idea of new qualities in evolution, does not this, despite Lewis's disclaimers, make their emergence entirely mysterious? Here the dualist might find his mark. Lewis claims that his scheme is not at all mysterious but this can only be in the sense that it is naturalistic and makes no appeal to 'supernatural' causes; but it certainly is mysterious in the sense that no *explanation* is possible of the emergent qualities nor, even, of why, for example, qualitatively identical DNA molecules should have the same emergent qualities. Creative the DNA molecules may be but they have all the spontaneity of the Guards on parade. The dualists might claim that their own account in terms of a creative, spiritual mind is superior because it can explain the emergence of new qualities. Or it may be that the dualist, like the mechanist, will reject the idea of emergence but, unlike the latter, accept the existence of undeniably mental events irreducible to mechanistic explanations. It is the existence of such events which leads the dualist to dualism.

We bake a cake and, as it cools, from nowhere a deep red icing settles on its surface. How do we explain this? By denying that it is a *magic* cake and instead saying that it is a *unique* cake where the flour and the currants have settled in just that one combination that allows for the *emergence* of red icing? Is this any more mysterious than the DNA molecule from nowhere obtaining brand new properties or the brain a coating of mentality? And if we try to lessen the mystery of the icing by postulating the existence of a ghostly chef, some departed Party member, perhaps, still anxious to do his bit, why would we think this more reasonable than conjuring up a god to paint on new qualities wherever in the universe they are needed?

If any content at all is to be given to ideas of 'emergence' or of 'hierarchies' then these ideas must be about what it is that exists at the one ontological level so that, for example, the dispute between the believer in emergent evolution and the mechanist is about whether or not vital forces or secondary qualities exist as well as quarks. This can be seen in Polanyi whose talk of mysterious emergent higher principles at one point becomes deflected into the advocacy of vitalism. Here the dispute is with orthodox Darwinians where Polanyi argues that rather than studying the origins of new populations one should try to account for the evolution of a single man by referring to that man's family tree which, he claims, 'includes everything that has contributed to the maturing of this human being' (Polanyi 1966:47). The point here is that, by denying the importance of commonly accepted environmental factors in human evolution, involving natural selection etc., Polanyi is, naturally enough, obliged to invent a different environment containing vital forces in order to account for this evolution; but these vital forces can then no longer be regarded as having a special ontological priority but must simply be bits of the universe interacting with other bits and, in particular, the complex chemical systems which are living organisms. This view, once teased out from the confusing talk of 'hierarchies' or 'emergence' and stated bluntly in its own right, can then be more coolly assessed.

TENSIONS

Modern biology, then, involves two fundamental metaphysical assumptions. The first is that, despite the useful retention of teleological forms of language, all causes of biological functional activity are efficient causes; and the second is that what, ultimately, exist to be studied by biology are structured collections of fundamental particles and their associated fields – *and nothing more*. There is the further issue of whether, as is sometimes suggested, the category of causality should be given up altogether but, leaving that aside, these two general views are logically compatible. However, when we turn to the special Darwinian explanation of the origins of living things – which, of course, has played some part in the downfall of strictly teleological accounts – there is the problem of whether *it* is compatible with the strongly reductionist accounts of biophysics. The question is not often asked but needs to be taken seriously. The theory of natural selection is, or at least, as originally conceived, was, concerned largely with explanation at the 'common-sense', macroscopic level and there is no guarantee that it will not suffer the fate of other theories of this kind that usefully miss the mark. As with the mechanics of gross bodies, the theory may be retained while the truth of the matter lies elsewhere, in among the strange interactions of what there ultimately is according to the quantum physicists. I examine this question in Part II along with two other difficulties for the fundamental assumptions of contemporary biological science: the problem of how on these knowledge is at all possible and the matter of how animal consciousness participates in a world seemingly designed to exclude it. The biological pot having thus been thoroughly stirred the reader will, I hope, be ready to savour the headier brew of the natural theology of Part III.

Part II
Problems

Chapter 4
Reductionism *or* Darwinism

UNGRATEFUL OFFSPRING

Reductionist theories have a habit of rounding on their parents. This was true of modern atomic physics which, arising out of a moderately common-sense Newtonian view, now presents to us a world quite beyond our capacity to picture. Newtonian physics, useful though it still may be for building bridges and predicting celestial orbits, has, in the matter of truth, failed us. It is not so often observed that the same is the case for Darwinism which, as itself a materialistically leaning theory, was at least a midwife at the birth of modern reductive materialism. In short, if reductive materialism is true then the theory of evolution by natural selection is false.

Some Darwinians have sensed a problem here and have tried to reassure us. Thus Ernst Mayr has claimed that evolution is 'consistent with the laws of the physical sciences, but it makes no sense to say that biological evolution has been "reduced" to physical laws'. This is because 'Biological evolution is the result of specific processes that impinge on specific systems, the explanation of which is meaningful only at the complexity of those processes and those systems' (Mayr 1978:39). If Mayr is not implying that evolution, in being 'consistent' with physical laws, both does and does not impinge on those laws then his argument must be that there is a quite new set of irreducible laws at a certain level of complexity, i.e. that at a certain level of complexity *new* forces or properties ('biological properties') come to be possessed by physical objects and these new forces or properties interact with the original ones.

This is clearly shown by William C. Wimsatt who explicitly defends the view that there is a two-way interaction possible between lower levels of atoms or quarks or whatever and higher levels of biological organisation. In the course of his discussion, where he takes as an example the evolution of termite colonies, he remarks as follows:

> the suspicion induced by the explanatory priority of lower levels is not dispelled by the substitution of natural selection for special creation as a mechanism consistent with lower level forces and explanations. It has led many to remain suspicious of the importance of functional considerations; they prefer to ignore them entirely in favour of the analysis of straightforward (lower to upper) 'how' questions, to treat selection as a disguised tautology rather than admit that there could be selection *forces* (which would have to be upper-level forces which could have lower-level effects) and to act as if selection of termite colonies is ultimately inexplicable in any other terms than as the solution to a gargantuan Schroedinger wave-equation or whatever the current 'lowest' level proposes.
>
> (Wimsatt 1976:246)

Against this view, Wimsatt holds that the forces of selection can have lower-level effects – presumably atoms find themselves pushed into new configurations by forces blowing in which are quite other than those that normally hold between them. The issue is smudged by his suggestion that those who hold the rival view must treat selection as a disguised tautology with the implication that it is only in this way that they can avoid recognising the upper-level force of selection. Leaving aside the question of what is meant by a force of selection, and whether it is in any way comparable to atomic forces, it is clear that someone who believes that the ultimate explanation of the existence of termite colonies is in terms of atomic particles is in no way committed, by this view alone, to the further belief that there is something logically odd about purported explanations in terms of natural selection. In fact, that person may believe that, because the ultimate explanation is humanly impossible (except in a very general way), we should hold on to the theory of natural selection.

When the reductionist looks closely at what is meant by a 'force of selection' they are able to press home their argument. We should not think of such a 'force' as in the same class as, say, a gravitational force or a centrifugal force or as coming into competition with such forces. In fact, when we get the whole story concerning selection forces we find it spelled out in terms of adaptation, differential survival, etc. For example, in the Valley of Falling Rocks tortoises with thick shells are better adapted than tortoises with thin shells and this fact will provide part of the explanation for the evolution of well-armoured reptiles in this region. This involves a bit of common-sense physics concerning which a reductive account could, in principle, be given. But the rest of this particular causal story, making use of the concepts of mutation, differential survival, etc., can also, without remainder, be reduced to the account in terms of fundamental particles.

We very frequently find, in expositions of the origin of life, the view that once the first living things have evolved, by purely chemical processes, then the quite new force of natural selection takes over the task of promoting further evolution. For example, Richard Dawkins, after taking us to the point where the basic biochemical 'building-blocks' were formed some billions of years ago, points out that a mere random shuffling of these blocks will not produce a complicated organism such as man. 'This is where Darwin's theory takes over from where the slow building up of molecules leaves off' (Dawkins 1976:15). It is as if, for the early stages of the biochemical soup, mere chemistry is sufficient; but as the soup starts to thicken a need is felt for the cook.

However, when Dawkins explains on what it is that the force of natural selection gets a grip, there does not seem to be available anything other than chemical or physical entities and forces which are perfectly capable of doing the job of bringing about evolution by themselves. According to Dawkins, natural selection gets to work once replicators are formed (these days DNA molecules but perhaps originally something else that was an evolutionary precursor of DNA). The important properties of replicators, which are supposed to pave the way for natural selection, are, he thinks, (i) that they act as templates, (ii) that they can split apart in such a way that each half is a further template and (iii) that they sometimes mutate. None of these properties involves the need for an explanation in terms of anything other than such things as the formation and splitting of hydrogen bonds and so on – or if it does, there is no reason to think that special *biological* forces will need to be invoked. Once having these properties, they are sufficient, in relation to the whole causal field about them, to explain evolutionary development.

We may suppose that DNA molecules of type-X are in equilibrium in the original primeval soup. If there is a mutation, i.e. a chemical change in one or more of these molecules, then this equilibrium may be upset and eventually a new one attained – but this, once more, is explicable (in principle) in terms of chemical kinetics. If the concept of natural selection is to be invoked it should be understood as a purely heuristic device which depends upon, without directly referring to, the realities of chemical interaction. This argument, once accepted for the case of DNA as one chemical among others in the primeval soup, can then be carried through to account for the whole of evolutionary development. The 'evolutionary problem', then, is not how natural selection got started but how a certain peculiar chemistry is possible.

TROUBLE IN MIND

There is, then, logical tension at the very heart of biology. I suspect that, if forced to make a choice between the two positions, most scientists would accept the reductionist view of the world as a restless sea of fields and particles with Darwinism floating as a purely heuristic foam on its surface. This world-view might seem worrying in its apparent implications for the notion of human dignity although, paradoxically, it might also once more arouse theological longings inasmuch as one might wonder at what now looks like the perfect design of the universe for the production of life. This issue I shall take up in Part III. For the moment I wish to press home two difficulties, one of which counts particularly against Darwinism and the other against reductive materialism. These two problems – which, in fact, are connected and to that extent each presses against both positions – concern, first, how the fact of our knowledge of things fits in with the theory of natural selection and, second, how consciousness can possibly find its place in the world described by reductive materialism. These issues light up a crisis in biology before which other heady disputes about punctuated evolution and so on pale into insignificance.

Chapter 5

Biology and knowledge

PERCEPTION AND SURVIVAL

In the eighteenth century Immanuel Kant, awakened from his 'dogmatic slumber' by his reading of Hume, devised the theory that our perceptions and concepts do not arise willy-nilly and from their own nature but are made to conform to certain innate a priori principles of the mind. The contents of our perceptual fields are laid out in a certain order in space and time not because that part of the world which lies outwith the mind is so constituted but because our minds supply the order and the a priori intuitions of space and time; and we believe that every event has a cause not because every, or even any, event does lie in such a relation but because the very constitution of our minds *constrains* us to think in terms of the category of causality.

Whatever were Kant's intentions, such a theory leads directly to scepticism, to the view of knowledge as mere conformity in innate prejudice. Nevertheless, Kant's view has received support from modern biology at least to the extent that there is evidence – both from direct physiological investigation and general evolutionary principles – that the brain is not a passive receptacle for, say, our sense impressions (which might then be said in some way to 'correspond' to external objects) but works them up in accordance with certain principles of its own. As with perception so with the intellect. The prerequisite for evolutionary success, with nervous systems as with any other organ, is survival value. This means, as Henri Bergson among others has maintained, that the evolutionary test of our concepts is the actions they make possible; and this in itself makes plausible the view that our brains, however pliable they may be, in the end constrain us to think in certain ways rather than others with no guarantee that how we think bears any relation at all to the truth. Harry L. Jerison has tried to make a virtue of this sceptical position without, I think, realising its devastating consequences for the theory of knowledge and the possibility of natural science:

> The 'true' or 'real' world is specific to a species and is dependent on how the brain of the species works; this is as true for our own world – the world as we know it – as it is for the world of any species.
>
> (Jerison 1976:99)

A little later he adds to this: 'The work of the brain is to create a model of a possible world rather than to record and transmit to the mind a world that is metaphysically true' (99). Perhaps, for example, we fill the world with minds – that is, before we become sophisticated and empty people of them – because our brains predispose us to think in personal categories; and our brains do this because belief in spirits, gods, etc. is linked with behaviour which helps us to survive as social animals. The link between concept and behaviour need not, of course, be a logical one; indeed, when, for example, one sees socio-biology denounced as 'sexist' or 'racist' – where the argument seems to be that socio-biological theories are untrue because they ought to be untrue – one is tempted to the belief that our brains are also predisposed to commit the is–ought fallacy.

The case for the brain's active role in vision has been stated, on purely biological grounds, by Gunther S. Stent (1974). Stent points out that there is much evidence for what he calls the 'selective destruction of information' as the nervous impulses pass in from the retinae of the eyes to the visual cortex, and that one can distinguish several 'levels of abstraction' as this occurs (Stent 1974:10). In particular, starting with the retinal nerve cells and progressing through higher levels of the nervous system, information from the objects perceived is progressively and selectively destroyed in such a way that the remaining information is of such things as parallel straight lines and hence, ultimately, surfaces. This all depends, according to Stent, on the peculiar circuitry in the visual centre of the brain. The details of this need not detain us but the moral springing from it will. This just is that, as Stent himself argues, such a view seems to imply a kind of Kantianism whereby the mind (in this case taken as the brain) imposes a certain 'a priori' structure on our percepts. In fact, Stent wishes to go much further and connect the facts of the physiology of visual perception with what he thinks is our intellectual predisposition to believe in Euclidean as against non-Euclidean geometry. It is here, I think, that he goes wrong. Stent argues as follows:

our own visual perception of the outer world is filtered through a stage in which data are processed in terms of straight parallel lines, thanks to the way in which the input channels coming from the primary light-receptor of the retina are hooked up to the brain. This fact cannot fail to have profound psychological consequences; evidently a geometry based on straight parallel lines, and hence by extension on plane surfaces, is most immediately compatible with our mental equipment. It need not have been this way, since (at least from the neurophysiological point of view) the retinal ganglion cells could just as well have been connected to the higher cells in the visual cortex in such a way that their . . . receptive fields form arcs rather than straight lines. If evolution had given rise to that other circuitry, curved rather than plane surfaces would have been our primary spatial concept. Thus neuro-biology has now shown why it is human – and all too human – to hold Euclidean geometry and its non-intersecting co-planar parallel lines to be self-evident truth.

(Stent 1974:13)

If Stent's argument is sound then we might also use it to explain why Aristotle, in considering alternatives to the parallels' postulate, dismissed them not as being logically impossible but as 'against nature' (Toth 1969); and why later investigators thought that they had disproved the possibility of non-Euclidean geometries because the conclusions following from the denial of the parallels' postulate, although not showing up any formal inconsistencies, seemed to them bizarre. However, I think these examples can be used to show that Stent is mistaken. For these thinkers found the denial of the parallels' postulate, and what followed therefrom, unnatural or bizarre just because it clashed with experience. This brings out the point that, even if it is true that visual perception depends on a kind of abstraction in the nervous system whereby nervous impulses are 'processed in terms of straight parallel lines', it is still certainly the case that what I see are straight lines and plane surfaces *and* arcs and curved surfaces. As far as deciding which sort of geometry to invent, curves in perception are as readily available to me as straight lines. Nor, of course, need we think that things would be different if the relevant nervous connections involved arcs: presumably our perceptual field would still contain straight lines as well as curved and our choice of geometry would, to that extent, still be undetermined.

However, we can dig rather deeper in our criticism and unearth a basic confusion underlying Stent's suggestion. When he speaks of straight lines and arcs, in his description of the circuitry of the visual system, he is, of course, still speaking of *Euclidean* straight lines and arcs. Suppose we consider these *Euclidean* arcs as they appear in perception. What is true is that we can take the uninterpreted axioms of a particular non-Euclidean geometry – that is, we take a purely formal system so that even to call it a 'geometry' is to use this term in a quite different sense from that used when we are talking about real triangles, say, drawn on a piece of paper[1] – and then we *interpret* these axioms *as* arcs so that, for example, the Euclidean arcs are now *defined* as straight lines. This will lead to such exciting concepts as parallel straight lines meeting or there being more than one straight line passing through a point and parallel to a given straight line; but this is *only* because 'straight line' in the basic axiom is interpreted as, for example, the *Euclidean* line as it appears on a sphere. Indeed, it is by interpreting the axioms of a non-Euclidean geometry as a special case of Euclidean geometry, e.g. as the geometry of the surface of a sphere or a saddle-back, that the former is shown to be consistent (on the assumption that Euclidean geometry is consistent). But, what we want in the case of a being who would think 'naturally' in terms of non-Euclidean geometry is not a master of mathematics in this way but someone whose brain cells have non-Euclidean *spatial* connections; or, to put it in a different way, someone whose perceptual field was, in itself, so to speak, non-Euclidean. This is not merely a matter of their perceptual world being one of curves rather than straight lines – as if they were a sentient bubble in a world of bubbles – but one, which we cannot picture to ourselves, where parallel straight lines do meet and the arcs are, in themselves, non-Euclidean. It is only in such a world, where all straight roads lead to Rome that start from it, that one would find an Aristotle who would think that Euclidean geometry is unnatural.

His confusions notwithstanding, what Stent says is still suggestive in that it implies, correctly I think, that there is a close connection between what we perceive and what we think; and we must still take seriously the idea that our brains have evolved so as to predispose us to perceive and think in certain ways rather than others. D.M. Armstrong once asked: 'What is perception?', and he continued by saying: 'A flood of light is thrown on this question by asking "What can somebody who can perceive do, that somebody who cannot perceive cannot do? What *powers* does perception add?"' (Armstrong 1961:105). From our point of view this is a good way of looking at the question because it is a very *biological* way with the emphasis on how perception is linked to the organism's behaviour – the important thing as far as survival is concerned. But having asked the question in this spirit, we cannot now come easily to the answer which Armstrong gives, that what perception allows us to do is to discover facts about the environment. What perception in the end allows us to do, if we are lucky, is to survive but what else it allows us to do as a means to that end is not necessarily straightforwardly determined. As Robert L. Trivers has remarked, 'the conventional view that natural selection favours nervous systems which produce ever more accurate images of the world must be a very naive view of mental evolution' (Trivers 1976:vi). Consider colour vision. On Armstrong's view we should have to conclude that we are finding out about the colours of things as we look about the world and, indeed, at the time he wrote *Perception and the Physical World* Armstrong was a direct realist concerning colour. Yet, as J.J.C. Smart (1963:69–71) has pointed out, if the physical details of colour vision are taken into account it is very difficult to believe any such thing. For example, according to the trichromatic theory of colour perception there will not normally be a simple one to one relationship between the information carried to the eye by light waves and the object's surface which we are claiming to be of a certain colour. It is very hard, then, to believe that the surface is that colour. If we take the view that the perception of colour is somehow illusory we can still go on to ask what it is that this illusion enables us to do, how it helps us survive. My own suggestion, which I shall not spell out in detail here, is that colour perception is purely and simply an aid to discrimination – what colour perception enables us to do is efficiently to pick out this object from that and this is what gives it its positive survival value. In Armstrong's analysis of perception, in terms of belief or tendency to believe, the perceptual beliefs that the various objects before us are of various colours are extra reasons for distinguishing them.

DARWINISM AND SCEPTICISM

Now the inevitable question arises. We have seen cause to think that in the perception of colour our senses, albeit for the best of reasons, lie to us. May not the disease be more deep-rooted than we like to think? Evolution in selecting our perceptual and intellectual abilities is not in the least interested in their capacity for truth but merely in whether or not they will help us to survive. To be adapted to the world does not imply knowing the world. It is the usual story: open the door a crack to the sceptic and he will storm the house.

There is a temptation to answer the sceptic in the following way. We have given reasons for thinking that some beliefs which in ordinary life we regard as indubitable – that, for example, roses are at least sometimes red – are in fact false. But this does not entitle us to conclude that *everything* we think true is false. As the stock answer to Descartes goes, because our senses sometimes lie it does not follow that they always lie. That we confess to some cracks in the edifice of knowledge does not give the sceptic licence to huff and puff and blow the house down.

But there is more to our question than merely to start the hare of abstract scepticism and upon our answer to it depends the very rationality of our belief in Darwinism. If the truth of Darwinism implies that evolution would not produce rational creatures capable of arriving at justified true belief about the world then we have every reason to disbelieve the theory. We may argue that it is possible for creatures having knowledge to evolve because there are such creatures, i.e. ourselves; therefore Darwinism must be false. If it is said that we must simply accept the implication that because Darwinism is true we do not have knowledge (and this is sometimes put forward in a disguised form by redefining 'truth' as, for example, that which leads to practical action or in terms of 'simplicity') then the answer is that even if the theory is true it remains the case that we can have no good grounds for believing in it. David Lack has made the point here:

> Darwin's 'horrid doubt' as to whether the convictions of man's evolved mind could be trusted applies as much to abstract truth as to ethics; and 'evolutionary truth' is at least as suspect as evolutionary ethics. At this point, therefore, it would seem that the armies of science are in danger of destroying their own base. For the scientist must be able to trust the conclusions of his reasoning. Hence he cannot accept the theory that man's mind was evolved wholly by natural selection if this means, as it would appear to do, that the conclusions of the mind depend ultimately on their survival value and not their truth, thus making all scientific theories, including that of natural selection, untrustworthy.
>
> (Lack 1957:104)

Lack's account of the problem suggests three questions:

(i) Can a purely physical thing, such as a brain, be said to think and to arrive at knowledge?
(ii) Is the brain's capacity for knowledge compatible with its contributing to the organism's chances of survival?
(iii) Could evolution by natural selection result in a brain with the capacity for knowledge?

Notice that there is point in asking questions (ii) and (iii) only if the answers preceding them are affirmative. I shall consider the questions in the order I have given them.

(i) The assumption I shall make here is that if we are Darwinians we should also be materialists. This has been denied by some thinkers who wish to retain the Darwinian theory of evolution while at the same time holding on to a non-materialist theory of mind because they think, for example, that the existence of consciousness is an undeniable fact which cannot be explained in terms of purely physical principles. Their solution has been to embrace epiphenomenalism, the view that the brain throws off mental states as a kind of smoke that lacks causal efficacy. Brain state A causes brain state B and *also* mental state a. But mental state a is idle: it does not act back on any brain state nor does it cause any further mental states which must themselves be thrown off by future brain states.

The merit of the theory is that it is fully compatible with Darwinism inasmuch as we need not think of the mechanism of evolution as anything other than natural selection acting on chance mutations. It is, however, open to a fatal objection. We cannot now regard the origin of consciousness as an evolutionary advance that gives to its owner a wider range of responses to its environment. It cannot do this because, by hypothesis, consciousness is idle, it does nothing. Nor can natural selection select a certain consciousness. All it can do is select a certain adaptive response to the environment and thus, also, the nervous system which is responsible for that response. As consciousness has no effect *on* the world, it cannot be selected to *fit* the world. If this is the case, there is no reason to believe that consciousness gives us a true account of the world – it is merely the silent murmuring of the brain as the latter goes about its business. The implications for the possibility of knowledge are obvious and disastrous.

Sir Alister Hardy (1975:Ch.3) has seen the difficulties associated with epiphenomenalism and has attempted to overcome them by giving the mind, as a conscious agent, an active role while, at the same time, still trying to account for evolution by Darwinian selection. The idea is that new exploratory behaviour by an animal, particularly if it is copied by its fellows, may in itself lead to new selection pressures. For example, suppose a bird, in a situation where there is strong competition for food, experiments with a new food source – perhaps it holds a twig in its mouth and digs out insects from beneath the bark of a tree – and suppose also a high proportion of that species copies the action. In the changed circumstances brought about by the birds' new behaviour quite new possibilities for evolutionary change are evident so that, for example, by natural selection a new kind of beak better suited for holding twigs becomes established.

Hardy's speculations about the possibility of evolutionary change caused by spontaneous or learned behavioural changes are interesting and we might conjecture that this kind of thing has been especially important for human evolution. If he had given his account of such evolutionary changes in purely materialist terms there would be no problems. However, Hardy thinks of the minds which initiate such changes as non-material things which somehow interact with the brains of animals. Now if Hardy were serious about his theory being consistent with Darwinism then, leaving aside the general question of whether postulating non-material causes could be consistent with it, we are no nearer to solving the sceptical issue. For there is no question here of mind somehow trying to work itself out in a general purposeful way so that in intending to achieve a state of knowledge it somehow *wills* the evolution of human beings – so that, so to speak, it constructs *Homo sapiens*. The bird, in picking up a twig, wants a feed, not the evolutionary modification of its descendants although this follows as a result of its action; and early humanity in making its tools and competing in war, etc. caused but did not intend the further evolution of intelligence. The overriding consideration here is that natural selection is regarded as the agent which picks out the relevant mental states with an eye to their survival value and there is still no guarantee that a non-material mind selected in this fashion would be capable of knowledge. Hardy might argue that it is only by postulating the existence of consciousness that we can make sense of the claim to knowledge: yet he has still to show how natural selection would select the particular *kind* of consciousness that would do the job. This is confused by him when he gets carried away by his theory so as to declare:

> The organs, the parts of the body – the limbs and feet, claws, teeth and beaks, tentacles, eyes and other organs of sense – are all tools or instruments carved out of the physical world by the mental element of the universe (to which consciousness and the Divine are related) by means of the behavioural selection I have discussed; the constantly varying DNA genetic code supplies the changing material for this selection to work upon.
>
> (Hardy 1975:212)

In fact, this is a far cry from the theory which he originally proposed and is more like a peculiar argument from design with Mind or God actively selecting the characters of organisms, as humans selectively breed dogs or pigeons, and as such has little in common with the theory of natural selection whose truth we are assuming.

(ii) Is the brain's capacity for knowledge compatible with its contributing to the organism's chances of survival? Lack's argument is as follows:

(I)   'Man's mind was evolved by natural selection.'

Therefore
(II)   'The conclusions of the mind depend ultimately on their survival value.'
(III) If the conclusions of the mind depend ultimately on their survival value then they do not depend on their truth.

From II and III:
(IV)   The conclusions of the mind do not depend on their truth.

Therefore
(V)   'all scientific theories, including that of natural selection, [are] untrustworthy'.

Lack's argument has two overlapping parts: the first, steps (I) and (II), arguing that the conclusions of the mind depend ultimately on their survival value; and the second, from (II) to (V), going from 'The conclusions of the mind depend ultimately on their survival value' to the sceptical conclusion concerning the possibility of scientific knowledge. This means that even if we block the sceptical conclusion (V), by showing that the brain's capacity for knowledge is not incompatible with its having survival value, we have still come only part of the way in demonstrating the viability of the Darwinian theory of evolution. For to show that a given characteristic has survival value is not to show that it is the result of natural selection nor that natural selection could bring about such a characteristic. Natural selection implies survival value but survival value does not necessarily imply natural selection. For example, the theory of the divine special creation of organisms will also explain why they are adapted to their environments.

I am not sure how Lack wishes his argument to be taken: whether he thinks that any brain built for survival will not be built for truth or that only brains forged by natural selection will have this disability. If he is making the general claim then it can be shown to be mistaken. There is no logical tension between the demands of survival and truth in that the concept of survival does not imply incapacity for truth. More than this; to speak generally of survival value is not say *how* the organism is fitted to survive. There is a multitude of ways in which living things achieve this and this raises the possibility that the capacity for truth might be one of them. Knowing about the world might be one way of surviving in it. In other words, why should not man's brain simultaneously serve the interests of both survival and knowledge?

(iii) Assuming that a purely physical organism of about our complexity could arrive at knowledge (and would not, for example, also need to have a non-material mind), and assuming also that the capacity for knowledge is not necessarily disadvantageous and might be positively advantageous, we can go on to ask whether the Darwinian theory allows for such a capacity. As a first step let us once more look at what Lack thinks follows from the theory of evolution by natural selection. This is 'that the conclusions of the mind depend ultimately on their survival value and not their truth'. What does Lack mean by this? One thing he might mean by saying that the 'conclusions of the mind' have this ultimate dependency on their survival value is that our existence as thinking animals has been *caused* by evolution by natural selection. In so far as he is merely saying that our thoughts do ultimately depend on something or other, in the sense that they have ultimate causes, then I do not see why his argument warrants scepticism. Our thoughts might be said to depend ultimately on natural selection or the primeval nebula or God's original creative impulse – or, indeed, on all of these – but this recitation of the remote causes of our thoughts does not seem to have anything at all to do with their soundness.

I take it that there is more to Lack's argument than this. Part of what more there is to it may lie in the consideration that there is something about the nature of natural selection as a cause of our thoughts that should arouse our suspicions. A reasonably competent and good god, we might think, could piece us together in such a way that our brains were able truthfully to deal with the world – and this is just because of the particular causal properties of the god which result in our purposeful *manufacture* – but there is nothing about natural selection as a cause to entitle us to such high hopes. If the theory of natural selection is correct then it is very highly improbable that truth-seeking, and – finding, organisms – as we believe ourselves to be – would evolve.

At first sight this argument has an intuitive plausibility. A closer look reveals a lack of the Cartesian clearness and distinctness which would allow such an intuition. This is because, in speaking of the improbability of the evolution of organisms such as ourselves, we may be thinking of all or any of a number of things. We may, first of all, be impressed with the sheer complexity of human beings, and particularly the complexity of the human nervous system, and the doubt may be that natural selection could be responsible for such a complicated being. It might be sufficient to explain less impressive examples of evolution, such as the adaptive radiation of the finches of the Galapagos Islands which Lack has, himself, closely studied and interpreted along orthodox Darwinian lines (Lack 1947), but surely not the more awe-inspiring examples of adaptation. The point, then, is quite general: How can orthodox evolutionary theory possibly account for very complex adaptations? The question is a good one and has its own complications; e.g. it involves questions of how greater and lesser degrees of evolutionary complexity are to be recognised, problems about the apparent need for very highly improbable concomitant variations for the evolution of complex structures and so on. However, I shall assume that this question, or group of questions, can ultimately be resolved in favour of Darwinism, perhaps along the lines suggested by Frazzetta (1975). I shall add to this, because it will be important in what follows, that the explanation of complex adaptations will probably involve the citation of somewhat peculiar circumstances, such as the evolution of neoteny, or the colonisation of a hitherto unoccupied environment, such as the land or the air, upon which or within which evolution is able to work.

If the problem is not the general one of explaining the evolution of sheer complexity then it may be that of explaining the evolution of a particular complex organism, in this case the human organism. The point may be that if we consider the Darwinian theory in its generality, as an explanation in terms of natural selection acting on random mutations, then it implies that the evolution of creatures such as ourselves, with our very special brains, is very unlikely. Is this Lack's worry? If it is, then it can be soothed by agreeing with him that if we consider the Darwinian theory in its generality only (or perhaps just the general theory plus a statement about the early conditions on Earth which allowed natural selection to get a foothold) then the evolution of this particular creature, man, must be seen as very improbable. An angelic intelligence knowing only that much about Earth would not look for souls to save upon it. But then the answer would seem to be that *any* example of a complex adaptation that we care to name is highly improbable if we consider the general statement of evolutionary theory only and do not take into account the specific conditions from which it has arisen. We may put the matter this way. It is not that the modern version of Darwinism does not allow for the evolution of highly improbable complex adaptations – it does and with the addition of certain other assumptions may even be said to predict that they will occur – but what it does not, by itself, predict is any *particular* improbable adaptation. To understand why any such adaptation exists requires looking at the concrete circumstances (in themselves, perhaps, highly unlikely when considered in the abstract) from which it has evolved. In this sense evolutionary investigations are very much historical studies.

The full answer to Lack, then, will involve looking at the actual historical circumstances of man's evolution and showing, in this way, how this improbable event came about. If we have some idea of just how improbable this evolution is we might also combine this answer with a prediction that similarly intelligent life will not exist elsewhere within a sphere of a certain number of cubic light-years around Earth. It might still be thought that there is some cheating going on here in that to explain man's evolution we have to throw in a handful of evolutionary factors in a most unlikely combination. This objection would be sound if these evolutionary factors were merely plucked from thin air just to save the Darwinian theory from having to face jarring facts; but it will not hold if it can be shown, through fossil studies etc., that the supposition of this odd combination of factors is not an *ad hoc* invention but actually corresponds to the facts. Even if the evidence for the details of man's evolution remains slim we might still remain confident that the Darwinian account holds if it can be shown that it works well elsewhere for similarly remarkable evolutionary developments where the evidence is available. Thus it has been argued that the peculiar adaptive features of birds – their big, efficient brains, their feathers, their high aerobic metabolism, etc. – were evolutionary possibilities because, among other things, of the particular characteristics of their dinosaur ancestors which, contrary to the older accounts, are thought to have been feathered and endothermic. In fact, in this account birds are now classified as modern dinosaurs (Bakker 1975). If the evidence really is strong for the dependence of bird evolution on such a fortuitous combination of circumstances – and even more so if other examples can be cited, such as the origin of eucaryote organisms from procaryotes (Margulis 1971) – then we might have some justified confidence that similar accounts are possible where the evidence is weaker.

Fortunately, it is no part of my job to deal with the details of man's evolution which, in such areas as the nature of sexual dimorphism in our species and even with regard to trivial matters of language, have become the matter of political controversy where ideology and ignorance make the loudest noises. I shall simply assume that an account of this evolution, consistent with Darwinism, can be given. However, even though this be the case we are not yet out of the conceptual thicket: Lack might agree with all that has been said so far but still insist we have not touched the core of his argument. I said earlier that simply to cite natural selection as cause, of some sort, of our thoughts has no bearing on the question of whether those thoughts are true or false; and, accordingly, Lack's argument was diverted into one of the possibility or probability of biological complexity. But his words will, I think, bear another interpretation. That is, when Lack speaks of our conclusions 'depending ultimately' on their survival value he perhaps means that, like the Vicar of Bray, we reach our conclusions with an eye to their usefulness rather than their truth – an ill made a virtue of by the pragmatists. For upon what is it that our conclusions *should* depend? Given that our interest is in arriving at true conclusions, the answer is obvious. Our conclusions should depend ultimately on – that is, should be validly derivable from – *true premisses*; and now the contrast with conclusions derived from premisses which are time-serving is inevitable. Because the premisses from which we start are selected for their usefulness, rather than their truth, the 'conclusions of the mind' will be true, if at all, only accidentally. This talk of premisses having survival value rather than truth as their chief virtue does not, of course, really entail their deliberate choice by Machiavellian individuals. It is just to take seriously, what we noticed earlier, that before we embark on our intellectual adventures our brains, as it were, supply us, in perception and perhaps in the a priori categories of thought, with the basic premisses, or framework, for our thinking; and where this basic framework has been selected because it is useful not because it is true. It is just this suspicion that Darwinism leads to a kind of materialistic Kantianism.

Some have tried to find a way around this problem by emphasising the historical nature of man and ignoring his biology altogether. Certainly, the historical account will get us some way but, unless the biological issues are squarely faced, we will end up with mere historical relativism. It is not enough to show how historical development has taken place – how, for example, economic or geographical conditions affect intellectual possibilities – although this is important in its own right. What has to be shown also, and this lies behind the historical account and is prior to it, is how the human brain was capable of embarking on this historical development bearing in mind that it was not evolved for it. The point is that we cannot think that the human brain's *potential* for cultural development is what constituted its original evolutionary advantage – that lay merely in its ability to cope with the environment it *then* found itself in – yet that potential must have been there as an accidental by-product of the biological adaptation.

As the story is usually told, the original evolutionary development, which allowed for the later historical development, was that of man's great intelligence which in turn was connected with the evolution of language and his ability as a tool user. This last was perhaps connected with the fact that he was a predator come late on the scene and had to develop novel ways of obtaining prey if he were to survive the intense competition of other predators (Alcock 1972). Whatever the details, the fact of the historical development of man helps us to find at least a partial answer to our original problem. At the very least it enables us to explain why our actions and our concepts are not glued to that former grassland environment in which our species originally evolved; and we might argue that although the mere fact of historical change will not, in itself, explain the human capacity for scientific knowledge it is at least a necessary condition of it. Certainly there would have been no theory of natural selection, for example, if human beings had remained at the cultural level associated with their original occupation of the grasslands.

Given all this, how, still, are we to escape relativism or scepticism? For the cruder kind of 'Darwinism', as used to explain the 'adaptation' of whole societies to their environments, no attempt is made to recognise this problem, let alone deal with it. Alexander Alland, for example, thinks that in our study of society we should not bother with what the people in that society think but only with their 'actual behaviour':

> Certainly from the point of view of evolutionary studies, the actual model or *cognitive map* which determines behaviour is irrelevant. The evolutionist is concerned with the interrelationships between actual behaviour and environmental parameters. If he has a good working model of the behavioural system, this is enough for research purposes.
>
> (Alland 1967:167)

Even with the more sophisticated view of Richard Dawkins (1976: Ch.11) where ideas (called by him 'memes') are thought of as quite new replicators, existing in and being selected by the environment provided by human culture (regarded as a kind of primeval soup), the question of the *truth* of these ideas intrudes itself. If we allow that the discovery of true propositions is possible then there is no reason why there should not be, for Dawkins's scheme, societies which, in valuing such propositions, place emphasis on their selection. But given the general Darwinian theory, just how is the selection of true propositions possible? This problem is particularly acute for Popper whom Dawkins mentions approvingly for the light he has thrown on the 'analogy between scientific progress and genetic evolution by natural selection' (Dawkins 1976:204). Not only is Popper's general philosophy of falsification a sceptical one – because it allows only for the elimination of false propositions and not the discovery of true ones (or, we might say, merely for the survival of those propositions which are not eliminated) – but the fact that he wishes to include among the theories an organism has about the world such things as innately determined perceptual beliefs (Popper 1972:142) must lead to the sceptical issue asserting itself. For such 'theories' will be rooted in the organism's biology and that being so they will have been selected for their biological value and not because other rival hypotheses have been falsified. Popper might claim that the biological origin of these beliefs is irrelevant and that they can still be criticised and, perhaps, falsified; however, if, as seems plausible, such beliefs were to include some with reference to basic categorial features of experience, e.g. concerning the existence of things in space and time, it is hard to see how this criticism and falsification could occur. With what categories does a brain criticise its own categories?

'All instruction given or received by way of argument proceeds from pre-existent knowlege', so Aristotle (1921:71a) tells us. It seems to me also true that, for each of us, the original 'pre-existent knowledge' is given us in perception – that it is the *world* so given us that enables us to make further advances in knowledge. If this be said to be old-fashioned empiricism it is, nevertheless, powerfully supported by recent researches in palaeo-neurology which suggest that the great increase in brain size in mammals in general, and more particularly in our own species, has been very largely concerned with the evolution of improved perceptual abilities (Jerison 1973). If we are to avoid the biological relativism latent in Popper's talk of innate theories and quite explicit in Jerison's account, earlier noted, of perceptual models which are not 'metaphysically true' – a relativism which, nevertheless, paradoxically somehow makes an absolute of biological knowledge – then we must insist that, in some respects at least, perception does put us in touch with the world.

Perhaps we can argue that evolution, even by natural selection, would not leave a creature like ourselves completely devoid of a correct view, in perception, of the world. Even if we take the view of Bergson, who as strongly as anybody emphasises that perception serves the end of action rather than truth, it seems that we can still say *something* about the world.

> The distinct outlines which we see in an object, and which give it individuality, are only the design of a certain kind of *influence* that we might exert on a certain point of space: it is the plan of our eventual actions that is sent back to our eyes as though by a mirror, when we see the surfaces and edges of things. Suppress this action, and with it consequently those main directions which by perception are traced out for it in the entanglement of the real, and the individuality of the body is re-absorbed in the universal interaction which, without doubt, is reality itself.
>
> (Bergson 1911:12)

We can see that even though perception is, in a sense, illusory according to Bergson, inasmuch as 'reality itself' is 'the universal interaction' (elsewhere 'the Whole'), it must still reveal to us the seams in the Whole where action is possible. For ourselves, more pluralist than Bergson, we may note that in our account of the illusoriness of colour perception we suggested that the wholesale illusion of colour was an aid to the discrimination of objects; that is, it guided us to the real properties of things. We become acquainted with objects in the round, we might say: assuredly not as bundles of atoms and molecules but as space-filling things of certain shapes and sizes which we *now* know to be such collections of sub-microscopic entities. Such perceptual knowledge, we might surmise, would be of inestimable value to early man and, indeed, would be present in his primate (and probably much earlier) ancestors.

It is not enough to assert, merely in the general interests of the theory of knowledge, that perceptual acquaintance with such things as spatial properties is a fact. It must also be shown that such an assertion is plausible on Darwinian grounds. In this context it might be argued that in stressing the truthfulness of our perception of space (and, by extension, time and perhaps such things as causal relations etc.) I have simply begged the question against the sceptic. If, as I have suggested, colour perception is illusory but serves the interests of the human organism why is the same not true of the perception of space? One thing we might emphasise in reply to this is, what we earlier noted, that perceptual knowledge has not been shown to be incompatible with survival value so that we might have some hopes of a demonstration that at least some features of the perceptual field are not illusory. To this we may add that although we can give a plausible account of how the illusion of colour aids survival it does not seem that the same can be said of the perception of space.

Consider once more the theory that colour vision is an aid to the discrimination of objects. This might first be explained at the 'phenomenal level' by using the example of a multicoloured map where a child learns that Kent is coloured green, say, not because that county actually is green, or because that colour symbolises something, but simply so that it stands out from the surrounding counties (and at this level, of course, the objection will quickly be made that this presupposes that colours exist). But an explanation, still consistent with Darwinism, might be given where colour itself disappears from the account and the organism is considered as an object-discriminating machine which responds to various bundles of light rays in ways which improve its discrimination.

The same kind of reductive account cannot be given of the perception of space and time if only because this account will itself presuppose their existence, e.g. in the explanation given of the perceptual areas of the brain, and because the Darwinian theory cannot be coherently stated unless with reference to space and time. Moreover, it is difficult to see how an active organism such as man could successfully move around in space unless his sense organs gave him an accurate account of spatial properties. To use the language of Smart (1963:85), perception of space (and time) is much less *anthropocentric* than that of colour; and we might speculate that the perception of qualities such as heat is intermediate in this respect.[2] If this intuition is correct then we may conclude, against Thomas Nagel (1974), that we do know something, from the inside as it were, of the perceptual fields of other very active organisms such as bats. We cannot imagine what 'illusions', corresponding to our 'illusions' of colour, the bat's 'sonic radar' subjects it to but the spatiality of the world the bat becomes acquainted with through these illusions would be very familiar indeed.

However, I should add to this that it seems to me that, as one's reductive account digs deeper, the Darwinian account in terms of natural selection etc. ceases to have application and we are dealing only with basic physical forces acting between fundamental particles. Whatever quarks do, they do not compete. Similar remarks apply, I think, to the idea of space–time in general relativity where it might be said that our ordinary concepts of space and time, which are presupposed by Darwinian theory, are illusory (Smart 1963:Ch.7). In either case we have here to do not with the problem raised by Lack but with the different and very difficult problems associated with radical reductionism.

I shall not here take up these difficult problems nor shall I in this chapter face up to the problem of consciousness which I feel is, at this point, a pressing one. As a final remark I will point out that even if it can be shown that Darwinism allows for the correct perception, in our species, of such things as the temporal and spatial characteristics of the world there is still a long way to go before we have shown how our brains, according to that theory, make science possible. Early man, if he thought about the matter at all, would be a naïve realist – objects for him would be just as he saw them, continuous lumps of coloured stuff. We see things as he saw them but we refuse to believe what we see. This implies, paradoxically, the capacity to *criticise* the a priori structure of our perceptual world. Here, perhaps, lies the truth behind Cartesian scepticism and its accompanying dualism. There must be some part of man (which Descartes thought was the immaterial soul) capable of the awareness of, but also of standing back from, the deliverances of the senses. We but open our eyes and a world of coloured objects floods our brains but, as Descartes saw, by inwardly stepping back from it, we can refuse it assent.

'I know I exist. I do not know that my body exists. Therefore I am not my body.' It is easy to laugh at this argument of Descartes's and demonstrate its invalidity by a formally equivalent parody. Yet good insights sometimes beget bad arguments and it may be that Descartes was on to something important. This 'I', which in some direct way knows itself and is in general the knowing subject, cannot be the body because it is able critically to take deliverance of the body's products, sensations. As we are doing our best not to be dualists we must say that there must be some part of the human brain able to do what Descartes's incorporeal mind can do.

This essentially critical capacity, this ability to say 'No' to the deliverances of the senses, and, indeed, to any other bits of a priori wisdom the human brain may throw up and of which we can become aware, is itself bound up with the evolution of language – and the problem of accounting for this evolution on Darwinian lines can be illustrated by Lenneberg's remark that no one knows how long language has existed nor how it is related to brain size (Lenneberg 1967:Ch.6). Nevertheless, language, as again Descartes saw, is a very human thing. I will not argue that the capacity for critical thought lies entirely within language – animals other than man can, in a way, think – yet thought of any sophistication must be indebted to it. Consider, once more, this ability to refuse assent even to what presses most closely upon us. By turning our attention away from the thing, as it presents itself in perception, and to its propositional expression in language, then it is easy to negate this proposition. 'Some things are coloured', we say, looking about the world, but having said it we may look at our expression, in itself, and convert it to 'No things are coloured.' As Whitehead (1978:5) remarked: 'The negative judgement is the peak of mentality.'

Chapter 6
Consciousness and its objects

METAPHYSICS AGAIN

Modern biology, both in its acceptance of the theory of natural selection as the motor of evolution, and in its strong tendency towards ontological reductionism, is materialist in its metaphysics. Organisms, it is assumed, are complex biochemical machines and nothing more; and it is commonly believed that the biochemistry will turn out to be nothing over and above the absolutely fundamental physical particles (the quarks or whatever) in certain complex relations. Life at its evolutionary beginning was but peculiar chemistry and it is difficult to see, on that assumption, how modern evolved life can be anything other than more complicated peculiar chemistry. Humans appear in this story, but only towards the end, in a short footnote, recording a brief redistribution of the fundamental particles and forces.

But a theory must, if it is intellectually viable, account for all the relevant facts. And, as we have seen, when embryonic modern materialism emerged during the Renaissance there were, even then, certain facts concerning the existence of secondary qualities and the existence of consciousness that did not sit easily with it. It has once more become fashionable – particularly among some feminists, I notice – to sneer at the attempts of Descartes and other thinkers to resolve this intellectual tension by resort to dualism, whereby consciousness and the physically lame secondary qualities are tucked away in a non-material mind. But this view at least recognised the problem and, as A.C. Crombie (1964) has argued, was, for its time, scientifically progressive. As it were, it got consciousness and the secondary qualities out of the way while scientists were investigating the physical structure of the world, including the living things it contained. In this respect we might notice that, in supposing the interface between brain and mind to occur in the pineal gland,

Descartes's version of dualist interactionism delayed to the last moment, so to speak, their causal communion, thus leaving open a purely physiological approach to the nervous system.

Whatever is the case for other animals, human beings – at least some of us some of the time – are conscious. It is this fact, and others associated with it, that has, from Descartes on, provided the kernel of the objection to reductive materialism. In an imaginative way the objection was put by the great rationalist philosopher and scientist, Gottfried Leibniz, in his denial that 'perceptions' could be accounted for materialistically:

> We are moreover obliged to confess that *perception* and that which depends on it *cannot be explained mechanically*, that is to say by figures and motions. Suppose that there were a machine so constructed as to produce thought, feeling, and perception, we could imagine it increased in size while retaining the same proportions, so that one could enter as one might a mill. On going inside we should only see the parts impinging upon one another, we should not see anything which would explain a perception.
>
> (Leibniz 1973:para.17)

The great virtue of this example of Leibniz is that it brings out clearly the point that there is nothing (relevantly) more to such a system than a set of parts *mechanically* impinging upon one another. By getting inside it one can just *see* that that is all there is to it. In a way that, as a pioneer of computer logic and manufacture, Leibniz would approve, we can update his example by imagining ourselves wandering around the inside of a giant, complicated computer and finding that, no matter in what detail we are able to trace the connections between its components, nowhere do we stumble across a consciousness within such a 'thinking machine'. Even if it prints out a sound version of the ontological argument for God's existence, it is all logic and no awareness – certainly, we would not find among its busy circuits the feeling of 'a guilt greater than which cannot be conceived' which Professor Malcolm (1960:60) thinks is necessary for a full understanding of that argument. In case we are overawed still by the detailed physics of modern computers with electrons streaming between high-tech transistors, we can take advantage of the point, emphasised by the 'functionalists', that abstract computer logic can be concretely embodied in hardware of many different kinds. Imagine, then, walking around the vast, purely mechanised, digital computer, worked by elephant-power and composed entirely of pulleys, springs and ropes, the remains of which A.K. Dewdney (1988) claims have recently been discovered on the island of Apraphul.[1] No sign there of consciousness will be found among its motions or its creakings. Similarly, if a human brain is just such a machine (where, as in the film *Fantastic Voyage*, we might imagine ourselves shrunk to microbe size and inspecting its inner workings) there seems nothing to explain our 'perceptions'.

THE ARGUMENT DEVELOPED

Leibniz's argument can be developed, and its force appreciated, by looking at a response to a popular attack on reductive materialism. In the formulation of J.B.S. Haldane the argument[2] is as follows:

> if my mental processes are determined wholly by the motion of atoms in my brain I have no reason to suppose that my beliefs are true. They may be sound chemically, but that does not make them sound logically. And hence I have no reason for supposing my brain to be composed of atoms.
>
> (Haldane 1930:209)

According to this argument the materialist hypothesis is self-refuting because, although it might be true, it cannot be *reasonably* stated.[3] If true it implies that no reasons can be given for *any* hypothesis. However, it is not clear whether the force of the argument lies in the supposed determinism of the materialist theory – and in this case, of course, the argument could be reformulated for purely mental or spiritual beings if their successive states are also held to be causally determined – or whether it lies, rather, in the thought that brain substance is the wrong kind of *stuff* of which to say it is right or wrong. Only mind-stuff, on the latter view, is reasonable or reasoning stuff. Possibly, the two theses are run together in that matter, unlike mind, is held to be the wrong kind of stuff because it is subject to causal determination and so unable to *choose* reasons for its arguments.[4]

Whatever the exact nature of the argument we can see that it hinges on the idea that materialism cannot be true because all material processes (including brain processes) are 'blind'.[5] This formulation has the virtue of immediately bringing to mind the objection that we have no reason to accept the premiss that all physical processes are blind because the materialist's contention just is, or should be, that certain complex physical processes, pre-eminently those of the brain, are *not* so disadvantaged. Margaret Knight, for example, has argued that an electronic brain can be trusted

> because we know that its operations proceed in accordance with mathematical laws. To put it differently, mathematical laws and relationships have their counterparts in the functioning of the calculators. Similarly they have their counterparts in the functioning of the human brain.
>
> (Knight 1952:102)

Similarly, Popper has claimed that Haldane's argument, as originally formulated, will not work because computers, besides obeying the laws of physics, 'may nevertheless work in full accordance with the laws of logic' (Popper and Eccles 1977:76).

Now one is tempted to retort that everything in the universe in some sense obeys mathematical and logical laws. The motion of a stone rolling down a mountainside can be caught in an equation and even a kettle of boiling water can be said, unless we are Hegelians or Marxists of a certain kind, to accord with the law of non-contradiction. Clearly, Knight and Popper mean something other than this. What they mean is, roughly, that bits of matter can be brought into such relation with each other that the whole can be regarded as a kind of concrete embodiment of a mathematical or logical calculus. For example, we might say a machine works in accordance with logical laws if its parts in some way 'map' the laws of the propositional calculus (or, we might say, if the machine's components are a possible interpretation of the *abstract* propositional calculus). Thus, whereas in logic textbooks we have to deal with variables that stand in for propositions that can be either true or false, so in our machine we may have switches (or valves) that can be either on or off; and where in logic we have the truth values of the logical relations defined in terms of the truth values of the propositions they relate, in the machine we shall have the final state of one of its parts determined by the way the switches are connected. For example, the logical relation of implication holding between any two propositions, P and Q, is always true except when P is true and Q is false; and this might be interpreted in the appropriate part of the machine as the electric current (or stream of water or whatever) always proceeding except when switch (valve) one is on (open) and switch (valve) two is off (closed). This, of course, would merely be a function of the arrangement of the wires or water pipes.

The question of what it means to say that a machine obeys the laws of logic is a difficult one. In passing we may note that whereas Knight thinks that the notion implies that materialism is a satisfactory theory, Popper, who as we have seen accepts the same notion, believes that it shows, on the contrary, that materialism must be false. The point I wish to make is that, if the account given above is even roughly correct, then *all* we have in a computer, and in the human brain in so far as that also is regarded as a computer, is the concrete embodiment of a logical calculus. As such it is *not* a piece of logic nor, even when we turn on the current, does this embodiment of logic *do* logic. What we have, of course, attached or built into these 'logic machines' are 'recording devices' of various kinds which, for example, flash on a screen the number of times a certain operation occurs. In this last case we may say that the machine has done a sum for us, e.g. $2^{10} \times 1.5^{-6}$, but we only say this because the display on the recording device is such that it saves *us* doing the sum. If there had been a different recording device attached to the same wiring then we might have said that the machine was singing a song or presenting a colourful visual display.

To introduce the notion of a recording device is to draw attention to the fact that the inputs and outputs of calculators can be labelled in various ways. At its simplest this labelling may be merely a matter of calibration as when we have a calculating device consisting of a number of glass cylinders of equal diameter. If cylinder A, which is filled with water to mark three, and cylinder B, filled to mark five, are together emptied into cylinder C then we *may* interpret this as 3 + 5 = 8; and, in this case, the calibrations are simply ways of labelling certain aspects of the initial and final stages of the process so that it saves us doing a calculation. Even this simple device may be used as a multipurpose computer merely by changing the labels. If all the numerals standing for even numbers are rubbed off and replaced with the word 'true', and all those standing for odd numbers replaced with 'false', then we can now do some simple logic. A little thought will show that a combination of 'true' and 'true' or a combination of 'false' and 'false' from A and B will yield the result 'true' in C, while any other combination will yield 'false'. This is the defining condition for the logical relation of *equivalence* which is true if P and Q are both true or if they are both false but false for any other combination; so that we can use our 'machine' to do simple exercises in logic.

Is the device *really* doing mathematics or logic or any other of a myriad things we might suggest merely by changing the labels? In one sense, of course, it is doing none of these things. All it is doing is going through a number of states and ending up with a purely physical result that can be labelled in some way. In this sense we can say that the sum 3 + 3 is not the machine's problem but ours. The machine is not in the least worried about the problem although we should be and, particularly when we consider a more complex computer, make sure it is properly constructed so that *we* get the correct answer. However, people do say that such machines think, calculate, etc. and there is no harm in this as long as we know what we are doing when we say such things and, in particular, if we take note of the fact that what such machines are said to be doing depends on *our* interests not theirs. The nature of our interests is shown, as argued above, by what labels or recording devices we attach to the various bits of machinery that save us the trouble of thinking or calculating.

Now the difference between humans and machines here is shown by the fact that the former are, at least often, authorities for their own case. If someone says that he is thinking about logic rather than mathematics then it will generally, although not always, be rash to dispute this. People very often can be said to know what it is they are doing (irrespective of what anybody else may think about the matter) and this is bound up with the fact that human beings are *conscious*. We can bring this out by looking at Roland Puccetti's argument that it would make sense to say of certain complicated machines that they think (Puccetti 1968).

Puccetti imagines a future when cars are driven not by people but by what he calls Super-Self-Directing Automatic Drivers (Super-SDADs) which are mechanical units attached to the steering wheels, gears, etc. of their respective cars. The Super-SDAD has a model of the town it is driving in in its 'memory banks' and is able to direct the car from any given point in the town to any other point. Besides other bits of sophisticated behaviour, such as being able to respond to traffic lights, the Super-SDAD, as Puccetti puts it, 'learns from experience and is able to solve unforeseen problems' (Puccetti 1968:32). Now should we say of such a machine that it thinks? That we should is shown, Puccetti believes, by the following scene:

> The owner says into the speaker: 'Sixteenth and Vine Streets, please!' They sit back and relax. But at the corner of Fourth and Vine the car comes to a slow stop. The passenger asks, 'What's the matter? Isn't it working? Why doesn't it go on?' The owner replies: 'Wait a minute. *It's thinking*'. After a brief period the automobile changes gear, turns to the left, and proceeds up Fourth Street in a northerly direction. 'You see', comments the owner, 'it's going to try another route to escape that heavy downtown traffic.'
>
> (Puccetti 1968:32)

This shows, says Puccetti, that if the future contains such marvellous machines then the people of that time may correctly say that they think. Suppose he is correct in this (and in my view people will be, and already are, saying of much less complicated machines than this that they think), we can still ask about *what* it is that they are thinking. Again, it seems to be the case that what the machine in the car is thinking about, i.e. what *counts* as being the object of its thinking, is decided *for* it by some sentient being. The situation is the same as for the less complicated machines we considered earlier except now we do not speak simply of labelling inputs and outputs. The machine, while retaining exactly the same brain with the same 'memory banks', the same logic network, etc. (and it is here, I take it, that the *thinking* is supposed to go on)[6] may be wired up to slightly different inputs and outputs and then may be said to be thinking about its moves in a game or thinking about solving a problem in geometry and so on. The same considerations apply to the descriptions Puccetti gives of what the machine is *doing* and of which he says, 'if the above operations are not of thinking, then what are they instances of?' (Puccetti 1968:33). Among the several things he thinks the machine did are: '(1) scanned its memory store for experiences of route conditions at that time and in that place; (2) recollected that here traffic becomes heavy'(Puccetti 1968:33). A change of interest on behalf of the machine's owner, and a slight re-wiring of its input and output, and the above descriptions might become: (1) it scanned its memory store for weather conditions in the various sea-lanes at that time and that place and (2) recollected that here the sea is heavy. Indeed, in order to relieve the boredom of passengers, the Super-SDAD might, at one and the same time, be connected both to the car's controls and to the illuminated panel of a game. In this case, the one logic circuit might be said to be thinking, at the same time, of both quickly reaching St Paul's Cathedral and beating the *Cutty Sark* to Australia.

Puccetti thinks that ' "Thinking" is attributed to the machine in a perfectly neutral way, so far as consciousness is concerned'(32) although he believes that it is an open question whether or not we should regard it as conscious. Now if the Super-SDAD is conscious then we cannot, as we have done, play fast and loose with its thoughts. What it is thinking about is what it is conscious of thinking about. This is true no matter how *we* use its circuits for our own ends. Wire up its input and output as we will then, no matter what purpose of ours it serves, if it is conscious of thinking about sailing the briny seas, then *that* is what it is thinking about. If someone does claim, then, that a particular machine is conscious then we may always ask, 'Of what is it conscious?' or 'What is it thinking about?' where the answer to these questions is not given in terms of our interests. But then there seems to be no answer to these questions because, apart from the problem of discovering just what the consciousness of a particular thing is, it does not seem to make sense to say that such things as logical networks are conscious. They are just bits of matter standing in and doing a job for us.

It is important to see that exactly the same argument applies to the human brain if it also is regarded as something like a logic machine. Suppose the brain of someone is active and that we, as super-scientists, observe the various impulses in one region of it and *interpret* them in a certain way – e.g. we may decide to treat them as the axioms of a logical calculus. By then, by means of a suitable apparatus, observing the brain impulses as they emerge at some other region – and by 'tagging' them in some way – we might find a solution to a complicated logic problem. But the person who owns the brain is not, unless by some extraordinary coincidence, doing logic – they might be thinking about horse racing or enjoying a walk. The tagged brain currents as they surface in a particular part of the brain are, for us, the solution to a problem in logic (or any of a number of things according to how we tag them) but the brain was not solving a logic problem, it was simply moving to an end-state which is somehow connected with, say, walking. As with the Super-SDAD, it does not seem to make sense to say that the logical networks of the brain (i.e. the bits of brain that we *interpret* as bits of logic) are conscious.

That the reply to the anti-materialist argument – that all material processes are blind – has taken the form of pointing out that computers, and by supposition brains, contain material processes that are not blind stems, in particular, from the successes of computer technology. It is tempting, and perhaps correct, to think that in order to do logic (in the sense outlined above) material systems must contain embodiments of logic, i.e. logic networks of some kind; and it is then easy to think that logic networks must underlie or are a number of, if not all, mental activities. As we have seen, such an approach does not touch the problem of consciousness. However, it is as if this problem gets lost because of the overwhelming impression one may have that logic or mathematics really is being done by computers. It is not as if the logic networks are entirely passive affairs, like a diagram with lines joining premises to conclusions, of the structure of an argument. Electricity courses along the connections from point to point – conclusions seem literally to flow from premises. But once the misleading metaphors are isolated it is not difficult to see that although the logic networks of brains and computers are active systems – so that we can say, in a highly metaphorical sense, that logic gets done – their activity is not that of the conscious working out of a problem.

THE SENSITIVE MIND

Someone might agree with at least part of the above argument yet insist that it does not bring down reductive materialism. What it shows, it might be said, with its reference to the way a logic network can be connected to quite different sorts of inputs and outputs, is that it is a mistake to attribute mental qualities to an internal 'brain' – or to such a brain alone. The moral to be drawn is that our account of mental attributes should be pushed in a behaviourist direction with emphasis on what the organism or robot (say) overtly does. Thinking, for example, even conscious thinking if the idea of consciousness is allowed, largely comes down to how the organism behaves.

I have used the word 'largely' in the last sentence because some proponents of the mind–brain identity theory have tried to reach a compromise between a purely 'internalist' theory of mentality and the behaviourist account by espousing a *dispositional* analysis of mental states. D.M. Armstrong (1968), for example, regards mental states as brain states *apt* to produce behaviour of certain kinds. A problem with this, apart from the question of deciding what is *the* potential cause of behaviour, is that it does not make sense to speak in the abstract of 'a state apt to produce so-and-so' – one has to take account of the causal field[7] within which the state lies, which would mean in the concrete case of a human being taking account of the way his brain is connected up so as to produce behaviour of a certain kind. Here, once more, the decision as to whether we have a mental state, and what it is, depends entirely on the manifest behaviour.

The drift towards behaviourism, or near-behaviourism, might seem inevitable unless something can be made of the notion of the non-reducibility of consciousness. It was the fact of consciousness, it will be remembered, that I tried to emphasise by pointing out that people were very often authorities in their own case; and it was this fact, I claimed, that stood firmly in the way of reductive materialism. However, because I was particularly concerned to deal with supposed computer analogies for the human mind I picked on *thinking* to try to make the point; and the trouble with this is that thought, as at least sometimes expressing the 'propositional attitude'[8] of belief, seems peculiarly susceptible to a behaviouristic or dispositional analysis. And consciousness, as the notion appears, for example, in the distinction between conscious and unconscious beliefs, may be similarly handled or, indeed, its existence denied altogether. Colin McGinn has brought this point out by contrasting propositional attitudes with what he calls sensations:

> We are not inclined to suppose that propositional attitudes are, like sensations, defined by a distinctive phenomenology.... In the case of sensations we seem to be taking up the first-person perspective, considering what it is like for the subject of the sensation and ignoring, or regarding as secondary, how a person's sensations are presented to others. In the case of propositional attitudes it seems more natural to accord central importance to how the attitude figures in shaping a person's propensities to act; the dispositional properties of propositional attitudes seem internal to their nature.
> (McGinn 1982:8)

As a matter of fact I think the important matter of consciousness can be brought out in connection with thinking. This is especially so if we do not regard cognition as necessarily involving, revealingly, the purely mechanical, unthinking 'thinking' that Bertrand Russell somewhere complains ruined his brain when he proved the theorems of *Principia Mathematica*; and if, instead, we remind ourselves that thought often enough involves mental imagery or, even, the considered perception of objects, natural or contrived. However, I agree that the case is more easily and obviously made for perception where it is clear that a range of 'items' we are conscious of is a fact too stubborn to conjure away with incantations based on the latest discoveries of physical or physiological science. This is what H.H. Price was getting at in his classic, albeit much criticised and now much ignored, account of what goes on when, being fully alert and in conditions of good lighting, we see a tomato:

> When I see a tomato there is much that I can doubt. I can doubt whether it is a tomato that I am seeing, and not a cleverly painted piece of wax. I can doubt whether there is any material thing there at all. Perhaps, what I took for a tomato was really a reflection: perhaps I am even the victim of some hallucination. One thing however I cannot doubt: that there exists a red patch of a round and somewhat bulgy shape, standing out from a background of other colour patches, and having a certain visual depth, and that this whole field of colour is directly present to my consciousness.
> (Price 1932:3)

Surely Price is right – under such conditions it would be madness to deny 'that this whole field of colour is directly present to my consciousness'. However, such madness has been enthusiastically embraced by modern philosophers drunk with their knowledge of science. Jerry A. Fodor (1981), for instance, in an article on 'The mind–body problem' for the *Scientific American*, manages a Cook's tour through some of the major positions taken on the issue with but scant mention of consciousness and is thus able quickly to dismiss classical dualism whose strength precisely is that it seriously tries to account for this fact. There is, he admits, the difficulty for the view known as functionalism of the 'qualitative content' of perception but this immediately gets directed into a puzzle about causality. Again, there is J.J.C. Smart (1970) who some years ago presented us with the first of a series of desperate ingenuities in support of his materialist faith. Gaze through newly polished spectacles at a whole kilogram of brightly lit tomatoes and still Smart was prepared to deny that you make conscious contact with bulgy, coloured patches. What is it to have an after-image according to Smart?

> When a person says, 'I see a yellowish-orange after-image,' he is saying something like this: '*There is something going on which is like what is going on when* I have my eyes open, am awake, and there is an orange illuminated in good light in front of me, that is, when I really see an orange.'
>
> (Smart 1970:60)

Now, of course, what the ordinary person who talks of seeing a yellowish-orange after-image is saying is nothing at all like the second proposition Smart attributes to them; and if the ordinary person, God bless them, did in wonderment venture the thought 'There is something going on which is like what is going on' etc., this expresses a *further* proposition. The whole point of Smart's account, given a spurious logical rigour by being presented as a 'topic-neutral' *analysis*, is to deny the existence of the obvious, of what have been called the *qualia* of perceived qualities such as colour. One can see a kind of madly logical progression from such a view to the 'eliminative materialism' of Richard Rorty (1970) which regards talk of beliefs, pains, etc. as superstitious 'folk psychology' on a par with the 'beliefs' in witches and things that go bump in the night. In the non-superstitious age of the future one might more properly say 'My C-fibres are firing' than 'I am in pain'. I suppose that if to complain of pain is mere folk psychology then the attempt to eliminate the already non-existent object of the complaint is but folk medicine – if only the word could be spread, the savings for the public health system on pain-killers alone would be enormous.

Regretfully, the obvious truth to which Price directs us in his admonition to gaze at ripe tomatoes in good light can be lost if we allow ourselves to be distracted by misrepresentations or by issues which are beside the point. R.J. Hirst (1959), for example, thinks that Price is *here* arguing that the objects (traditionally called sense-data) which are present to consciousness are things which differ from material things or the surfaces of material things. Price, he thinks, has argued that because, in perception, 'no one material thing is indubitably present', and because a sense-datum (e.g. a coloured patch) is indubitably present, therefore the sense-datum cannot be a material thing (Hirst 1959:32). Now this argument, Hirst claims, depends on the hidden premiss 'What is indubitably present cannot be identical with what is not indubitably present' and he has no difficulty in showing the falsity of such a proposition (32).

I shall not go into the details of Hirst's argument but simply make the point that he has badly misunderstood Price. The latter is not indulging in the Argument from Differential Certainty, as Hirst calls it: rather he is trying to draw to our attention a very important matter of fact that occurs when we perceive something and he is doing this not so much by argument as by inciting us to get into a perceptual situation (or, at least, to imagine ourselves in such a situation) and seeing this matter of fact for ourselves. He is saying get in a position where you can see a tomato in all its glory in bright light etc. Now look at it. Even though you can doubt all sorts of things – e.g. you may think that perhaps it is a wax model rather than a real tomato – you surely cannot *seriously* doubt that present to your consciousness is a red, bulgy patch. The admonition is: look and see.

Again, if we wish to make reference in this way to what is given in consciousness it is important that we do not allow ourselves to be distracted by irrelevancies. In an important article Price has pointed out that one way in which we might formulate a 'sense-datum terminology' which is neutral between ordinary perception, illusion and hallucination is to make use of the idea of *appearing* and 'appearing verbs' such as 'looks'; so that, to use his example, we might say 'There appears to be a pool of water over there which glitters' where this description is neutral as to whether we are dealing with perception, illusion or hallucinations (Price 1964:11). But, as Price says, 'common sense philosophers' have tried to cut the ground from this approach, in so far as it attempts to speak of appearances as *objects*, by their analyses of the concept of appearing. These analyses differ but we may consider just one of them – what Price has dubbed the probability sense of appears. According to this, to say, for example, that the sun looks oval (when it is near the horizon on a misty day) is simply to say 'it is as if the sun were actually oval and I were seeing it to be so' (Price 1964:11).

This kind of analysis may be correct; this may be what we mean when we say 'The sun looks oval'. But if, as these philosophers wish, we stop here then the effect is to turn our attention from important experiential facts and restrict it to questions of language only. In this way we are first distracted, and then hypnotised, by these linguistic analyses. The irony is that common-sense philosophers have, themselves, accused sense-datum theorists, such as Price, of being hypnotised by language. Thus it is alleged that the sense-datum theorist illicitly assumes that, because we can speak of the oval appearance or look of a thing, as well as of a thing's appearing or looking oval, there must be an oval *thing* which is the appearance or look. The truth of the matter is, once more, that Price and thinkers like him base their belief in oval appearances not on matters of grammar but on what they find in experience. Price, in speaking of the person seeing the oval-looking sun, puts the matter as follows:

> His experience is as it would be if he were seeing an actually oval object in the veridical sense of 'see'. But again we have to ask *how* or in what respect his experience is like that. And we shall have to answer that the quality oval is in some sense presented to him. Or we could say that this quality enters his experience (not just into his thoughts or the propositions he entertains). It enters into his experience, or has a place in his visual field, in just the same way as the quality oval itself does when he sees a physically oval-shaped object, an oval-shaped cloud for instance, in normal conditions.
>
> (Price 1964:13–14)

PERCEPTION AS BELIEF

If one wishes to draw attention to this most intimate yet still strange fact of the consciousness of sensible existents then there is not much more one can do than appeal, as Price does, to experience. It is such a basic sort of fact that it is impossible to define it in terms of anything else and, indeed, attempts to do this invariably come to grief. For example, even philosophers who have wished to defend the notion have mixed it up with questions concerning incorrigibility where it is said that when we are directly conscious of a sense-datum we have incorrigible knowledge of at least some of its properties; and this supposedly absolutely incorrigible knowledge is then taken as a defining feature, or a criterion, of the relationship of being directly aware of sense-data. The whole notion of being directly conscious of sense-data (or, as it is often put, of *sensing* sense-data) can then be attacked on the grounds that there is no such thing as incorrigible empirical knowledge. Any empirical proposition can sensibly be doubted.

There is, perhaps, a sense of 'knowledge' which would lead us to say that in being directly aware of a bulgy red patch we *know* that red patch. This would be a meaning of the notion that concerns the intimacy of the contact between the self and that sensible datum of which it is directly aware – this is a bit like the biblical sense of 'know' where a man and a woman sexually know each other. But this sense of 'know', although it may be the one traded on in the argument against the direct awareness of sensory items, is not the one required by that argument. This is indicated by the fact that *what* it is that can be doubted when one contemplates one's sensory field is a *proposition* concerning that field; and this indicates that what we have to do with here is something different from, say, the bulgy red shape that is being sensed, i.e. we have to do with a 'propositional attitude', e.g. a belief that expresses the supposed knowledge. The correct view, then, and the answer to this argument against the possibility of direct awareness, is to distinguish carefully between the relation we have to sense-data when we sense them and the relation we have to sense-data when we have beliefs (expressible in propositions) *about* them. Because I am sensing a red patch it does not follow that I am believing there is a red patch; nor is it impossible, even in the best conditions for sensing, that I have false beliefs about my sense-data. Perhaps, for example, the part of my brain or mind responsible for belief is schizophrenically separated from the part responsible for sensing. As I earlier suggested, under the conditions described by Price it would be madness to deny that we are directly conscious of a bulgy red patch, but madness is not impossible.

In the above argument I have made use of the distinction between perception and belief and the distinction does seem to me self-evident. However, notoriously in the history of philosophy the two have been often run together as when Leibniz described 'perception' as confused thoughts and the British empiricists, going in the opposite direction, regarded thought as merely the association of sensory 'ideas'. Paradoxically, in the interests of supposedly empirical science, the rationalist notion of accounting for perception in terms of belief has been revived. I shall, then, briefly look at this theory in order, once more, to bring out the real character of perception.

D.M. Armstrong (1961:126–7) has put the theory as follows: 'all perception, whether veridical or non-veridical, involves the acquiring of a belief, or an inclination to believe, in an *existential* proposition to the effect, that a certain particular object has a certain property or properties'. Armstrong has put this view to work in several ways. For example, he is able to use it to explain perceptual illusions and hallucinations which come down simply to believing falsely that a situation is such and such or, at least, to having the inclination to believe that it is so. But the metaphysical merit of the theory, as Armstrong sees it, is that it sits nicely with a reductive view of the world. In effect, Armstrong is denying the distinction made earlier between sensations and propositional attitudes because, in his view, sensations are included in the class of propositional attitudes. As we saw, there is an initial plausibility in the claim that a dispositional or behaviouristic account can be given of such propositional attitudes – at the very least the troublesome 'qualia' supposedly encountered in perception are banished from the world.

One critical approach to this view is flatly to deny that in certain instances when something looks so-and-so one does have the belief or the inclination to believe that it is so-and-so. Frank Jackson, for example, tells us that when confronted by the Muller-Lyer illusion, in which two equal lines look unequal, he does *not* believe that they are unequal and, in fact, feels not the least temptation so to think of them; similarly, he says, when looking at what he knows to be a white wall through blue-tinted spectacles, 'I neither believe nor am inclined to believe that the wall is blue' (Jackson 1977:38). The trouble I find with Jackson's assertion that he does not entertain the relevant propositions in these instances is that, although I believe him, I do not see why the belief theorist should. The reason I believe Jackson is that I think that I can directly inspect the qualities given to me in consciousness (the 'looks') and simply see that they are not the same as the beliefs I may or may not entertain about them. For me, the case is no different for 'veridical perception' than for non-veridical: even if the wall is blue and looks blue and I believe it to be blue it is perfectly obvious, to me, that the patch of blue I am aware of is not the same as my belief concerning it. But the point is that the belief theorist does not accept any part of this account of sense objects and their qualities being given in consciousness. If he is right then the question as to the nature of perception is an open one and may yet be answered in terms of the entertaining of beliefs of a certain kind.[9]

It is precisely because Jackson does not bring against the 'analysis' of perception in terms of belief a positive reference to experiential facts that he is not able, at this point,[10] effectively to deal with it. He is, in fact, able to embarrass the account given by Pitcher (1971:34) of a white wall looking blue – where it is said that we have a suppressed inclination to believe that it is blue – but this is largely because of the unfortunate interpretation Pitcher gives of 'inclination to believe' where, as Jackson points out, he confuses it with 'wanting to believe'. There is, of course, no question that, because a wall looks blue, necessarily anybody wants it to look blue. But if we look at the ordinary account of what it is to be a suppressed belief or inclination to believe – which involves referring to a *sometime* belief or inclination to believe (Jackson 1977:39) – then Jackson simply begs the question. He says of the Muller-Lyer illusion and the white wall looking blue,

> there may never have been a belief or inclination to believe: for example, it was not that I was inclined to believe the wall blue when I first put on the glasses and then suppressed the inclination, rather I never had the inclination at all.
>
> (Jackson 1977:39)

But this is merely to *assert* that Pitcher's theory is false. In fact, as far as he has gone, Jackson cannot even handle a belief theory which dealt with non-veridical looks not in terms of suppressed beliefs or inclinations to believe but straightforwardly in terms of actual beliefs. This might hold, for example, that in the case of the white wall looking blue we have the perceptual belief that it is blue and *also* the belief that it is not blue. An account might then be given of why we tend to *act* on one side of the contradiction rather than the other. In the absence of an appeal to experiential facts all his argument amounts to, once more, is the *assertion* that he does not have such beliefs.

In affirming against the belief account of perception certain experiential facts which it does not take account of, it is useful to refer once more to the question asked by Armstrong (see Chapter 5): 'What can somebody who can perceive do, that somebody who cannot perceive cannot do?' One thing such a person can do is contemplate certain objects and their qualities, e.g. bulgy red shapes, as they enter consciousness. Armstrong would deny that such a thing is possible but the answer to this is that perception just as clearly *does* allow the contemplation of such objects as it allows one safely to cross the road.

One feels a certain embarrassment at this response to reductive theories like Armstrong's just because, reflecting the character of the perceptual consciousness it appeals to, it is so short and direct. It is true that there are ways of making the appeal to the given look more complicated but, in the end, they come down to the same simple insight. This is the case, for example, with an argument used by R.G. Swinburne (1986) against Armstrong's view that we can account for the evident differences between the senses by making reference to the particular sense organs by which we obtain perceptual beliefs. We can imagine, says Swinburne, someone whose optic nerves are connected to the auditory centres of his brain so that when he looks at coloured objects he hears notes of various kinds.

> He would then be able to acquire beliefs (true and justified) about the colours of objects, by the operation of his eyes. But the character of his sensations which mediate these beliefs would be entirely different from the character of our sensations which mediate our beliefs about colours – which difference we may naturally express by saying that he has no visual sensations, whereas we do. Although he acquires beliefs about them by the operation of his eyes, he does not *see* the colours.
>
> (Swinburne 1986:35)

The virtue of Swinburne's imaginative thought-experiment is that it forces one to contemplate the qualitative differences- and therefore the actual experienced data, themselves – when one sees something as against hearing a sound. But the intuition underlying the story just is, once more, the appeal to evident experience. Armstrong would, I think, here just grit his teeth, dig his toes in and, in the interests of what he thinks science tells us, carry on determinedly denying the obvious. However, even he, in the earliest formulation of his belief theory of perception, revealingly made concessions to the idea of directly perceived sensory items when he criticised the rival reductive theory of J.J.C. Smart. Imagine, says Armstrong in the course of that criticism, that colours are suddenly wiped from the world and replaced by brand new qualities that, in the relations they bear to each other, 'map' the relations between colours (Armstrong 1961:180). We can, I think, make sense of Armstrong's fantasy but only on the assumption of the fact of direct awareness. Consider the colour *green* and the new 'colour' *greeb*. How, without making the assumption of direct awareness, can we make sense of saying that 'The leaf is green' and 'The leaf is greeb' express different propositions? It cannot be argued that the difference between green and greeb is established by the relations they bear to other members of the ranges of qualities to which they belong because, by hypothesis, these relations are identical. Any difference between the meaning of 'The leaf is green' and 'The leaf is greeb' must depend on the qualities green and greeb to which their names point; and the names can do the pointing only if we are in touch with examples of the qualities.

If colours were suddenly wiped from the surfaces of things and replaced by this new range of qualities then (if we remember the good old days) we would be in possession of knowledge concerning the relations between the new and old ranges. Indeed, if we were to come across a box of magic paints in which colour had been replaced in this way then we could paint a scene in which green leaves lie side by side with greeb ones; and we could then discover, by direct inspection, the relations which green and greeb bear to each other. But this, once more, seems to imply that we are acquainted with these qualities in their own right. The relations exist because of the nature of these qualities and it is plausible to say that we can come to know the relations only if we know these natures. If this be denied by arguing, once more, that our knowledge of green and greeb would be simply that they lie as terms at the opposite end of a number of relations, then it is difficult to explain why we cannot, in our imaginations, *construct* the relevant relations and so imagine what a quite new series of 'colours' is like. And this we plainly cannot do. I suggest that why it is so plain that we cannot do this, and why we would not spend more than a few seconds contemplating the endeavour, just is because we *know* that knowledge of the relations between such qualities is gained only if we are acquainted with these qualities. If this were not the case then there is no reason why, in principle, we could not give detailed accounts of the 'colours' existing in other, possible universes – or, indeed, why we should not be able to give detailed descriptions of what the visual world of the honey bee might be like.

I shall conclude this section by making this appeal to anyone seriously contemplating the belief theory of perception: do you really think, to take the case of visual perception, that any proposed set of beliefs could match the richness of experience when you see something? Suppose a wiggly line is drawn on a piece of paper. Just what are the propositions the percipients are supposed to entertain when they look at it? Is it merely, 'There is an x such that x is a line and x is wiggly'? This does not seem sufficient – there is much more than that presented to consciousness. Well, is it 'There is an x and x is a line and x is black and x curves up at the beginning and then reaches a maximum from which it descends again . . . '? As a matter of fact, I think that whatever list of propositions is put forward the visual scene escapes it – and I can just *see* that a particular list of propositions is insufficient by inspecting a *line* in my visual field and not by comparing it with some longer *list* – but the point is that for the belief theory to do justice merely to inspecting a wiggly line seems to require a massive number of propositions. If this is true for looking at a line then just how long a list of propositions would be required to catch the awareness of a tree in autumn with its leaves, some green and some gold, shimmering in the wind?

THE PERCEIVING SELF

It is important in bringing forward the fact of consciousness to falsify the theory of reductive materialism that we are clear about the complex nature of this fact. There is, first, the question of the contents of consciousness, of *what* we are aware, where these may be such items as pains, coloured patches, etc. and which themselves are impossible to reconcile with the reductive account. But, second, there is also the fact that these objects do stand in that most peculiar of *relations* to selves that we call consciousness and this, itself, consistently escapes the net of relationships we are presented with in neurophysiology.

The matter is confused by those thinkers who see the difficulty the fact of consciousness raises for the usual neurophysiological account of humans but who then reduce it to the first problem only, of accounting for the objects of consciousness. Thus the physiologist Sperry has argued that a full account of the brain must take account of consciousness as a fully existent, causally potent, emergent 'property' of the higher nervous regions; yet when he comes to give examples of this property they are all of what would normally be taken to be objects of consciousness in themselves and without reference to the relation they bear to the subject of consciousness.

> the primary thesis . . . may be taken to imply something like the following: As we look around the room at different objects in various shapes, shades and colours, the colours and shapes we experience, along with any associated smells and sounds, are not really out where they seem to be. They are not part of the physical qualities of the outside objects but, instead, like hallucinations or the sensations from an amputated phantom limb, they are entirely inside the brain itself. The perceived colours and sounds, etc. exist within the brain

not as epiphenomena, but as real properties of the brain process. When the brain adjusts to these perceived colours and sounds, the adjustment is made not merely to an array of neural excitations correlated with the colours and sounds but to the colours and sounds themselves.

(Sperry 1969:535–536)

For Sperry, the problem of fitting consciousness into an account of the brain comes down merely to giving an account of the causal interactions of 'sensations' among themselves and with the rest of the neural network; and these 'sensations' are, themselves, taken as emergent *properties* of the brain. Even though Sperry's model of the brain contains more than the usual reductive account – and to that extent deserves praise in taking account of certain facts ignored or explained away by the reductionist[11] – it is still, in a sense, mechanistic in that it is concerned only with the interactions of bits of brain-stuff and leaves out of the picture the more basic fact of what has been called the 'shining forth' to the self in consciousness of these emergent properties of the brain.

It should perhaps be said that nothing I have so far argued necessarily commits me to the dualist view whereby it is supposed that a non-material, purely spiritual substance, the self or mind, somehow 'occupies' the material body. Such a theory might seem more likely when we take into account the fact of consciousness but, nevertheless, we might still toy with the idea that the self as that which is conscious of pains etc. is a material thing or system. However, even if this latter suggestion is taken up it should be emphasised that reductive materialism still falls before it. Suppose, for example, one were to postulate the existence in the brain, of a special 'organ of consciousness'. How, if the mechanics or the chemistry or the physics of this organ are also given (and there is not merely the vague supposition of such an organ without any idea at all of how its function is performed), could this in any way touch our problem? One might explain that the nerve cells from the various sensory areas of the brain send their filaments to this organ of consciousness, whose own cells react in special ways to the incoming electrical currents, but at the end of the day consciousness once more slips the net and all one would have is an account of something that in some respects might *simulate* a conscious being.

It would have to be said that the brain, besides possessing the ordinary physical properties postulated by the physicist, *also* has the *extra* property whereby it is able to enter into the relation of being conscious of certain things. In fact, something like this was suggested by Joseph Priestley who argued

> that the powers of sensation or perception and thought, as belonging to man, have never been found but in conjunction with a certain organised system of matter; and therefore, that those powers necessarily exist in, and depend upon, such a system.
>
> (Priestley 1965:113)

This hypothesis Priestley recommends as the simplest, to be favoured above the idea of an immaterial mind, 'till it can be shown that these powers are incompatible with other known properties of the same [material] substance; and for this I see no sort of pretence' (113). Whatever the merits of Priestley's suggestion it is clear that it is not compatible with what are usually put forward as supposedly science-based reductionist theories. This illustrates the point that in discussing reductionist theories one should be careful of speaking too generally and should specify just what kind of theory is being considered. Of course, if one attributes mental qualities to the fundamental particles, themselves, after the manner of Whitehead or Teilhard de Chardin, then, at least on the face of it, there seems no reason why one should not have a peculiar reductionist theory which includes the mental. But this is not the kind of reductionism which is under discussion.

Part III
Natural theology

Chapter 7
Biology and cosmology

'THE FITNESS OF THE ENVIRONMENT'

Not all is metaphysically rosy in the garden of biological theory. As we have seen, the impetus given to reductionist theories by Darwinism can be turned back on the latter view. There is no such thing as a *force* of natural selection – even though biologists often speak as if there is one – and the only real forces are those between the fundamental particles, no matter in what complex configurations they participate. We have also observed that, even in taking the theory of natural selection at face-value, problems emerge concerning the possibility of knowledge and these, when connected with the obvious fact of the consciousness of human beings, are an embarrassment for both Darwinism and reductive materialism.

The possibility of a natural theology, which we thought we had firmly disposed of in our first chapter, re-emerges. There are here splendid opportunities for those seekers after watery mysteries who eagerly seize upon the bare fact of logical tensions within science in order to assail us with their various ill-thought-out views. But it *is* the case that the fact of human consciousness cries out for an explanation and does not receive it within the main body of biological science – unless, indeed, vague gestures towards ideas of emergence count as such. One can, then, have some sympathy for those thinkers who invoke the special actions of a god to explain the coming into existence of consciousness within the course of evolution or of embryonic development;[1] and on their behalf we might answer to the sneer that on this hypothesis we have to do with a mere 'god of the gaps' that we have here not a mere crack to be papered over but a yawning chasm. Recent times, however, have seen the attempt to revive a full-blown version of the argument from design and it is to this attempt, which brings together both biological and the most abstruse cosmological considerations, that I wish now to turn my attention.

Some years ago the physiologist L.J. Henderson (1913) investigated the complex conditions necessary for life in his book *The Fitness of the Environment*. In this work, taking advantage of the science of his time, Henderson showed how the possibility of the evolution of living things depended, in a detailed way, on the special properties of such things as the water molecule and the carbon atom. Henderson did not, himself, make use of these fascinating facts to base an argument for God's existence – although he was sympathetic to natural theology as keeping alive genuinely *scientific* issues that would otherwise be ignored – but it is by appealing to such considerations, and tying them in with the latest theories in cosmology, that the modern design argument has been set going.

Before looking at this argument in more detail I wish to set aside, perhaps more brusquely than it deserves, an allegedly a priori reason for believing 'that it is rather improbable that a universe chosen at random would be suited to intelligent life' (Forrest 1982:3–4). Peter Forrest gives it as follows:

> Simplicity is *a priori* more probable than complexity; and the greater the complexity the lower the probability. (If that were not so, it would be irrational to believe the simplest theory compatible with the data.) Now, although science continually shows us that reality is simpler than we might have thought, it is nonetheless the case that the laws of chemistry and the environments required for life are complex ones. *A priori*, it is much more probable that a universe would not contain this sort of complexity than that it would. Consequently, it is *a priori* improbable that a universe chosen at random would be suited to intelligent life.
>
> (Forrest 1982:4)

I lack Forrest's confidence in assigning a priori relative probabilities to more or less complex *universes*. However, let us agree with him that it *is* rational 'to believe the simplest theory compatible with the data' and then note the following problem. He admits that science has shown that 'reality is simpler than we might have thought' while still maintaining that the universe is improbably complex. Well, what are we to make of that? I take it that in believing that science has shown us that the universe is a bit more simple than appears at first sight Forrest is a realist about science, that he thinks science shows in what respects reality has this simplicity. That is, Forrest must believe that science shows us something of the universe as it really is – its basic laws and so forth. Now if this is so then considerations of simplicity can take us no further. This is because any further account, e.g. in terms of God, of these actually existing basic laws would *add to* the complexity of the universe in the sense that, for example, the system God plus world is more complex (and therefore more improbable) than the world taken in itself. I shall argue later that what in fact often happens with theistic explanations is that talk of the basic laws of the universe, or of the real causal properties of finite things, is a smoke-screen and all, or nearly all, real activity is taken as belonging to God alone. Simplicity is supposedly gained but at the high cost of disposing of what it is that the theist set out to explain, the razor wielded being Sweeney Todd's rather than Occam's.

A prioristic estimations of probability aside, it remains true that intelligent life exists and that the universe seems peculiarly suited to its development. The universe began, we are told, in an immensely hot big bang fifteen thousand million or so years ago and during its expansion has cooled and congealed into galaxies of stars. It is arguable that solar systems are essential if the conditions for life are to be met; but why is it that ordinary matter, itself necessary for the formation of stars and planets, exists at all? Why is it that there is some strange 'flaw' in what physicists call 'CP (charge-parity) symmetry' so that the elementary particles of matter were not destroyed by their antiparticles, leaving a universe of light but no substance? Robert K. Adair has put the matter as follows:

> It seems that, at a time somewhere before the first millionth of a second after the universe was born in the fiery ball known as the big bang, matter and antimatter probably existed in equal amounts. There were almost exactly equal numbers of particles and antiparticles, all in thermodynamic equilibrium under conditions of enormous pressure and temperature.... Then, as the universe expanded and cooled, most of the particles found their corresponding antiparticles and the pairs annihilated each other. If the CP symmetry were exact, only the very few particles and antiparticles that had by chance not found annihilation partners would be left. But the symmetry was slightly flawed, and an excess of about one in a billion protons and one in a billion electrons survived to form, in the fullness of time, galaxies, stars, planets and ourselves.
>
> (Adair 1988:30)

We exist today because the particles of matter of which our bodies are made could not find partners in the annihilation dance of thousands of millions of years ago. According to Adair we must postulate the existence of a weak or very weak force that accounts for the 'violation' of CP symmetry but, whatever the physical explanation, it is beginning to look as if somehow things had been *arranged* so that the present complex universe of matter eventuated.

The above is but one example of a whole series of coincidences, involving basic physics, which have to be met before the evolution of life is possible. It is because of the delicate balance of basic physical forces that the universe expands at just the rate to allow the formation of planetary systems suitable for life. Slightly different values of these forces and the universe would have collapsed quickly and lifelessly back into its singularity or, alternatively, expanded speedily into a barren homogeneity. If certain nuclear constants were a bit different then the carbon atom, essential to the sort of life we know, would not have been 'cooked up' in the interiors of stars or, if formed, would lack its amazing capacity for almost limitless combination. The list of finely balanced physical conditions necessary for conscious life to evolve is long and impressive.[2] The question is, What to make of it all?

ANTHROPIC ANSWERS

What some thinkers make of it all is that, literally, someone did make it all, i.e. that some god or gods designed and put the universe together. This hypothesis I shall discuss in some detail later but, before doing so, I shall examine an attempt to avoid the issue. It is sometimes claimed that there is nothing surprising in the observed fact that the universe is orderly, fit for the development of intelligent life and so on because if it were not there would not *be* observers making these observations. Taken as a supposed answer to the design theory, and not merely as a resigned acceptance of the complex structure of the world, this gets us nowhere. All it does is repeat the fact that there is a complicated world containing observers.

If the fact that sentient beings, e.g. humans, exist really were taken as an *explanation* of the existence of the universe then the explanation would, as J.J.C. Smart (1987:113) puts it, be 'back to front'. This reply should be obvious but may not be so because of any of a number of reasons. First, sometimes arguments of the type under consideration come with a quantity of distracting scientific detail which serves to divert attention from their peculiarly inverted structure. This might be the case, for example, with G.J. Whitrow's attempt to demonstrate that the three-dimensionality of space 'is the unique natural concomitant of certain other contingent characteristics associated with the higher forms of terrestrial life, in particular of Man, *the formulator of the problem*' (Whitrow 1955–6:31) because three dimensions are required for the development of a complex nervous system.[3] Second, arguments of this kind are often logically valid, or can be easily made so, and this may confusingly lead to the belief that we therefore have a *causal explanation*.[4]

Third, in recent times there has been much fuss made of a so-called cosmological 'anthropic principle' which can, with care, be used to reach interesting conclusions but is easily confused, once more, with causal explanation. The anthropic principle, which unfortunately now names a potage of disparate things,[5] was originally formulated by Brandon Carter (1974:291) in a so-called weak form, as follows: 'What we can expect to observe must be restricted by the conditions necessary for our presence as observers.' Stated thus the principle might guide research in several different ways. It might, for example, inspire the search for those conditions which are explanatory of our existence as observers – and here the case is logically no different, unless we are predisposed to idealism, to other instances, e.g. galaxies, whose conditions we might be led to seek. On the other hand we might be interested more in the epistemological side of the anthropic principle and emphasise the selectivity of our observations. This again may lead to interesting conclusions, e.g. as to why we observe the universe to be as big as it is, which depend upon acknowledging our necessarily special, privileged spatio-temporal position in the universe. There is, in fact, a powerful critical use of the epistemological side of the principle which, at the same time, is peculiarly open to ontological abuse. Thus an effective criticism has been made of an argument of Dirac which concludes that the universal gravitational 'constant' is, in fact, decreasing. In essence Dirac was puzzled by what seemed a strange 'coincidence' between the age of the universe, measured in the 'natural' units of the time light takes to cross a nuclear distance, and the ratio between the gravitational and electromagnetic forces. Both yield enormous numbers of magnitude 10^{40}. Dirac hypothesised that the numbers were, in fact, equal and, in order to retain the equality as the age of the universe increased, suggested that gravitation decreased in strength with time. Against this the anthropic principle has been used to argue that intelligent, carbon-based organisms are bound to live at a time when the age of the universe is of the same magnitude as the ratio of gravitational to electromagnetic forces.[6] There are arguments, based on such considerations as the stellar synthesis of the heavier elements, to show that the time required for the evolution of human-like intelligence must be of the order of magnitude of the time a star like the sun remains on the main-sequence.[7] Paul Davies, whose account of the issues involved I have here been following, brings the argument to its conclusion:[8]

> Now the lifetime of a star can be estimated from the theory of stellar structure. It depends both on the strength of gravity, which holds the star together, and the strength of electromagnetic forces which controls how efficiently energy is transported through the star and radiated into space. The details are complicated, but when they are worked out, it turns out that the lifetime of a typical star, in natural subatomic units, is precisely the ratio of the strengths of the two forces – 10^{14} – give or take a factor of ten or so. The conclusion is that *whatever* number this ratio might have been, intelligent creatures would only be around to wonder about it when the universe had existed for roughly this same number of subatomic time units.
>
> (Davies 1980:172)

Such arguments can be valuable in sorting out what coincidences of values are *merely* that from those that cry out for a more profound explanation, be that physical, metaphysical or whatever. Also, they may guide speculation in a more substantive manner as in Brandon Carter's suggestion that the coincidence of the lengths of time for biological evolution and solar stability implies that evolution on Earth has been rather fast – with the further implication that intelligent life is rare within the universe (Carter 1983). However, the danger is that, because, in some sense, the human observer is brought in in the explanation of these large-number coincidences, the observer is then also, by a wholly illicit extrapolation, brought in to 'explain' the physically more basic fine-tuning of constants that, in fact, really explains the existence of knowing subjects.[9] And all this is reinforced by the tendency, already rampant among quantum physicists, to lapse into idealism in their explanations of events on the atomic level.[10]

THE JOKER IN THE PACK

Among those thinkers who do not lapse into these strange parodies of Kantianism or theism, who believe it is physics that explains physicists and not vice versa, there are some who appeal to the notion that there are many universes in order to explain why it is we inhabit this one. There is still the appeal to a 'selection effect' – that *of course* we find ourselves as thinkers and observers in a universe fitted to produce thinkers and observers – but there is now no suggestion that somehow it is us observers who do the selecting. It is universes that 'select' in that some, among the perhaps infinite number of them, are physically fit for the evolution of sentient life. Naturally enough we find ourselves in one of them.

Stated thus bluntly, with no underlying account of why the individual separate universes exist, the 'world-ensemble' theory provides no explanatory comfort whatsoever. The situation is this. We have our own universe with planets occasionally, if not always, producing life; and, to escape explaining this fact, we surround it with a host of other universes, most limp and halting efforts and some, perhaps, bursting at the seams with creatures. But where is the comfort in such numbers? The logical situation is unchanged – *our* universe, the one that begat and nourished us, is put together with as unlikely a set of fine-tuned physical values whether it exists in isolation or lost in a dense scatter of worlds. So, then, by itself or surrounded by others, the existence of our universe still cries out for explanation.

The error here is getting us to think of our universe as just one card in a vast pack of cards and thus diverting our attention from the mystery of its existence to the contemplation of the probability of drawing it at random. And in case we are overawed still by such a slim chance we are further told that this already existing universe really chooses us. Only those who pick the joker live to tell the tale. If we were able, *à la* Forrest, to assign chances to the existence of universes then we might say that the probability of our one existing, just like that with no further cause assigned, is so-and-so (with 'so-and-so' presumably being some very low number). This is a quite different matter to assigning a probability to choosing at random our universe, taken as existing, from a cosmic bag of them. If there is only one universe – this one – then the probability of picking on it is one; if there is a very large number of universes, perhaps an infinity, then one would be unwise to risk one's shirt on the gamble. But whatever the probability of finding our world among the one or the many, the probability of our world existing at all takes on its own value irrespective of whatever else independently exists. There is, then, something logically odd in conjuring up a dust of universes large and varied enough to ensure at least one world carries sentient life and we are still left with the problem of accounting for the strange fact that that is precisely what our world does.[11] Natural theology reinstates its claims.

Chapter 8
From world to God

DESIGN

So 'fit' is the universe for the evolution of life and intelligent mind that several modern thinkers – philosophers, physicists and others – have revived the ancient argument from design for God's existence and it is perhaps little wonder that Barrow and Tipler (1986) devote a long chapter to its history in their massive book *The Anthropic Principle*. The basic argument is as follows. There are many examples of order in the world which are brought about by the activities of minds, i.e. human minds. There is also the fact of the general orderliness of the universe as a whole. Therefore the orderliness of the whole universe (apart from the bits produced by human and other finite minds) is brought about by the mind of a god.

The argument can then be embellished in various ways by producing examples of the universe's 'design', such as those stubbornly fine-tuned 'coincidences' the anthropic principle is concerned with. It can also be developed by inferring what characters the god must have from the supposedly awesome fact that he put the whole universe together – and so 'he' is commonly said to be enormously powerful, knowledgeable and so forth. He is also commonly said to be a non-embodied mind because, among other reasons that might be held for this view, he is supposed to have brought about everything that is material or, at least, brought law to the material. I find myself doubly impressed here. I am mightily impressed by the facts and arguments presented to us by the cosmologists – although retaining a residual scepticism concerning how much we can really be said to know about 'the whole universe' – but I am also greatly moved by the immense logical difficulties involved in the argument from design and the god of its conclusion. I shall try to bring out first the problems associated with the analogy drawn between the minds of humans and that of God[1] and then, second, the difficulty of giving a coherent account of the relation God has to the world. These two issues, in fact, turn out to be closely connected.

AN EMBODIED GOD?

It has been commonly assumed, or asserted, that for the argument from design to have much force one must accept a dualist account of the nature of men and women – that is, one must hold that humans consist of a non-material mind interacting with a material body. As Peter Forrest (1982:6) puts it, on the assumption of dualism 'it is not antecedently implausible that gods exist. For we already have in our theory entities very like gods, namely our own non-material "parts".' I think that there is something to this contention; even so, as we shall see, the analogy between God and man ultimately breaks down. However, it has recently been contended *from the side of theism* that we should not accept a dualist account of either humans or God – all are essentially embodied persons. We can look at this in the context of a supposed reduction to absurdity of the design argument which attempts to show that the conclusion of that argument should be that God has a body just like man's. This comes out clearly in David Hume's *Dialogues Concerning Natural Religion* where the theist, Cleanthes, has put the argument as follows:

> Look around the world: contemplate the whole and every part of it; you will find it to be nothing but one great machine, subdivided into an infinite number of lesser machines, which again admit of subdivisions, to a degree beyond what human senses and facilities can trace and explain. All these various machines, and even their most minute parts, are adjusted to each other with an accuracy, which ravishes into admiration all men, who have ever contemplated them. The curious adapting of means to ends, throughout all nature, resembles exactly, though it much exceeds, the productions of human contrivance; of human design, thought, wisdom, and intelligence. Since therefore the effects resemble each other, we are led to infer, by all the rules of analogy, that the Author of nature is somewhat similar to the mind of man; though possessed of much larger faculties, proportional to the grandeur of the work which he has executed. By this argument *a posteriori*, and by this argument alone, do we prove at once the existence of a Deity, and his similarity to human mind and intelligence.
>
> (Hume 1962:143)

As presented by Cleanthes the argument is by analogy so let us look at it in this light. Comparing the order of the universe to the works wrought by humans 'we are led to infer', says Cleanthes, '*by all the rules of analogy*, that the Author of nature is somewhat similar to the mind of man' (my emphasis). It is, apparently, by making use of these 'rules of analogy' that, in the same dialogue, the sceptic, Philo, is able to show just how little we can infer concerning the attributes of the 'Author of nature', not even that he or it is an *author* rather than some kind of unknown cause of the world. Suppose we do allow 'that the universe, sometime, arose from something like design', as Philo puts it, we have no means of deciding what characters the designer possesses except by resort to 'the utmost licence of fancy and hypothesis' (Hume 1962:169). 'And why not become a perfect anthropomorphite?' Philo asks. 'Why not assert the Deity or Deities to be corporeal, and to have eyes, a nose, mouth, ears, etc.?' (168).

A recent attempt to answer Philo has been made by R.G. Swinburne, a modern Cleanthes as D.Z. Phillips (1985:91) has aptly described him, but one who, as a distinguished proponent of inductive logic, would be expected to be conversant with 'all the rules of analogy'. Let us take up the argument, far advanced, at the point where Swinburne has produced an argument for mind–body dualism for the case of humans. Humans are essentially minds or spirits but the human condition is such that minds are in interaction with their bodies ('soul-cases' as nineteenth-century English slang revealingly called them). The ontological analogy with humans then easily proceeds: God, likewise, is a spirit. Philo, argues Swinburne, (1972:199) is guilty of the 'supersimilarity fallacy'[2] in suggesting that God is corporeal; he has not taken account of the differences as well as the similarities in comparing the human and the divine situations. God being responsible for the order of the whole physical universe, apart from those tiny bits that are the concern of embodied persons, there is, as it were, no room for his body.

If we accept the dualist account of human persons then we might think Swinburne's response is well taken. But suppose, for whatever reason, we are not happy with dualism, that we think persons are essentially embodied, yet we still wish to retain the analogy between God and man – could we not, without falling into the supersimilarity fallacy, maintain that God has a body? Could we not make sense of the view that the universe is God's body without then feeling committed to directing our finest instruments to the search for his brain or his arms and legs? This position has recently been taken by Grace M. Jantzen who wishes to eschew dualism while, at the same time, retaining as much as possible of the conceptual apparatus of traditional Christian theism:

> a whole new creative possibility is opened for theology when a holistic model of human personhood is explored. If human personhood and particularly the relationship between the mental and the physical in human persons is still to provide an analogy for the relationship between God and the world, as I shall suggest it does, the analogy will no longer point towards a God existing independently of the world and interacting with it like a majesty from on high, because we can no longer think of our souls, the analogate, as being essentially different from our bodies and ruling over them. Rather, the relationship between God and the world will be much more intimate, and his attributes of power and knowledge will not be forces externally applied, as we shall see.[3]
>
> (Jantzen 1984:9)

Jantzen is aware that the initial, instinctive reaction to her view is likely to be hostile but reminds us that here our instincts are, in fact, steeped in a dualist philosophical tradition. She therefore asks for, and is entitled to get, a fair hearing for her revisionist theology.

Something that immediately strikes me about her espousal of this down to cosmos deity is the lack of interest she shows in the details of God's neuroanatomy. We can, I think, sympathise with her rejection, as silly, of the response that would have us search for God's liver or limbs, but the issue is more pressing when we are told that God has a mind, that he is a thinking, perceiving, willing being. For, despite all the difficulties associated with the mind–body problem, it remains the fact, fully acknowledged by Jantzen, that in us humans brains are necessary for behaviour, that a complex nervous system is a condition of mentality. Yet when she comes up against this problem she simply first of all dismisses the idea of God's brain on theological grounds – which need not detain us – and then, second, levels the charge of 'bad philosophy' against those who would pursue this line of thought:

> It does not follow that brain is *necessary* for mind: conceivably there are things without brains which nevertheless are (or could become) conscious. Would we be prepared, for instance, to rule out *a priori* the possibility of developing robots which acquired consciousness? Or to say that if there is conscious life on other planets it *must* be of the same organic structure as our own? Unless we have *defined* mental activity as activity dependent upon a brain of specific

construction, there seems no possible way that we could know in advance that things made of very different hard- or soft-ware from ourselves could not have consciousness and other mental abilities.

(Jantzen 1984:69–70)

This is rather too quick. In the above passage Jantzen is trying to counter an argument of Edgar Wilson (1979:56) who, after considering the correlation found between intelligence and brain size and complexity, concluded that 'This strongly suggests that brain structure is a necessary condition . . . for mind.' Now if we regard Wilson as maintaining that a necessary condition for mind is a brain of the organic type evolved on Earth, then Jantzen's argument has some force. Robots might one day be conscious and perhaps the crewmen of flying saucers already are. But this gets us nowhere towards showing that a complex brain or nervous system – or at least a complex something-or-other – is not a necessary condition for mind; and, in fact, everything we know empirically about the dependence of mind upon matter leads to the conclusion, tacitly admitted by Jantzen in her reference to hard-ware and soft-ware, that mind is always embedded in a complicated material structure. Think up the most bizarre conscious creatures possible short of God – wise nuclear plasma organisms, perhaps, living at the centre of the sun – then, in order to make your story in the least bit credible, you must tell us, or allow us to assume, that they have their own nervous systems adapted to their material circumstances. By what miracle, then, is God alone exempt from this otherwise quite general condition?

Intertwined with the fallacious argument that because this or that kind of complex nervous system is not necessary for consciousness therefore none at all is, is a different strand of thought which somehow, by osmosis, lends its seductive subtlety to its mate. This now concerns the *meaning* of concepts involving consciousness as is shown by Jantzen's eager dismissal, as 'nothing more than an empirical generalization' (Jantzen 1984:69), of the correlation of brains and minds; and by her protest that the issue is not to be decided on a priori grounds or by definition. The argument is, I take it, that whether or not a complicated nervous system is empirically necessary for mind it is not a *logically* necessary condition. Minds, then, are necessarily embodied (I shall not stop to enquire as to the kind of necessity involved here) but, even so, we can imagine the minded body as brainless and, as a matter of fact, that is the condition of God's presently massive organism. Jantzen's god is thought of in the image of the Straw Man of *The Wizard of Oz*.

People are what you meet. Jantzen's approving reference to Antony Flew's slogan (Flew 1967:12) suggests she thinks that the necessity of body for mind can be shown by some sort of 'conceptual analysis' although she is not explicit about this. If this is so then we should note that such analyses, in stressing the conceptual irrelevance of neurophysiology for mental concepts, tend in a behaviouristic direction; and we might then raise questions, in the spirit of that same philosophical tradition, concerning the meaningfulness of thinking of the *universe* as a body. What sense is there to the idea of a body that has no environment in which to display itself? And how do we meet this embodied person, God? Surely not as astronomers gazing through telescopes or biologists peering through microscopes. In the still of the night, perhaps, or in the calm meadows of England or the wild bush of Australia? But this is like saying you have met the woman whose lock of hair you chance upon hidden in a book or that you are acquainted with the person whose liver cells you are examining as a pathologist.

I shall not pursue this line of criticism further – partly because I think so-called conceptual or logical analysis often resembles free-association more than logical enquiry – but, instead, shall look more closely at the 'mere' empirical generalisation concerning mind–brain correlation that, supposedly, has the mind of God as an exception to the rule. According to Jantzen, like us God perceives and thinks and acts – only more so. Take perception: the way God perceives the universe is said to be like the way we sense states of our bodies, from the inside as it were. God, we might say, feels the entire universe as we feel the aches in our bones. But now, unlike the human story of our pains and vertigoes and so on, the tale of God's feelings is a mere history with no depth of physiological explanation possible. This is puzzling enough in its own right. We feel, some of us, that if the universe really is God's body then there must be something about the 'go' of it that explains how God senses it; and if there is no physical explanation for God's sensations, nothing corresponding to nerve conduits or association centres, then, in desperation, we might seek explanatory relief in dualism. There being nothing about the physical universe to explain its perception of itself – in the way that, for example, Professor Armstrong's mind-body identity theory explains how the human organism perceives itself – it is natural to seek the explanatory 'mechanism' in something wholly other than the universe. The idea then naturally emerges of God as an immaterial spirit standing over and above the universe he sightlessly watches and this notion at least seems to have explanatory virtues that incantatory appeals to 'holism' (Jantzen 1984:9) conspicuously lack.

It is, I think, fair to say that Jantzen's concept of an embodied god is dualist to the extent, at least, that it involves an absolute experiencing finding satisfaction in the eminently experienceable. But we can force it even further in the direction of dualism. Let us recall just how detached God's mental capacities are from the particularities of his body. Just now he is omniscient, omnipotent, etc. and with a galaxy-studded, granulated body some thousands of millions of light-years across. Some few thousands of millions of years ago he was a 'mighty atom', an immensely dense, hot, largely unstructured ball but then, as now, he was omniscient, omnipotent, etc.; and so he will be in the distant future when, perhaps, his body will be a diffuse mist of electron–positron pairs. There seems little point in seeking the *grounding* of such powers or capacities in any one of these time-slices of the universe, never mind in all of them, and they therefore float quite free of their supposed material base. However, matters are much more puzzling than even the above account suggests because Jantzen thinks that the laws governing the constituents of the universe are, themselves, decided upon by God who can, if he wishes, at any time change them. God's body, then, comes out as a kind of metaphysical amoeba whose form is decided by the drop of a fiat. It seems clear that if there are material things whose particular powers and liabilities are given, and at will changed, by some general law-deciding power then this latter, in dualistic fashion, must stand ontologically above the purely plastic matter it manipulates. It is an unmovable mover shifting the world as it sees fit.

EQUIVOCATION AS ANALOGY

Let us, then, return to the dualist view of human persons and their bodies and God and the world. We observe now the astonishing fact that the puzzling fine structure of the universe that allowed for the emergence of the human mind is explicable by recourse to a great spirit that is analogous to those minds that have so emerged. At both ends of the analogy we have pure non-material minds that consciously and thinkingly bring order to the material world. The argument for God's existence is based on an analogy that could not be simpler or clearer. But is that really the case? An examination of this question will show that, even on the dualist assumption, in its most important aspect the comparison between the minds of humans and the mind of God is not at all close; and the vast dissimilarity between them, not to be papered over by references to a supposed 'supersimilarity fallacy', saps the strength of the design argument. We have, in short, equivocation masquerading as analogy.

I can bring out the supposed character of the analogy between the god and humans, and the hidden complications it enshrines, by looking more closely at the argument for the god's non-embodied existence. Swinburne's formulation leads us directly into the complexities of the issue:

> if a person brings about directly the connections between things, including the predictable connections between the bodies of other persons and the world, there is no region of the world, goings-on in which bring about those connections. The person must bring about those connections as a basic action. His control of the world must be immediate, not mediated by a body. So the dissimilarities between the two kinds of order necessarily lead to the postulation of a non-embodied person (rather than an embodied person) as a cause of the temporal order in nature.
>
> (Swinburne 1979:149)

The god, then, brings about the order of the world *directly* or *immediately*; his actions in this respect are *basic actions*. We might say that whatever he does he does *just like that.* Here the comparison and contrast is with humans who can also do some things as basic actions, just like that, but who can do other things only by doing something else first. Suppose Mr Smith pokes out his tongue. A 'personal explanation' of this as a basic action would be roughly as follows: Mr Smith had the intention that his tongue poke out and tongue-poking is among Mr Smith's basic powers so out poked his tongue. Again, suppose Mr Smith brought about, as a mediated action, his failure at an examination. A personal explanation might be, roughly: Mr Smith intended to bring about his failure *as a consequence* of performing the basic action of expressing independent thoughts in his examinations; expressing independent thoughts was among his basic powers; and expressing independent thoughts had the consequence of so enraging his examiners that they failed him.

It is, then, supposedly by means of this straightforward analogy with human basic actions that we have some reason for believing in, and understanding, the god's dealings with the world. Now I think that the distinction between basic and mediated actions does reflect something of the way we ordinarily speak about what ordinary and even extraordinary embodied persons do although I also think that the vulgar distinction is much too rough and ready for the fine metaphysical work Swinburne requires of it. And except when he is trying to show the conceptual possibility of non-embodied action, where he has recourse to such fantastic examples as Uri Geller let loose amongst the cutlery, all the instances of human basic actions to which he refers are firmly embodied ones. This ordinary way of speaking gives the illusion, particularly if we are in a metaphysical mood, that because personal *explanations* of basic actions are so simple in form *what actually goes on in the world* when someone does something like poking out his tongue is also a very simple matter. 'Tongue, poke out', I say and then, so we think, *really*, just like that, with nothing else at all involved, out pops my tongue. Apart from questions of grandeur, human tongue-poking is on a level with God's drowning of the world.

Things are not that simple. Let us start where we think we know something about what is going on, at the human end of the analogy. It is just not true, in general, that when, as we say, a human wills a basic action that we have a simple causal situation – that is, it is not in general the case with humans that basic actions flow directly, as it were, out of their intentions. Tongue-poking and singing are enormously complicated businesses. Leaving aside the fact that the basic actions of highly skilled humans, such as jugglers, require an enormous amount of dedicated training – so that we wonder just how they came to be able to do such things just like that – we know that quite ordinary basic actions involve complex causal chains involving the nervous and muscular systems. This has disastrous consequences for the strength of the analogy with the god's actions which are taken, in being basic, as being basically causally simple. The strength of the analogy being thus sapped, the argument, from that analogy, to the god's existence is correspondingly weakened. Stories of Uri Geller bending spoons and starting up watches might convince us of the meaningfulness of the concept of what we might call an absolutely basic action, but his exposure as a mere conjuror should remind us of the weakness of the design argument.

Later, when discussing why he thinks the theory that the god brings about the correlation between brain events and mental events is superior to the rival materialist account, Swinburne (1979:173) remarks, 'There is a very natural connection indeed between an agent's intention to bring about X, and the occurrence of X; for the intention has written into it one thing with which it is naturally correlated: its fulfilment.' But just what is involved in this 'natural connection' between an intention to bring about X and the occurrence of X beyond the two facts that (i) the intentions of agents are frequently fulfilled and (ii) in some sense the intention 'mirrors' the event that is its fulfilment? There is here no implication, which the fully fighting fit design argument requires, that there is a simple causal connection between the intention and the event which fulfils it.

It is here that we must remember the dualist presupposition of the design argument: human persons, at least while they are here on Earth, are supposed to be dualities of body and spirit although they are *essentially* spirits. Does this not prove the strength of what seemed to be a weakling of an argument? In one respect the analogical argument is improved inasmuch as the first and second terms of the analogy have the same ontological status – they are both spirits. But in metaphysics, as in life, there are swings and roundabouts and what is gained for the ontological analogy is at the expense of the analogy of action. The god, by analogy with human persons, is supposed to produce most of the order in the world. However, it turns out, on the assumption of dualism, that humans never, as far as we know, produce *anything* as a basic action. The essential premiss of the design argument is false.

Consider a man who raises his arm. On the assumption of interactionist dualism, the relevant causal story is as follows. The man, as a spirit, has the intention of raising his arm and while having the intention (or shortly after) his spirit interacts with his brain thereby bringing about a complicated sequence of physical events which results in his arm rising. The direct causal effect he has on a tiny part of the world, perhaps only a neuron or so in his brain, is not a basic action for *that* is not what he willed. Nor is it normally a mediated action because humans do not usually intend bringing about brain activity and are rarely aware of it. In fact, it is beginning to look as if everything humans do, even what are *usually* regarded as basic actions, is brought about by the unintended consequences of having intentions so that, forced into the mould of the dualist theory, the *ordinary* distinction between basic and mediated actions shatters.

There is a subtle equivocation, involving two quite different meanings of phrases such as 'direct action', whereby this tragic loss of the design argument's premiss is concealed. One meaning, the official one, is bravely out in the open while the other, surreptitiously introduced, skulks in the conceptual shrubbery of dualist metaphysics. The first meaning, the overt one, refers to the quite ordinary way we can speak of human persons doing things just like that – hand-waving, nose-picking, leg-scratching and so on – where no reference is made to, or assumption made of, a supposed simple causal directness in bringing about these activities. The other meaning, the covert one, does have this reference; it concerns the direct causal action of spirit upon matter. Swinburne needs to run these two concepts together just because he wants to arrive at the conclusion of a god who *by* intending to produce a state of affairs X in the world directly causes that state of affairs. As I put it earlier, the god intends state of affairs X and state of affairs X just directly flows out of his intention. 'Hand rise,' I say and my spirit interacts with my brain – potassium and sodium ions move across nerve and muscle membranes, currents flow, muscles contract and expand and *eventually* my hand rises. 'Let there be light,' said God and there was light – *really*, just like that.

There is a nice example of this particularly pernicious equivocation in an earlier article where Swinburne tries to answer the charge that the argument from design should lead to the conclusion that the god is unaware of what he brings about in the universe in the same way that humans are normally unaware of the changes they induce in their brains. This supposedly does not follow 'because of the pervasiveness of the natural order' (Swinburne 1972:200).

> Since the god is postulated as the cause of all regularities in the world (other than the few produced by human agents) there are no other regularities left by which what he produces directly can cause natural laws. If an agent is to produce some effect indirectly, he can only do so by producing something directly which then goes to produce its effect in accordance with a natural order independent of the agent. So if we take the analogy seriously and postulate a similar cause acting similarly, an agent acting intentionally, this rules out postulating a similarity between causes in the respect that they bring about an effect intentionally by bringing about some effect unintentionally. The god must be aware of what he produces directly.
>
> (Swinburne 1972:200)

The argument is revealingly similar to Swinburne's proof, which I gave earlier, that the god is non-embodied; and this brings out the point that in both demonstrations the distinction between direct and indirect action, as it appears in the premises, has to do with the immediacy of causation and not with the direct consciousness of what is to be brought about. The god directly or immediately causes (nearly) all physical regularity: that is why he must be non-embodied. It is only because of equivocation that we can conclude that this direct causal action of the god on the world means that he 'must be aware of what he produces directly'. In fact, it is easy to think of examples where the god in directly intending something, e.g. the composition of a 'mental poem', unintentionally, but with causal directness, stirs the world.[4]

GOD WILLING

Even on the assumption of the dualist theory of the human constitution, there is, it has been argued, very little in common between the ways humans produce order in the world and the way the god is supposed to produce it and this has led to the conclusion that the argument from design, considered as an inductive argument, is very weak. It should also caution us against too easily drawing inferences concerning the nature of the god and his modes of action. Here, also, in this rarefied metaphysical atmosphere, highly intelligent bluff common sense is left gasping. Let us look at this notion of a god who can do things simply by willing them and let us slip from the idea of a god as mere law-giver (we shall return to it later) to the full-blown Christian conception of God as 'maker of heaven and earth'. How much do we understand of this doctrine and what can we infer from its bare enunciation concerning God's attributes? Swinburne thinks there is no problem at all concerning the meaningfulness of the doctrine of the creation of the world from nothing:

> Human beings do not have the power to bring matter into existence (given that we construe 'matter' in a wide sense which includes energy). It is, however, fairly easy to picture what it would be like for them to have such a power. If I could just by so choosing produce a sixth finger or a new fountain-pen (not made out of pre-existing matter) I would have the power to bring matter into existence.
> (Swinburne 1979:139)

Human beings do not, as Swinburne notes, have these marvellous powers to bring things into existence but, he claims, it makes sense to imagine them as having them. Similarly, then, it makes sense to say that God made the whole universe. But what is it that we understand of this 'picture', even for humans? Certainly, we can form a picture of someone willing something to exist – a cold bottle of Stein lager, say – and we can imagine a sample of that something appearing before him, out of thin nothingness. And we *are* imagining it to be a real bottle of beer which materialises, not an hallucination – it slightly increases the total mass of the universe and, who knows?, by doing so might eventually bring about the reversal of the cosmic expansion. So we have the willing and an example of what is willed coming into existence. But there is still the question: Should we describe this picture as one of somebody just willing something into existence? Did that person's willing *bring about* the existence of that which suddenly springs into existence?

I can throw some doubt on the supposition that we should describe such strange goings-on in this way by telling a story of my own. Here somebody, in the forthcoming period of general prohibition, desperately wills a packet of Senior Service cigarettes to appear and one materialises in the cell he occupies in the rehabilitation centre. So far my story is like Swinburne's but now it takes a different turn. Whereas in Swinburne's tale the extra finger or fountain-pen is brought into existence by the willing, in mine the unrepentant smoker is just lucky. As he is doing his craven willing the cigarettes just happen to pop into existence for no reason at all, 'by chance'.

Well, what is the problem? Swinburne has his story and I have mine. The problem surely is that our respective stories are so alike as they start off that there seems no justification for their quite different endings. *Either* the extra finger growing out of my forehead was caused by my willing it *or*, for no reason at all, like Topsy it just grew. Can we change the story a bit to weigh the balance somewhat in favour of Swinburne's causal description? Suppose every time a certain person wills a fountain pen to exist one appears so that we have to dig him from beneath a mound of them. The regularity of the coexistence of the willing and the materialisation might appeal to Humeans but I still feel inclined to dig my heels in and parallel the beginning of the new story while saying that every time a pen appears it does so by chance.[5] The point is, my story seems to make sense and, if it does, how do we choose between it and Swinburne's seeing that they are not relevantly different so as to allow for these quite disparate descriptions of what is happening? If there is this difficulty in imagining humans wishing pens or digits into existence, what are we to make of accounts of God bringing about the universe?

One reason we may be inclined to accept, without further ado, the causal description of these strange, imaginary happenings is the 'match' between the content of the intention and the physical occurrence. Someone wills a fountain-pen or a universe and a fountain-pen or universe springs into existence. Therefore, one may be inclined to believe, it is the willing that has caused these things to exist. We would not, I think, be as readily inclined to accept the idea of a causal connection where this 'match' does not occur. Suppose, for example, someone tries for a fountain-pen but instead gets Goldilocks and the three bears. Or suppose that there is no intending anything at all, that the person is an unfortunate to whom these things just happen – he goes for a bushwalk and the track behind him is littered with rusting cars and empty beer cans. We would be much more inclined to think that in this sort of fantasy the connection between person and occurrence is casual rather than causal.

I suppose that the reason we would be reluctant to accept a causal description in the latter kind of story – apart from the fact that we just know that going for a walk in the woods never does have such consequences – is that there is, as it were, a lack of proportionality between the supposed cause and effect.[6] This is bad enough when a person is supposed to will one thing and instead gets something quite different but it is intolerable when he is imagined to bring things into existence while thinking of, or willing, nothing whatsoever. There is, at the very least, no possible explanation of the sheer complexity of, say, volumes three to five of *The Encyclopedia of Philosophy* if these are supposed to be brought into existence by an unreflecting albeit perambulating mind.

Given our reluctance to allow the application of causal descriptions in these bizarre stories we might turn an equally sceptical eye on the original tales of people deliberately willing fountain-pens or worlds into existence. True, we have what I called the 'match' between the intention's content and the thing intended but we saw earlier that this implies nothing at all about a simple causal connection between the two. If we appeal to our basic intuitions concerning causal connections we might find something very odd indeed about the notion of someone just willing a complicated piece of matter, such as a finger, into existence. Suppose someone objects to the story I told earlier – of a person regularly, but by chance, getting a fountain-pen every time he willed one – that such a steady accumulation of pens could not 'just happen', that it must have been caused. My answer would be that I already know that as, indeed, I know that not even one pen would appear in that way. But, I would add, neither do I believe that the pens *would* appear in the way Swinburne suggests just because they could not have such a cause as he suggests. *The* cause of the supposed profusion of pens is said to be the will but that does not have the necessary machinery for the job.

The argument adduced above should give reasons for the proponent of natural theology to pause if not altogether give up the chase for a spiritual ground of the world; but, having considered the matter, he may still defend the meaningfulness of the claim that very simple happenings, such as mere willings, may be the causes of the existence of complex things such as big toes. After all, intuitions as to the essential nature of the causal relation may differ.[7] Again, it might be said that the concept of causality is complex and that the theist is entitled, for the purpose of their argument, to separate one conceptual thread from the normally closely woven web[8] – the more so, perhaps, because they are concerned with cosmological issues.

So be it. But now, standing out starkly against the background discussion of what counts as a causal explanation, is the question of how we determine what properties God must have that enable him to make a universe. He is said to be very knowledgeable. Why so? In the fantasy of the man who wills the growing of an extra finger there is no hint that any extraordinary knowledge is involved. Presumably, in order to make sense of the supposition that it was that particular thing he willed, we must assume that he has some general knowledge of fingers, but there is no further suggestion that, say, he had also carefully studied *Gray's Anatomy*. Why, then, do we assume that God, in willing a universe, must know such a lot? Finger- and universe-growers are, as far as we know, both unskilled labourers.

We must put to one side the reply that stories of humans willing things to exist are meant only to demonstrate the meaningfulness of the idea of God's creation of the universe and that they play no part, beyond that, in the argument for that creation and the attributes of God necessary for it. The stories show the meaningfulness of the notion of creation by being *models* of it. This is forgotten when the argument turns to the issue of God's attributes when the basic model is taken to be that of ordinary humans intelligently going about their business. God is then thought of as a poet[9] or a master-craftsman and his properties determined accordingly.

Here it might be urged that, rather than lapsing into sceptical impotence, we should closely examine this difference between the two ways of bringing things into existence – by production and sheer willing – in order to make some plausible guesses concerning, say, the kind and the extent of knowledge necessary for creation. We might start by wondering how much descriptive content must be associated with, for example, the intention to bring a watch into existence. Is it like strongly hinting that you would like a watch for Christmas and leaving the details concerning the kind of time-piece – whether it is a pocket- or wrist-watch, Swiss or Japanese, and so on – to the good sense and taste of a benevolent friend? That does not seem right for in the bare willing of a watch, with no preferences stated, there is nothing to explain why you get a digital rather than an analogue piece, why it needs a battery rather than working by clockwork. And what if you got a miniature sand-timer or sun-dial with wrist-straps attached? Perhaps, then, in willing something into existence we should be a bit specific about it.[10] How specific? The electric, digital watch we will and get is pear-shaped and stamped 'Made on Sirius IV'. Would these latter characteristics also have to be represented in the description we give of what it is we intend to bring into existence? And then, of course, the watch must be made of something – of stainless steel or kryptonite or whatever. Would we have to specify what that something is and, if so, what would that involve?

We might use the following somewhat tenuous argument. In the usual case of human manufacture there is a product, e.g. an axe-head, and a raw material, e.g. an unstructured stone. There will be knowledge of some of the properties of the raw material and also of those properties of the product which are, or support, its desired characteristics; and there will be knowledge of how to get from the one set to the other. But this knowledge is incomplete which raises the question of how technology is possible. How did Stone Age man, knowing nothing of how the properties of hardness, brittleness, etc., depend on molecular structure, make his tools? The answer, of course, is bound up with the fact that things have their own ways of acting, some of which we can come to know and take advantage of. What, then, of the willer of fountain-pens? Producing them from nothing he needs no knowledge of raw materials and the technology for making pens from them. Taking account of this great difference in the way things are brought into existence, we might be led to conclude that the relevant knowledge possessed in the pure volition or production of pens is only of the pens. But how much knowledge?

Some, and perhaps all, of the desired properties of the manufactured object will depend on other properties it possesses, e.g. the ductility, etc. of crystals is explained by their quantum-mechanical properties. Therefore, in making such things the manufacturer must, knowingly or unknowingly, include these other characteristics in their make-up. (He could not, for example, make a red paint unless it were a substance of a particular molecular constitution which accounts for its redness.) But whereas the ordinary manufacturer may remain ignorant of these other properties that must exist if the desired characters are to eventuate, it is arguable that the 'wilful manufacturer' must know all about them. Unable to depend on the independent action of raw materials to produce, say, a thing of a certain unknown molecular structure which results in redness, he must, himself, directly produce that structure; and it is now very tempting to say that in order to do so he must know all about it and how the colour red depends on it. It looks as if the reason no human can will things into existence is that no one, not even Stephen Hawking, knows enough about the fundamental constitution of matter. This, it might be argued, is where things are different with God. As creator of the universe he must have known every fine detail of its inner constitution. There is, of course, the problem of how it is God comes by this profound knowledge of universes but, given the hypothesis of the creation, we can infer that he must have it.

But now, once more, and even accepting an argument of the sort just outlined, have we really understood the notion of creation by bare willing? Do we think that a scientist who came to know everything there was to know about hydrogen would thereby be one whit closer to bringing even a single atom of that gas into existence by some kind of purely mental breath? Is there, then, something else God knows that we do not? Is there a special skill or know-how which he possesses? The trouble here is that we are unable to conceive what it could possibly be. It cannot be special knowledge of how to manipulate pre-existing stuff – because in cooking up universes there is a marked lack of ingredients – so we seem to be left with something like a peculiar quality associated with God's willing. We might say that there is a great strength or intensity associated with God's willing but, on reflection, we still do not see how that will explain the existence of worlds. What, in the case of gods, distinguishes powerfully wilful from strongly wishful thinking? All this brings us closer to the question of what kind of world God creates.

Chapter 9

And back again

THE WORLD WILLED

What, then, of the universe? What is its ontological status and what, supposedly, is the relation it bears to God? In the last chapter, in discussing the problem of finding out just what God's attributes are, the assumption was made that the universe was created holus-bolus, out of nothing. This view may, itself, take two quite different forms and, indeed, may even be challenged by a rival picture, stemming from Plato's *Timaeus*, that God does the best he can with a recalcitrant, pre-existing matter which can never quite be brought up to scratch. The latter cosmology, also, may take several different turns, each with its own logical peculiarities. The whole issue, then, of the relation of God to the world, and the bearing this has on the question of their ontological dependence or independence, requires closer examination. It will be convenient, in undertaking this, to revert to the facile but flawed analogy between man and God.

It was argued that we are liable to be much too impressed by the supposed ontological analogy, where both terms are taken as spirits, and that we should examine closely the question of *how* exactly humans and God do things. It is not merely a matter of grandeur – if that – that God brings order to the universe while Wren could only manage such edifices as St Paul's Cathedral and the Royal Naval College. If we look at the causal stories involved in the two cases, the analogy falters. Consider a human who is doing something that introduces order into the world, e.g. filling in a tax form. According to the dualist interactionist account, what happens when a human person wilfully and successfully fills in a form is that their mind consciously forms an intention to perform this action and, also, as a separate matter, causally interacts with its brain. The brain, in the usual physiological story, then sets up impulses in the appropriate nerves which cause muscles to contract etc. and eventually the form gets filled in. We might present the matter diagrammatically, as in Figure 1.

God does not have a brain although this is not supposed to put him at a disadvantage. The whole universe, near enough, forms the field for his activity. But how shall we depict this activity of God moving the things of the universe? As a first attempt let us show God's stirring of the world as in Figure 2.

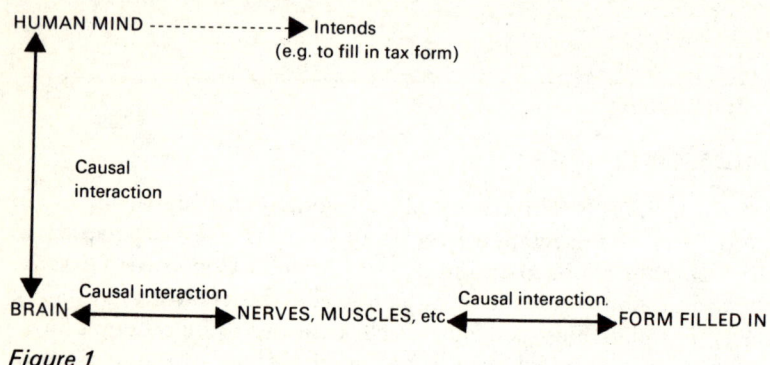

Figure 1

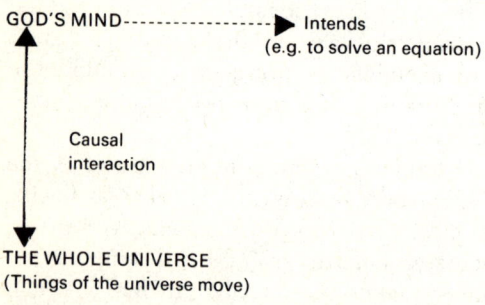

Figure 2

In constructing Figure 2 I have, I hope, followed the rules of analogy. The causal stories, which are what the argument from design is about, are as close as I can get them allowing for the vast differences between God and humans and their respective fields of endeavour. God, then, on this account indulges in some intentional activity or other (e.g. doing a bit of mental arithmetic); and also, but separately from the intention, the spirit of God interacts with the world, bringing about the orderly progression of its members.

The orthodoxly pious will recoil in horror at this picture of the relation between God and world and it is not difficult to see why. First, there is the point, touched on in the last chapter and now made quite explicit in the diagrammatic representation of God's *interaction* with the world, that we have no analogical base for depicting a correspondence between the content of God's intention and the happenings in the universe. The causal analogy is with the way human spirits, when intending things, interact directly with their brains and, of course, even when intentions are realised the correspondence is not, at least usually, with the brain state *quite unconsciously* produced on the way to that realisation. We have no reason to believe, as far as the analogy with humans goes, that God is aware of what he brings the universe to, or even that he knows the universe exists as he goes on with a sort of spiritual whistling in the dark. But, second, it is also clear from the diagram that, whether or not knowingly, God *interacts* with the universe, i.e. the universe is taken as an independently existing system capable of acting back on God; and this, again, will not appeal to the religiously orthodox who will insist on the absolute sovereignty of the creator over the world.

It is just here, of course, that the proponent of the design argument insists that the leap by analogy to the mind of God has, as its springboard, the evident fact of the *designing* minds of men and women; and, as we have seen, the jump ends in murkier logical waters than we might, at first, have expected. One person's charge of supersimilarity fallacy is answered by another's of equivocation. However, let us proceed directly to the diagrammatic representation of the position which is, I suggest, something like Figure 3.

The diagram looks simple but, in fact, I had to pause to think just how best to picture God's relation to the world. But I hope that, however else it may fail, Figure 3 does show that whatever it is that God does emerges straight out of his will – there is no other 'moment' of God's mind which does the interacting with the world and which may, or may not, match up with the intention.

The problem arises when we look at the far end of the causal relation, the term I have labelled 'UNIVERSE'. How are we to take that? Straightaway we should notice that there is an ambiguity hidden by the definiteness of the arrow proceeding out of the will of God and embedding itself in the universe. This, to effect a first classificatory division, either may mean that the universe is, itself, created 'out of the

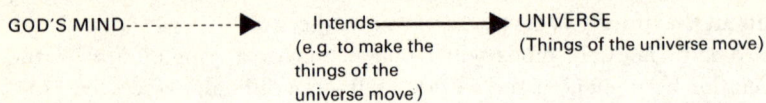

Figure 3

will of God', where the model is of a Uri Geller producing whole cabinets of cutlery from nowhere; or the notion may be, rather, of God as a spoon-bender writ large, the mind that acts wilfully and designedly upon the world as given.

Let us start with the latter idea of a god bringing order to a pre-existent universe. The view seems simple and straightforward enough, if we allow ourselves to be trapped by mental imagery, but, in fact, is fraught with complications and difficulties. We should at once distinguish two different accounts of what it is that God is acting upon. There is, first, the essentially platonic idea of the world as made up of formless matter to which God brings the order which, in itself, it entirely lacks; but, second, the concept may be of a universe which has some structure to it but which, nevertheless, requires a few deft touches from the mind of God to bring it up, or closer, to some standard or other. In the furnace of the metaphysical imagination these two models often melt and run together.

The first view is quickly disposed of. Nothing can be done for a world that has nothing. If we think of God as trying to act on the 'matter' of the universe then all we can do is sympathise with his frustration as the universe remains totally unresponsive to his intimations. In particular, lacking causal properties, the absolutely dull and passive, stuffingless matter cannot *interact* with God or anything else never mind what prodigious blaze of energy is directed at – and unresisted through – it. None so deaf – even to the word of God – as those who cannot hear.

It may be objected that this argument relies on the assumption of interactionist dualism which we long ago discarded in favour of creationism, the view that God freely creates things. Could not God, then, improve this laggard of a universe by adding something to it? But what? Causal properties? How is this to be achieved – how does even God make such properties stick in a substratum that inherently can support nothing? You cannot pull out and then put back the causal properties of inert things as if they were the matchstick legs of a child's plasticine beetle. If God is to create the order for a universe then he will at the same time create the universe that is so ordered; and other absolutely listless worlds, if such there be, will sleep their time away, ignoring, and ignored by, God and his living creation.[1]

The other picture is of the universe with its own inherent properties and structure but needing a little help to enable it to bring about some desirable state of affairs, e.g. intelligent life. Here, again, we should carefully specify *how* it is that God adds to the world so let us accept the conclusion of the design argument that he acts on the world by *creation*. We might imagine him improving on the details of the structure of the universe by adding little bits here and there. For example, it may turn out that certain chemical steps essential for the evolution of life on Earth were physically impossible at the time and place they were needed unless some outside intervention was involved; and we might imagine God coming up with the chemical goods – although a rival hypothesis would be that the necessary substances were supplied by an extra-terrestrial intelligence that had evolved by a different, physically possible, pathway. If we stick with the hypothesis of the discarnate god then, unless we object to the very idea of creation from nothing, there is nothing logically objectionable to the idea of the world being brought to order in this way;[2] and the main objections to it are on grounds of elegance and simplicity. Rather than imagining God as thinking up bits and pieces to slot into the universe wherever they are needed it would, on these grounds, be better to think of him as creator of everything apart from himself.[3]

Similar considerations apply to the notion of a discontented god who intervenes in a much grander way in the affairs of a below par universe. Here the thought is of a cosmos with some general property or properties that are not up to scratch as far as producing some desirable end is concerned. Again, the 'fine-tuning' of the constants of nature comes to mind. For example, Bernard Lovell tells us that

> if the proton and proton reaction had been only a few percent stronger, then all the protons would have formed into helium in the first few million years of the Universe, and . . . a universe would have evolved which could never be comprehended by any form of intelligent life.
>
> (Lovell 1975:125)

Our universe, then, perhaps bubbled into existence from the basic space–time fabric and, failing to pass the critical scrutiny of a watchful god, had its fundamental forces adjusted to the benefit of future curious astronomers. Here we should steadfastly refuse to be seduced by the image of a god *interacting* with the basic particles or their force-fields and, in that way, in effect by the introduction of a further force, ensuring that the universe comes to something more exciting than, say, a vast expanse of inert gas. The god is supposed to wipe clean the basic constituents of matter, removing the offending properties that would bring about a lack-lustre world and replacing them with characteristics of the right values for a universe worthy of existence. We might note, without dwelling upon, the logical difficulties of such a view – e.g. can we really make sense of the notion of holding matter steady, as it were, while ripping out and replacing some or all of its properties? – but whatever the problems in that area, we might, in any case, think that the orthodox notion of creation is far more elegant.

MUCH ADO OUT OF NOTHING

The design argument tends inexorably towards the notion of God's creation of the world 'out of nothing'. The universe exists because God so wills it. However, as a kind of reflection of the different directions the doctrine may take when it concerns the bringing of order to a pre-existing world so, also, when we take up the idea of absolute creation, two quite different paths may be followed. Whereas originally we had the view of God as the bringer of order to a formless matter or chaos – where God is the source of all causal potency – so now, correspondingly, we have *theism* where the divine mind is thought of as directly causing, or creating, each and every state of the world (with the possible exception of the succession of states of other minds). And corresponding to the theory that God merely adds bits and pieces to an otherwise causally integrated universe – where these additions are themselves, once created, causally effective in their own right – there is *deism*, in which the universe is thought of as created or willed into existence but, once originated, as having its own self-sustaining powers.

As general cosmological theories theism and deism are logically incompatible so it is important to decide which it is that is supposed to be the conclusion of the design argument. Unfortunately, a great deal of the literature on the question of God's relation to the world – whether or not this is worked out in connection with the design argument – is much confused. Often, there is absolutely no sign the author is aware of the distinction of theories while, in other instances, sometimes in almost the same breath, they are presented together in an attempted metaphysical oil and water mixture. For example, in a popular presentation Adam Ford tells us of the existence and 'work' of the fundamental forces of nature only to write, in the very next sentence, of God's absolute creation and sustenance ('from moment to moment') of the world:

> This creating spirit, the eternal presence, is the field in which the reactions of fundamental forces have their being and weave their work. Creating and sustaining from moment to moment, the Spirit makes possible the emergence from matter of the spiritual dimension. Everything, every photon and every quark, every sparrow on the housetop and every hair of the head is absolutely dependent upon his sustaining loving power.
>
> (Ford 1986:72)

We have here an echo of the difficult theological distinction between the immanence and transcendence of God where it is held that he is *both* absolutely distinct from his creation *and* intimately involved in it. Ford's dilemma is that, on the one hand, he is so immensely impressed by what is going on in the universe that he wishes to tell us all about it in terms of the causal realities of the cosmos; while, on the other hand, he so desires to persuade us of the absolute sovereignty of God that he cannot believe that mundane entities are *really* causally potent or in the least self-sustaining. We can bring this into connection with the argument from design by making the Kantian point that that argument is dangerously liable to collapse into the cosmological argument. A thinker may be so impressed by the causal order of the world that he will try to explain, by God's creation, not merely the existence of causally interacting things but cosmic causality itself. God, then, is taken as *causing the causality* of things – which is to say that the causal powers of things are illusory and that everything is *really* brought about by the power of God. If we now bring under the same rubric the self-sustaining powers of 'contingent things' – if things are taken as having no staying-power, as it were – then we have the basis for an outright cosmological argument with its conclusion of God 'sustaining', i.e. creating, the world from moment to moment.

The uneasy coexistence of these conflicting strands of thought – of the respect for science as against the drive to explain away scientific laws, of deism as against theism – can be detected in, once more, the detailed arguments for God's existence of R.G. Swinburne. We saw earlier that when he was arguing for the meaningfulness of the creation of things from nothing Swinburne imagined the willing into existence of fully independent objects such as fountain-pens. Once brought into existence these fountain-pens carried on existing in causal interaction with other things, not needing a 'sustaining' will to keep them going. We might, then, expect this 'deistic' aspect of such imaginings to be carried over to the full-blown picture of the making of the universe. What in fact we get, dressed up, and concealed, in the jargon of the philosophy of science, is equivocation between the deistic and theistic positions. Interestingly, this occurs in the context of Swinburne's version of the cosmological argument.

What is it about the universe that the hypothesis of the god is supposed to explain? Speaking very generally we may say that the cosmological and design arguments lead to explanations of the universe's existence and order. But we need to be much more specific. In particular, we need to ask what sort of order is meant to be explained. Swinburne tells us that it is that order which we capture in scientific laws of succession. Now although he often talks in a positivistic, Hempelian way about these laws[4] he makes it clear that this is for the sake of convenience only and that he is really concerned with *the causal powers and liabilities of the things of the world*. It is the god's activity which is supposed to explain why things have the powers and liabilities that they do have.

What can it mean to say that God is the reason for, i.e. the cause of, the powers and liabilities of things? There is at least this degree of clarity in the hypothesis of deism, that the god in the beginning made an independent universe whose constituents had fully real causal properties. And it is in this kind of way that Swinburne writes when describing the wonderful causal order of the world which, he thinks, cries out for explanation: 'what the all-pervasive temporal order amounts to is the fact that throughout space and time there are physical objects of various kinds, every such object having the powers and liabilities which are described in laws of nature' (Swinburne 1979:139).

The show of realism in such statements is misleading. We tend not to see this just because of the fact that, in his versions of the cosmological and design arguments, Swinburne primarily uses the 'easier' (44) Hempelian account of the laws of nature and only after this briefly 'translates' it into the mode of powers and liabilities. Our focus is on the laws of nature regarded positivistically, *i.e. on mere regularities*, and the important causal issues lie blurred at the edge of our vision until God, as the cause of all apart from himself, is brought in to dominate the whole field. The picture is, then, of the universe as a bundle of regularities which are, in their entirety, brought about by the never-idle will of God.

I can bring out this point, along with the fact that Swinburne will not face up to its implications, by looking more closely at the cosmological argument as he presents it. What he is trying to explain is the following. There is 'the series of states starting from the present and going backwards in time, S_1, S_2, S_3, and so on' and 'there are laws of nature L which bring about the evolution of S_3 from S_4, S_2 from S_3, and so on' (120). This he represents diagrammatically (Figure 4).

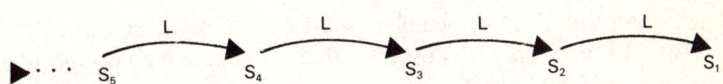

Figure 4

Now although he has said it is the 'laws of nature L which bring about the evolution' of one state of the universe from another, the hypothesis he really wants to entertain is that 'a person G brings it about at each instant of time, that L operates, and so brings it about for each S_{n+1} that S_{n+1} brings about S_n' (126). The situation, he claims, is as in Figure 5.

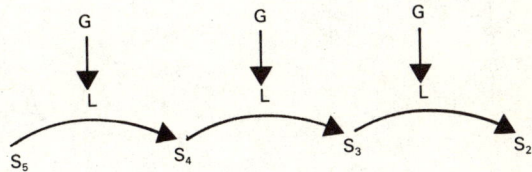

Figure 5

Already there are the seeds of an equivocation in these descriptions of how the universe goes on its way. I take it that when Swinburne says that God 'brings it about at each instant of time, that L operates' that he is thinking of the laws of nature purely descriptively, as mere regular succession of the states of the universe. It is not as if God makes the laws of nature which then go on to *act on* the states of the universe, drawing one out of the other. (In fact, Swinburne, himself, attacks this hypostatisation of the laws of nature.) The view must be, then, of God successively producing the states of the universe according to a pattern or plan, much like the successive images of a film are cast on a screen by a projector. On the other hand, there is, I think, something of a different view which gets partial expression in the talk of the laws of nature bringing it about that one state of the universe follows another. This is the 'translation view' that talk of the laws of nature should ideally be replaced by talk of the powers and liabilities of the things in the universe. And to look at laws of nature in this way is to espouse a naturalistic causal theory that is incompatible with the theistic hypothesis.

The confusion of views being presented is made more difficult to detect by the fact that in Figure 5 there is a further confusion of symbolism involved in including, in one and the same representation, the straight causal arrows descending from God and the curved ones, labelled L, connecting states of the universe. This is equivalent to running together Hempelian talk of regularities with talk of causal powers and has, quite misleadingly, led to the causal darts from God terminating in the *laws* bridging the states of the universe rather than

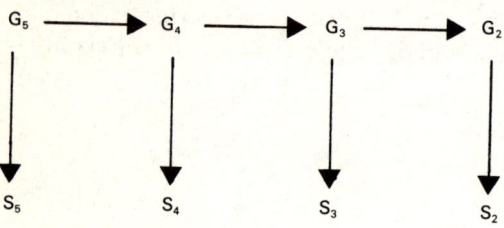

Figure 6

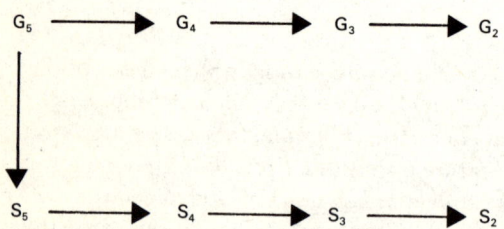

Figure 7

in those states themselves. This hides the fact, once more, that in theism, as against deism, it is God who is utterly, and without remainder, causally responsible for each and every state of the universe. This is the God of Descartes who, at each instant of time, 'sustains' the universe by creating the state appropriate to that instant. The revised picture of Swinburne's theism should, then, be as in Figure 6. This can be compared with the case for deism (Figure 7).

We are now in a position to see just how misleading Swinburne's account of the matter is when he gives his explanation in terms of powers and liabilities:

> Our supposition that there is a full scientific explanation of the existence of each state of the universe in terms of the action of an immediately prior state then amounts to the following. The universe at any given time t_n is in a state S_n. At each such time it has the power P to bring about its continued existence with whatever constant characteristics it has (e.g. same matter, or same quantity of energy), and a liability K necessarily to exercise P. Our supposition that a person G acts from without to conserve it in being is the supposition that G brings it about that it has the power P and the liability K. G makes it bring about its subsequent existence, and its subsequent possession of its permanent characteristics. At any time he could make the universe bring about different subsequent permanent characteristics or not give it the power to bring about its subsequent existence.
>
> (Swinburne 1979:126)

This passage is most puzzling. We have the contrast between a full scientific explanation of the states of the universe and the theistic explanation of these states. The scientific explanation refers to the power and liability of one state to produce the next and, unless we specialise in puzzles about causality, I think we can understand this. But then, to our astonishment, the supposed contrasting theistic view also makes reference to the causal powers and liabilities of the states of the universe. What is it for God to conserve the universe in being? According to Swinburne this means that God 'brings it about that it has the power P and the liability K'. But power P and liability K just *are* the universe's own power and liability to sustain (conserve) itself in being. It might seem, then, that to say that God 'brings it about' that the universe has these powers and liabilities is to say that he creates a universe, or, more accurately, a first state of the universe, which is self-sustaining – and this is deism. The only contrast between this explanation and the scientific explanation is that the former postulates an extra bit of activity at the beginning of things.

However, the concepts of power and liability will not remain steady. In the very next sentence, after having told us that the world has its own power and liability, Swinburne tells us that it is God who 'makes it bring about its subsequent existence'. Not only that but God 'could make the universe bring about different subsequent permanent characteristics or not give it the power to bring about its subsequent existence'. The very next state of the universe may contain a preponderance of honest politicans or, perhaps more likely, nothing at all. The talk of God *making the universe* do this or that – making the universe make its 'subsequent existence' or making it make its 'subsequent permanent characteristics' – is highly misleading. So is the picture of God withholding power, i.e. causal power, from the universe. Such language insinuates the view, still, that the universe has its own fully independent existence and that God makes it do this or that in the same way that we can make things do this or that, i.e. by entering into causal interaction with them. This is not Swinburne's real view. That is that God is the full and immediate cause of each and every state of the universe. It is as if what seemed to be wholly realistic talk about the causal powers and liabilities of things is 'translated' *back* into positivistic talk of mere regularities and then the *real* cause of these regularities is sought in God's will.

SCIENCE AND THEISM

If God is the full and immediate cause of everything apart from himself then the things of the world cause nothing. This exemplification of the law of non-contradiction cannot, as with Austin Farrer, be got out of the way by referring to it as 'the paradox of double agency'. Here, as with Kierkegaard at his worst, paradox just is contradiction. Have we, then, grounds for choosing between the rival hypotheses of theism and deism?

In fact, on the assumption of scientific realism, theism very quickly falls just because it ultimately denies the real existence of the causal structures of the world. The fire that, as we say, flickers and burns does neither. God makes fire-state one in flicker-pose X to be followed by fire-state two in flicker-pose Y and correlatively wood-states one and two in their appropriate poses. The world, on this hypothesis, is not even a blooming buzzing confusion for there is neither bloom nor buzz about it.

The position is very close to that of the clear-headed Berkeley who makes his mistakes without trappings. There is the same sense of a boneless universe poised on the tip of God's will and the edge of nothingness. There are regularities in this flickering existence, which we may gratefully make use of in going about our business, but they are, themselves, supplied from outside along with the flicker. The only causes, the only *real* causes, are spiritual ones and they are causes by production or creation. Indeed, with its every detail determined by the will of God, and its potency mere fanciful boast, by what right do we call this vast outpouring a universe rather than a sheer imagining?

The argument from design has its roots in a sense of wonder at the complex order of things. It is, as Kant (1963:A623, B651) remarks, 'the oldest, the clearest and the most accordant with the common reason of mankind.' But we find that as the argument proceeds to a theistic conclusion the natural causal order of things is illusory. The scientist may draw our attention to the delicate 'fine-tuning' of the constants of nature necessary for the evolution of life and consciousness; we may be told of the interactions of galaxies and the birth and death of stars; but by the time we come to the cosmological conclusion of the design argument these stories are revealed as just that, mere stories, the real springs of the world being the wills of spirits. The conclusion devours its premiss.

THE EMPIRICAL CONTENT OF THEISM

But if theism has such disastrous implications why is it that acute thinkers like Swinburne do not see them – or only half-see them? At least part of the answer lies in the fact, as pointed out by John Anderson, that even abstruse metaphysical views have an associated empirical content. Thus Anderson gives the example of Berkeley's criticism of Locke's notion of substances which *support* their accidents. We know what the word 'support' ordinarily means, as when we speak of a man's braces supporting his trousers or an enthusiast supporting a political party, and it is this ordinary meaning which misleads us into mistakenly thinking we understand the really quite mysterious notion of accidents held up by substance. As Anderson (1962:90) puts it, 'the common relation gives us no help in the understanding of the metaphysical one, but the use of the common word tends to confuse our minds and makes us *imagine* that we have understood something.'[5]

Something similar is true of the idea of God *sustaining* the universe. We know the ordinary use of 'sustain' – doctors and nurses sustain the health of their patients and the gutter press sustains ignorance and prejudice – and this leads us to think we have fully grasped the view of an absolute sustaining of the world. We need not claim, in this case, that there is no special metaphysical notion of sustenance but merely that the ordinary use intrudes when the unfortunate consequences of the espousal of the metaphysical notion make themselves felt. For when we examine this metaphysical absolute sustenance of the universe we find that it is the sustaining of its very existence and this bears little resemblance to a kidney machine sustaining the life of a patient, which is to say, sustaining the patient in a certain state. If the machine is turned off the patient will die and we might portentously describe this as the patient 'going out of existence' – but we would not expect a sudden inrush of air to fill the body-shaped volume vacated by the corpse. Discard the ordinary images, then, and examine the idea in its own right and we will find that this 'sustaining' of the states of the universe by God just comes down, as we have seen, to his immediate *creation* of each and every one of them. This must be the case because no state of the world has, in its own right, the power to produce another. God, then, is not doctor to the world because the world is not an independently existing patient. It is the wholly epiphenomenal glow of God's mind.

DEISM AND THE NOTION OF 'THE WORLD'

What, then, of deism? There is at least this sense to the notion: that the god it tells us of is one who makes a wholly independent universe with its own causal structures amenable to scientific investigation. In the context of the argument from design, the astonishing facts concerning the 'fine-tuning' of nature's constants do really play their part in bringing about the complexities of sentient life and are not mere show. On the other hand, we must not forget the weaknesses in the analogical argument that leads to the view of such a god producing the universe by a sheer willing that it be so. We have no experience of things being willed into existence – unless, revealingly, we are thinking with Berkeley of the imaginative production of mental images – nor, if we do accept the deistic hypothesis, have we much in the way of grounds for inferring the properties of God.

However, I wish now to look at the problem of creation from the side of the world, as it were, taking for granted that the notion is intelligible and well-founded and even allowing God his traditional attributes of omnipotence etc. There are, as we shall see, still profound difficulties in the way of understanding just *what* it is that God creates or can create although, as perhaps some comfort to the orthodox, we may be able to clear up the notorious theological problem posed by the evil in the world.

It is an interesting fact that in several modern versions of the design argument emphasis is placed on the necessity of the universe being just as it is – at least within narrowly confined limits – if it is to be fit for the production of life. Whereas in the past sceptics could wonder at the efficiency or wisdom of a god who produced such a vast universe just to house a few, perhaps only one, flowerings of intelligent life, now the findings of science are used to argue that things had to be that way. Billions of years of time resulting in billions of cubic light-years of space were needed for the formation of the relevant chemical elements and the subsequent evolution of sentient organisms. The idea seems to be that God was rationally compelled to design the world the way it actually is.

But now the thought arises that God, as omnipotent, can do anything so why could he not have designed a much different, and perhaps much better, universe? It is here that we must remember that the hypothesis under consideration is that of deism which emphasises the *independence* of the universe once created; and we need to make the point that the God of deism, even though omnipotent, can make only what it is possible to make. This means that God can make only those worlds that *can* exist independently of him. He cannot simply dream up any kind of structure whatsoever and then by fiat *make it* have the robustness necessary to stand on its own. We can see this by referring to the work of the theologian Thomas F. Torrance who, after claiming 'As it was created out of nothing the universe might have been quite different from what it is', later goes on:

> Regarded in itself the universe is what it is, this one and only universe which has come into being, but considered from the side of God's free creation it is only one of all possible universes since it might have been very different. This means that we must think of God's relation to the universe in terms of an infinite variability bound up with his unlimited freedom and rationality. As such God remains the free creative ground of the universe even though by bringing it into existence he has actualized one possibility among all the others which has the effect of ruling out the others as really impossible or at least entertainable. This is the only kind of 'necessity' that the universe has, that it cannot now be other than it is.
>
> (Torrance 1981:22)

I do not at all see how it follows from the supposed fact that the universe is created from nothing that it could have been other than it is. It is revealing that Torrance speaks of the universe 'regarded in itself' but then immediately asks us to consider it 'from the side of God's free creation' when it becomes merely the *actual* universe God makes out of a range of *possible* ones. How do we really know *from the side of possible universes* how many there are, whether one or many or perhaps an infinity of them? It is no use here appealing to the side of God's creativity, because the properties a world has, *including its capacity for self-sustenance and the causal interaction of its constituents*, belong to it, the world, in its own right. On the hypothesis of deism God makes the universe with *its own* properties fit for its own causality and we have no evidence that other properties could do the same or a similar job. In case it still be insisted that God, being omnipotent, could construct a universe of a certain 'basic structure' – e.g. with fundamental particles of a certain kind – and then over and above that determine how it goes causally, then the answer once more must be that this is but a diguised way of espousing a non-deistic position. There is the collapse back into theism or an unstable interactionism.

What, after all, does this talk of 'possible worlds' of us philosophers and theologians come to? The idea is of God having before his mind a list of the detailed ground-plans of all such worlds, any one of which he can realise. But we also think we know something of what is on the list besides the universe we happen to inhabit. We picture to ourselves, *or so we think*, a world in which an intelligent bi-pedal rabbit is blown to pieces and immediately reconstituted and we may be bolstered in our faith in this as a possible world because we can see moving cartoon images of such goings-on on television or at the cinema. What does this amount to? Surely no more than that we can imagine such things happening and can express them in non-contradictory propositions. The proposition 'Bugs Bunny has just now been squashed flat as a pancake' is compatible with 'In three seconds time he will be his old self again'. In fact, we may even see him filling out like a balloon and returning to his original lovable shape. Bugs Bunny, then, is, as the jargon goes, logically possible which is to say that there is no logical contradiction in our concept of him or between the propositions in which we describe his behaviour. But is he *really* possible? Could he in fact exist?

We need a context. If Mr Bunny is to exist he needs a world in which to do so. Let us try to fit him into our universe. There he is on some distant planet, along with his friends and enemies, all of whom, like himself, are endlessly amorphous, can run on thin air and pull question marks from their heads. Well, what are these creatures *made of*? They seem to be sorts of mammals and birds and so forth so, if only they would stay still long enough to be opened up, we might expect to find brains and livers and so on within them. Could such delicately adjusted organ systems really be capable of such instant and profound changes and then return to their normal functioning states? Here the answer might be that they could if only they were made in the right kind of way of the right kind of stuff. Let us, then, get down to the nitty gritty bedrock and ask, 'What is the fundamental stuff of which these animals are made?' and, as we have placed them in our universe, let us first toy with the suggestion that they are made of the same fundamental constituents, the quarks, leptons, etc., as the rest of us. It is, I suppose, if we say it quickly enough, logically possible that the fundamental particles be brought together in such a way that the more outrageous cartoon characters go about their business in the real world.

But now we need to ask where these strange animals come from. Even though in some sense they have immense survival value no biologist would for a moment admit that they originated by the ordinary evolutionary processes of natural selection or whatever. They really are much too much caricatures of organisms for that. Perhaps we can imagine them as specially made by super technicians or directly created by God who, by a special act, intrudes them into our universe. Immediately we say that we once more raise the issue of whether or not there is any possible combination of the fundamental constituents of our universe which could act and interact in these bizarre ways and once more the answer is not to be sought in mere logical possibility, i.e. absence of contradiction. Whether or not such plastic structures are *really* possible depends not on abstract logical considerations but on the *real* properties of their constituents and their consequent potentialities. I can add that the scientifically minded persons I consulted, and could persuade to take the question seriously, firmly confined Bugs Bunny to the screen.

The difficulties bristle. We try the move of making these extraordinary creatures out of extraordinary stuff. Surely, we might say, if the ordinary matter with which we are acquainted will not do the job then we can always bring in some logically possible 'exotic matter'. Perhaps: but recall that we have placed this strange planet and its denizens in *our* universe and now I wish to know whether or not they are supposed to be in interaction with *our* matter. Suppose the answer is 'Yes', then how is the trick done? Ordinary matter, which is extraordinary enough, has, according to the design argument, been exquisitely crafted to the end of producing life. Must we expect it also to take on the burden of communing with wholly alien stuff thrust into its midst? We would have to tinker with our particles and fields, would we not?, to *adjust* them to the causal influences of this absolutely foreign material and we might wonder if this could possibly be done without upsetting the whole fine balance of things. Could God just *add* an extra causal property to matter? Or would not this 'property' especially designed to deal with aliens itself be alien and lack 'fit' with our world; or, at least, would it not require a redistribution and revaluing of those originally finely tuned characteristics that our cosmologists and theologians praise God for? On the other hand, if we were to place this extra 'bridging quality' on the other side of the divide with its roots in exotic matter then, *mutatis mutandis*, the problem of 'fit' would break out over there.

This rabbit and his associates are testing our imaginations and, perhaps, our patience. We can go on and on trying to place them in logically possible situations and still we have no guarantee that they are *really* possible. For example, we remove the problem posed by the supposed causal interaction of exotic with ordinary matter by cutting all causal links between the two – they go on in the one space–time world but in their own different ways without communion each with the other. Difficulties still arise. According to the physicists, space–time is not merely a yawning container into which things can be poured willy-nilly by God or by anyone else. The connection between space and time and matter – *our* matter including its associated fields of force – is much more intimate than that.[6] Space–time, it seems, is connected with the very form matter can take and we have little reason to think it can 'contain' just anything at all that we like to dream up.

Now the move will be to try to describe alternative 'possible universes' which shift for themselves in their own peculiar ways. When one of these is described to us do we really know how to assess the claim that God could have made it? Let us desert our cartoon friends and, with Professor David Lewis, briefly contemplate a rather pristine example of another universe. Here Lewis is describing the view that the proximity to truth of not quite true theories can be explained by reference to worlds where those theories *are* precisely true:

> For instance, we have the simple, approximate gas laws: and then we have correction terms. But if the correction terms were all zero, things wouldn't be too different.... The closest of the

approximate-gas-law worlds are pretty close to ours. That is why the approximate gas laws are close to the truth.

(Lewis, D. 1986:24)

In fact, in the interest of solving certain difficult problems concerning modality, verisimilitude, etc., Professor Lewis and other 'modal realists' are prepared profligately to confer existence on a multitude of possible worlds – and, in the case of Lewis at least, without seeking help from the notion of a creator-god. But let us ask, in the context of our discussion of deism, whether God *could* make *actual* an admittedly logically possible universe where gases always obeyed the 'simple, approximate gas laws' (the 'perfect' or 'ideal' gas laws as they are often called). Would such a world hang together, as it were? It is instructive, in contemplating this question, to consider what is involved ontologically in supplying the correction factors to the perfect gas laws in order to turn them into imperfect but real laws (in our world). One may try to arrive at these laws empirically (as it is sometimes put) by trying out different plausible-looking equations on lots and lots of samples of gases and seeing which provides the best fit. However, the more interesting investigations are theoretical ones concerning the basic constituents of gases. (In fact, even the 'empirical' investigations will involve background theoretical guesses or assumptions.) For example, if P is the pressure of the gas, V the volume and T the absolute temperature then the ideal gas law $PV = RT$ (where R is a constant) can be deduced from the theory that the constituents of gases are perfectly elastic, point-like 'billiard balls' which rebound off each other and the perfectly elastic walls of their container; and Van der Waals tried to supply correction factors b and a/v^2 by taking into account the fact that gas molecules come in sizes and that there are forces of attraction between them. These two real, not merely mathematical, factors work against each other, so to speak, the b (size) factor tending to reduce the compressibility of the gas and the close-range attractive force tending to increase it. This ruins the charming simplicity of $PV = RT$, replacing it with the fiercer $(P + a/v^2)(V - b) = RT$, but comes closer to describing the behaviour of real gases. But the assumptions of molecular size and attractive force go some way towards *explaining* why, for example, hydrogen gas never gets its simple multiplication sums right whereas carbon dioxide and other gases sometimes do.[7]

Let us set about picturing a possible universe in which a Sir Robert Boyle discovers, to his great satisfaction and the glory of God, that at all temperatures gases obediently and precisely obey the law named for him. Pressures and volumes *exactly* adjust themselves to each other so that their product remains steady. What are these gases made of? We think immediately, I suppose, of those, not tiny, but absolutely dimensionless points which make up for their lack of size by their immense strength and tenacity, forever jostling and rebounding from each other. It was, after all, from this hypothesis that the gas laws, which for our world are not quite laws, were first theoretically derived. Is this logically possible world possibly an actual world? If so, what is the causal 'go' of it?

We might stop briefly, in the company of Bishop Berkeley and John Anderson, for a session of head-scratching at this notion of a world of billiard balls of no size whatsoever. If the idea is found too objectionable then we can always replace it with one where the atoms of gas are very, very tiny balls, just this side of ideality, so to speak. (Actually, I should imagine that Daniel Bernoulli's assumption, in his original reasoning on this issue, was not that the gas-particles are dimensionless but that, being very small compared to the volume they occupied, their size could be ignored for mathematical purposes. This method of approximation works quite well for gases of low density.) Do we not, then, this problem aside, now have a picture of an ideal-gas universe?

But Van der Waals introduced *two* correction factors. What is this other one, the force of attraction effective in close encounters of the ideal kind? It also ruins the beauty of the interactions of the atoms as shown by the second bracketed expression of Van der Waals's equation – the atoms do *not* collide and rebound like perfect billiard balls in an eternal master-shot. The attractive force *intercedes* between them. Very well, then, remove it and let these immensely hard, elastic atoms collide face-to-face and fly away along their newly restored ideal paths. We are, after all, describing a possible universe built after its own plan.

Once more, at a distance, we glimpse the iceberg of reality in this otherwise friendly, warm sea of bare possibility. '. . . if the correction factors were all zero, things wouldn't be too different', Lewis wrote. But *things* would be different. In introducing attractive forces between the atoms or molecules of gases Van der Waals, whatever his intentions, was not providing only a needed but merely mathematical correction of the gas laws: he was saying something about how it is that the things of our world interact. He was, if you like, introducing an *ontological* correction factor; and we now know that we have to go beyond this position and consider, also, forces of repulsion without which the supposedly naked billiard ball points would not dart away from each other. Coming closer to modern physical accounts, we can envisage these points in space as surrounded by fields of force *which are what engage in the actual causal interactions*. In our world nothing, not even billiard balls, acts in the manner of (ideal) billiard balls.

If we were to relieve these miniscule dots of their fields they would indifferently sail straight past, or even through, each other. Such a universe would, in its basic particulate structure, be deterministically libertarian. Of course, in *our* universe things are much more complicated and mysterious. Its 'particles' are probabilistically fuzzy and are much too intimately bound up with their fields to be snipped out and set free. In one vision, at least, 'we can consider reality to be made up of a set of interacting fields (or better, one *unified* field) in Faraday's sense, where the field is the ultimate reality and the particles are quantum condensates of the field' (Adair 1987:49). Once more, the essential point is that this is the way our world goes on: it is because it is 'constructed' after this fashion that gases are fairly well behaved, that chemicals interact and life evolves. We do not know of other ways a world may proceed.

There is still the matter of bare logical possibility and I shall admit unhesitatingly that I can conceive of a universe where little, round, replete atoms interact 'manifestly by impulse', as John Locke put it. In playful mood, Sir Arthur Eddington (1935:11) once told us, 'When I think of an electron there rises to my mind a hard, red, tiny ball; the proton similarly is neutral grey.' The image is vivid and I can easily imagine such intrinsically coloured worlds as I can, indeed, ones where material objects of the naïvest of naïve realists trundle and others where phenomenalistic sense-data lawfully erupt. But, created or not, could such worlds exist?

I have made the distinction, in this discussion of universes, between 'logical possibility' and 'real possibility' and we can get something of a handle on the distinction in the following way. Among the designs of Leonardo da Vinci was one for a flying machine which was meant to take off by a bird-like flapping of its wings. It was always logically possible that such a device would fly as, indeed, it is that pigs might do so. But was it *really* possible? Leonardo would have thought so, I take it, because his design was based on the careful observation of actual flying machines – birds – so, unless avians need special vital forces as well as wings to stay aloft, there was a good chance that his was a workable contrivance. With its construction this century – made possible by advances in materials' science – we now know that this is the case. The point is that in claiming such real possibilities there is an expression both of ignorance and knowledge. The engineer, say, is not quite sure his invention will work before he tries it out – the explosion of the first hydrogen bomb might have destroyed the whole planet rather than merely vaporise an island and kill a few fishermen – but by appealing to his knowledge of the laws of nature, to similar, successful devices and so on, he has some reason to believe it will. The trouble with our grand cosmological speculations, where we think we have access to plans of whole universes, is that we do not know the rules of world-building. What plan could there be and to what principles would we appeal, what guarantees that the universe it attempts to model would, *in fact*, hold together causally? This is why we might feel obliged to make the appeal to this other kind of possibility, logical possibility, and, feeling the gap between it and the reality of things, try to glue it closed with God's immense strength. We forget that, once created, a world must go on in its own way and according to its own lights.[8]

THE AGONY OF THE WORLD

Our hopes for a proof of God's existence, initially raised high by observing the fitness of the universe for the production of life and consciousness, must now, in recognition of our ignorance, return to less exalted altitudes. Not only have the ordinary analogies of production and creation crumpled into the dust of equivocation, our notion of God's willing the world into existence becomes blurred on either side of the divide between creator and created. We do not really know what it is for a sheer willing to produce a world and nor do we know what worlds, apart from this one, are really possible. The facts cry out for explanation but the cry is in the dry wilderness of bare possibilities and the explanations are parched and desperate.

Now for the crumb of comfort. In the first chapter we saw a distinguished physicist puzzling over what he saw as the strange fact of cosmic untidiness, the grand doubling-up of the number of fundamental particles when only one set was needed for the 'manufacture' of stars and planets and life. But the universe is not, as according to the rationalist dream, a mere set of axioms from which theorems perfectly flow so why should we not expect a certain roughness about it? As we have seen, universes, even though conjured out of the pit of nothingness by the will of God, have to stand on their own; and it seems likely that a universe could not be made so that, for example, its *only* characters were those fit for the production of life. Even though all-mighty God would have to settle for compromise in the manufacture of an independent universe suited to some end – he would have to accept, in the interests of its cohesion, things about it towards which he is indifferent or which he actively dislikes in the same way that someone building a house may also provide nesting places for swallows and a home for cockroaches. Those extra particles, then, which so puzzled Professor Glashow in the manner in which they seemed parasitically to nestle among the more workaday ones, may simply be the inconsequential result of putting together interacting fields that produced the fundamental building blocks for the desired structures in the universe. Indeed, if certain modern cosmological theories are correct then matters may be much worse – in order to produce a desirable life-producing universe such as ours, God may have to create a 'supra-universe' which, by quantum fluctuations, bubbles forth an infinite foam consisting largely of useless ones.[9] I shall not discuss the possibility that, from the viewpoint of God, our universe is part of the cost of producing other more desirable worlds.

We have here the germ of a solution to the problem of evil, the question of how God's omnipotence and perfect goodness can be reconciled with the evident fact of evils in the world he created. In a letter John Cook Wilson made the point many years ago:

> We explain our own wrong or imperfect doing by ascribing it to our own causality and not to God's. Similarly we may explain the imperfection, which so troubles the argument from design as due to this other agency in Nature – not God. And I maintained it might be a mistake there to do what was usually done . . . attribute all that happened in nature directly to God as though it was his special province, forgetting that we have already made our own action our special province and not His.
>
> (Wilson 1926:866)

Here we have the clear recognition that the things of the world have their own agency; and if we combine this with the insight that, in creating such an independent universe, even God would have to accept the rough along with the smooth of it, then we get somewhere towards explaining the agony of it all. The universe must shift according to its own lights and, now we must add, according to its darknesses also. The travail of evolution, the immense waste and suffering leading to the supposedly admirable goal of human consciousness – itself, through carelessness as well as wickedness, source and recipient of much further suffering – all this might in some sense be said to be necessary for the realisation of that end.

There are crumbs that comfort but there are also tails with stings in them. Someone might be content, although with no good reason, to believe in God as designer of the universe and, further, gratefully embrace the solution to the problem of evil herein proffered. But, then, fideism, legless and begging crutches from reason, is, itself, one of the world's evils.

Notes

1 The decline of purposive explanations

1 But note the exceptions to this briefly discussed by Ernest Nagel (1961:407–8).
2 There is now evidence that there are at least three such sub-groups but no more than five (Cline 1988).
3 Darwin's own account, where he admits that 'we sometimes drank too much, with jolly singing and playing at cards afterwards' and confesses 'I cannot keep looking back to those times without much pleasure' is given in his autobiography (Darwin 1958:60).
4 This comparison is discussed by both Paley and Darwin. These days, of course, the eye is usually compared with a camera.
5 It is in stupidly (or maliciously) interpreting the modern theory of evolution in this way that the 'creationist' authors of a school textbook of biology are able to say that it 'may be compared to the climber on the side of an icy hill who in attempting to climb upward actually slips downwards 999 times to just one movement upward'. Naturally enough, given their premisses, the authors impeccably conclude, 'His net progress is downward, not upward', with the corollary that Darwinian evolution, in emulating this foolish behaviour, must similarly go downward (Moore and Schultz 1974:451–2).
6 According to Michael T. Ghiselin, it was on reading Malthus that Darwin realised the importance of thinking in terms of populations and, in particular, of 'the long-term effects of differences between individuals upon the composition of the population' (Ghiselin 1969: 59).
7 Smith got this example from Darwin who remarks

> We can no longer argue that, for instance, the beautiful hinge of a bivalve shell must have been made by an intelligent being, like the hinge of a door by man. There seems to be no more design in the variability of organic beings and in the action of natural selection, than in the course which the wind blows.
>
> (Darwin 1958: 87)

8 I do not wish to suggest that Harvey, in working out the function of the heart, explicitly compared it with any known pump of his time. The more

important clue seemed to be the *valves* (which had been described as such by Fabricius) of the associated blood vessels. There is some evidence that, *after* his basic work on the circulation was completed, Harvey compared the heart to a pump in the form of an early fire engine which had been introduced into London (Whitteridge 1971:169–72).

2 Biology and metaphysics

1 But on this see Rosenberg (1985:169–74).
2 Cf. Curtis (1975:9) who, in speaking of the importance of the theory of evolution, says: 'we begin to understand the *seeming* purposefulness of living things and their activities' (my emphasis).
3 In fact, this metaphor is revealing and shows that what are really doing the work of bringing about organic order in Bergson's theory are the 'original impulses' within the vital force, although Bergson brings them in ostensibly only to 'explain' cases of parallel evolution. Certainly, the 'choices' made by the vital force have absolutely nothing to do with the 'design' of organisms, either in intentional content or by causal connection; and, pathetically, Bergson's philosophy of nature, hailed as an epic of Heracleitean spontaneity, requires, under the guise of the original impulses, *moulds* into which to fit the things of the world. Equally pathetically, confronted with the real metaphysical content of their theory, Bergsonians retreat immediately behind their doctrine of 'intuition'.
4 However, the philosophical waters here are turbulent. Wittgensteinians, for example, would not accept the sharp distinction I have made between methodological considerations and the content of religious and scientific propositions because, they would say, the logical kind to which a proposition belongs may be shown by the way a person entertains it. That a religious person will not allow anything to count against their belief in the Last Judgement is not necessarily, on this account, an indication of bigotry or superstition but perhaps of the fact that their belief is not an 'hypothesis' – it may be more like a 'picture' they entertain to guard against temptation. With the Wittgensteinian D.Z. Phillips this view is bound up with the view of religion and science as quite separate 'language games', each with its own criteria of truth and meaning, so that it would be a mistake to look for connections between them of the kind relevant to this text. See, for example, Phillips (1976). I have criticised Phillips in Olding (1977).
5 Compare Mary Midgley (1985): 'Narrow-minded, conformist sceptics and immoralists are now a standard issue.'
6 See Lewontin (1972).
7 Cf. Gilbert (1982).

3 The stuff we are made of

1 For a suggestive account of this dialectical relation between different levels of theory in post-Galilean physics see McMullin (1972).
2 Cf. Lucretius (1951:47) who, in discussing Heracleitus' view that all things are fire, remarks, 'What grounds have we for taking away everything else

and leaving fire, any more than for taking away fire and leaving some other things? Either procedure appears equally insane.'
3 Quoted in Thorpe (1974:11).
4 But see Woolley (1988).
5 I leave aside as irrelevant to this issue the fact that the structure of a particular DNA molecule may be impossible in principle to predict because of quantum effects.

5 Biology and knowledge

1 Cf. Anderson (1962:6–11).
2 Cf. Olding (1968:63–4).

6 Consciousness and its objects

1 Naïve or quick readers should carefully note the date of publication of the article, the name of the island and the names of the 'chief investigator' (Robert L. Ripley) and his New York college (Charles Fort).
2 Haldane later retracted the argument.
3 Cf. the argument discussed on pp. 79–93 concerning the self-refuting character of Darwinism.
4 Thus the following version of the argument is given by Cyril Burt:

> Now let us ask how a set of physical changes, physically caused, could possibly 'correspond' to such conscious experience as seeing that an 'axiom' is 'self-evident' or to logical transition such as is implied by the simple word 'therefore'. If the whole sequence of statements were indeed merely the effect of a causal chain of physical processes, all blindly and mechanically determined, it would follow that the speaker could not help saying what he did; and his arguments, as reasoned arguments, could carry no weight. Why then should we take the smallest notice of what he says?
>
> (Burt 1975:56)

5 See note 4 above.
6 For the moment I ignore behaviouristic analyses of mental concepts.
7 For the notion of a causal field see Anderson (1962:126–31).
8 For the use of this expression see McGinn (1982:8).
9 Although the belief theorist may try to give a spurious rigour to his account by presenting it as an 'analysis'.
10 It should be emphasised that I am here referring to only one of a series of arguments used by Jackson against the belief account.
11 It should be said, though, that Sperry's theory is nowhere near as original as he seems to think; nor does he show any appreciation of the immense epistemological etc. problems it encounters.

7 Biology and cosmology

1 See, for example, Swinburne (1979:Ch.7 and 1986:198–9).
2 See, for example, Barrow and Tipler (1986).

3 This example is discussed by Smart (1987).
4 See, again, Smart (1987).
5 For several quite different definitions of the anthropic principle see Barrow and Tipler (1986:15–23).
6 See, for example, Barrow and Tipler (1986:15–23).
7 For an accessible account of the several generations of stars involved in the synthesis of the heavier elements, see Bennett (1988).
8 For a similar argument, with some of the mathematical details filled in, see Barrow and Tipler (1986:20–1 and 245–7).
9 And so the notion has been boldly proposed that the big bang at the origin of the universe eventually resulted in the evolution of conscious beings and the existence of these conscious beings somehow brought about the temporally prior big bang. (See, for example, Wheeler 1982.) We are here because the world is here and the world is here because we are here! I shall restrict myself to the tautology that nonsense, even when promulgated by eminent cosmologists, is nonsense.
10 See, for example, Shimony (1988).
11 However, the view here discussed should be distinguished from other 'many worlds' views, such as that of Everett, which are arguably more securely based in physical theory. (For an account of Everett's position see, for example, Barrow and Tipler (1986:472–89).) I have little to say about them here except, unless they are themselves taken as ultimate cosmological theories, they still leave unexplained why it is that, among the sets of physical values 'defining' universes of various sorts, one set seems peculiarly fitted for the evolution of life.

8 From world to God

1 I shall, henceforth, assume we are mainly discussing monotheism.
2 Swinburne also accuses me of the same fallacy.
3 But notice that Jantzen is not concerned in her book with arguments for God's existence.
4 In fact, I think that Swinburne does, momentarily, sense that there is something wrong with his argument because, immediately following it, he adds,

> There is, it should be pointed out, no necessity for men to be unaware of the effects which they produce directly. We shall with the progress of neurophysiology come to learn what the latter are and could no doubt then teach ourselves how to produce brain states.
>
> (Swinburne 1972: 200)

It is as if he thinks that, at present, the analogical base of the design argument is a bit weak because we have no examples of humans directly acting on their brains in the sense of intending so to act and the action springing directly out of the intention. But, he says, be patient. Wait for the progress of science and we will have such examples. It could easily be shown that the same confusion of meanings is at work in this description of what is going on when someone intentionally acts on his brain as in Swinburne's other accounts of direct action.

5 Cf. Baker (1986:41–2).
6 We can see this non-Humean intuition concerning causality in C. Perrault's criticism of 'epigenesis', the theory that embryological development is from an entirely homogenous egg: 'If the egg consists of homogeneous matter, as is presumed on this hypothesis, it can only develop into a foetus by a miracle, which would surpass every other phenomenon in the world' (Perrault 1680).
7 I would strongly resist the accusation that my own 'intuition', that the cause must be adequate in complexity to explain the effect, is merely a rationalistic confusion. Indeed, I should argue that rationalistic formulations, such as that the cause must have at least as much 'perfection' as the effect (Descartes), are rationalistic distortions of what is plainly the case.
8 An analogy might be drawn here with the physical notion of action at a distance where the requirement that cause and effect are contiguous is dropped. Cf. J.L. Mackie (1974).
9 Cf. Diotima:

> By its original meaning poet means simply creation, and creation, as you know, can take very various forms. Any action which is the cause of a thing emerging from non-existence into existence might be called poetry, and all the processes in all the crafts are kinds of poetry, and all those who are engaged in them poets.
>
> (Plato 1954: 86)

10 In Ursula le Guin's *Wizard of Earthsea* series (Le Guin 1968), wizards gain control over things by learning their magical names. But the arbitrariness of this comes out in the fact that dragons, who have their own magic, know a different set of names. To explain how the magic works, then, perhaps we have to postulate the existence of some great spirit who supplies the names but who, in doing so, is also in possession of their detailed definite descriptions.

9 And back again

1 Cf. Olding (1983:206–8).
2 But see 'Deism and the notion of the world', pp. 154 ff.
3 What, then, of such 'things' as numbers and laws of logic? I am aware of the issue but shall not here agonise on it.
4 See C.G. Hempel (1966).
5 However, I think it is arguable that Anderson, in his metaphysics, falls foul of his own strictures, e.g. as when in his unpublished lecture notes on Samuel Alexander he speaks of space and time 'working together'. Cf. A.J. Baker (1986:Ch. 7).
6 See, for example, Adair (1987).
7 On this see, for example, Partington (1966:35).
8 For a recent interesting discussion of the notion of logical possibility, see Mason (1988).
9 See, for example, Gribbin (1988:55).

Bibliography

Adair, R.K. (1987) *The Great Design: Particles, Fields and Creation*, Oxford: Oxford University Press.
—— (1988) 'A flaw in a universal mirror', *Scientific American* 258, 2: 30–6.
Alcock, J. (1972) 'The evolution of tools by feeding animals', *Evolution* 26, 4: 464–473.
Alexander, S.C. (1920) *Space, Time and Deity*, London: Macmillan.
Alland, A. (1967) *Evolution and Human Behaviour*, London: Tavistock.
Anderson, J. (1962) *Studies in Empirical Realism*, Sydney: Angus & Robertson.
Angross, R. and Stancia, G. (1987) *The New Biology: Discovering the Wisdom in Nature*, Boston: New Science Library, Shambhala Publications.
Aristotle (1921) *Posterior Analytics*, Book 1 (trans. Mure, G.R.G.), in Ross, W.D. (ed.) *The Works of Aristotle*, Oxford: Oxford University Press.
—— (1961) *Metaphysics* (trans. Warrington, J.), London: J.M. Dent and Sons.
Armstrong, D.M. (1961) *Perception and the Physical World*, London: Routledge & Kegan Paul.
—— (1968) *A Materialist Theory of Mind*, London: Routledge & Kegan Paul.
Avers, C.J. (1974) *Evolution*, New York: Harper & Row.
Baker, A.J. (1986) *Australian Realism: The Systematic Philosophy of John Anderson*, Cambridge: Cambridge University Press.
Bakker, R.J. (1975) 'Dinosaur renaissance', *Scientific American* 232, 4: 58–78.
Barker, A.D. (1969) 'An approach to the theory of natural selection', *Philosophy* 44, 170: 271–90.
Barltrop, R. and Wolveridge, J. (1980) *The Muvver Tongue*, London: The Journeyman Press.
Barrow, J.D. and Tipler, F.J. (1986) *The Anthropic Principle*, Oxford: Oxford University Press.
Bennett, G. (1988) 'Cosmic origins of the elements', *Astronomy* 16, 8: 18–25.
Bergson, H. (1911) *Creative Evolution*, London: Macmillan.
Bohm, D. (1961) *Causality and Chance in Modern Physics*, New York: Harper Torch Books.
Brierley, C.L. (1982) 'Microbiological mining', *Scientific American* 247, 1: 42–51.
Burt, C. (1975) *E.S.P. and Psychology*, London: Weidenfeld and Nicolson.
Cairns-Smith, A.G. (1985) *Seven Clues to the Origin of Life*, Cambridge: Cambridge University Press.

Canfield, J. (1964) 'Teleological explanations in biology', *British Journal for the Philosophy of Science* 14, 56: 285–95.
Carter, B. (1974) 'Large number coincidences and the anthropic principle in cosmology', in Longair, M.S. (ed.) *Confrontation of Cosmological Theories with Observational Data*, Dordrecht: D. Reidel Publishing.
—— (1983) 'The anthropic principle and its implications for biological evolution', *Philosophical Transactions of the Royal Society of London* A300: 347–63.
Charlesworth, B. (1982) 'Neo-Darwinism – the plain truth', *New Scientist* 94, 1301: 133–7.
Clark, A.J. (1984) 'Evolutionary epistemology and ontological realism', *Philosophical Quarterly* 137, 34: 482–90.
Clark, R.E.D. (1966) *Darwin: Before and After*, London: The Paternoster Press.
Cline, D.B. (1988) 'Beyond truth and beauty: a fourth family of particles', *Scientific American* 259, 2: 42–9.
Cohen, M.L., Heine, V. and Phillips, J.C. (1982) 'The quantum mechanics of materials', *Scientific American*, 246, 6: 66–79.
Copernicus, N. (1959) 'Narratio Prima', in Rosen, E. (trans. and ed.) *The Copernican Treatises*, New York: Dover Publications.
Copleston, F.C. (1955) *Aquinas*, Harmondsworth: Penguin Books.
Crombie, A.C. (1964) 'Early concepts of the senses and the mind', *Scientific American* 210, 5: 108–16.
Cummins, R. (1975) 'Functional Analysis', *Journal of Philosophy* 72, 20: 741–65.
Curtis, H. (1975) *Biology*, New York: Worth Publishers.
Darwin, C. (1958) *The Autobiography of Charles Darwin* (ed. Barlow, Nora), Glasgow: Collins.
Davies, P. (1980) *Other Worlds: Space, Superspace and the Quantum Universe*, London: J.M. Dent & Sons.
Dawkins, R. (1976) *The Selfish Gene*, Oxford: Oxford University Press.
—— (1988) *The Blind Watchmaker*, Harmondsworth: Penguin Books.
Deutscher, M.J. (1968) 'Popper's problem of an empirical basis', *Australasian Journal of Philosophy* 46, 3: 277–88.
—— (1983) *Subjecting and Objecting: An Essay in Objectivity*, St Lucia: University of Queensland Press.
Dewdney, A.K. (1988) 'Computer recreations', *Scientific American* 254, 4: 96–9.
Dirac, P.A.M. (1937) 'The cosmological constants', *Nature* 139, 3512: 323.
Dyson, F. (1985) *Origins of Life*, Cambridge: Cambridge University Press.
Eddington, A. (1935) *The Nature of the Universe*, London: J.M. Dent & Sons.
Farrer, A. (1966) *A Science of God?*, London: Bles.
Fiddes, J.C. (1977) 'The nucleotide sequence of a viral DNA', *Scientific American* 238, 12: 55–67.
Flew, A.G.N. (1967) 'Introduction', in Flew, A.G.N. (ed.) *Body, Mind and Death*, New York: Macmillan Co.
Fodor, J.A. (1981) 'The mind–body problem', *Scientific American* 244, 1: 124–32.
Ford, A. (1986) *Universe: God, Man and Science*, London: Hodder & Stoughton.
Forrest, P. (1982) 'Anthropic answers and the existence of god', *Proceedings of the Russellian Society* 7: 1–10.
Foster, M.B. (1934) 'The Christian doctrine of creation and the rise of modern natural science', *Mind* 43, 172: 446–68.

Frazzetta, T.H. (1975) *Complex Adaptations in Evolving Populations*, Sunderland, Mass.: Sinauer Associates.
Galloway, J. (1988) 'The fallacy of the unselfish gene', *New Scientist* 117, 1602: 67–8.
Gardner, M. (1985) *Whys of a Philosophical Scrivener*, Oxford: Oxford University Press.
Geach, P.T. (1977) *Providence and Evil*, Cambridge: Cambridge University Press.
Ghiselin, M.T. (1969) *The Triumph of the Darwinian Method*, Berkeley: University of California Press.
—— (1974) *The Economy of Nature and the Evolution of Sex*, Berkeley: University of California Press.
Gibson, J.J. (1968) *The Senses Considered as Perceptual Systems*, London: George Allen & Unwin.
Gilbert, L.E. (1982) 'The co-evolution of a butterfly and a vine', *Scientific American* 247, 2: 102–7B.
Glashow, S.L. (1975) 'Quarks with colour and flavour', *Scientific American* 233, 4: 38–50.
Grene, M. (1974) *The Understanding of Nature: Essays in the Philosophy of Biology*, Dordrecht: D. Reidel Publishing.
Gribbin, J. (1988) 'Bubbles on the river of time', *New Scientist* 120, 1612: 52–5.
Haldane, J.B.S. (1930) *Possible Worlds*, London: Chatto & Windus.
Hardy, A. (1975) *The Biology of God*, London: Jonathan Cape.
Harre, R. (1970) *The Principles of Scientific Thinking*, London: Macmillan.
Harrison, R.G. (1977) 'Parallel variation at an enzyme locus in sibling species of field crickets', *Nature* 266, 5598: 168–70.
Hawking, S.W. (1988) *A Brief History of Time*, London: Bantam Press.
Hempel, C.G. (1966) *Philosophy of Natural Science*, Englewood Cliffs: Prentice-Hall.
Henderson, L.J. (1913) *The Fitness of the Environment*, Gloucester, Mass.: Smith.
Hirst, R.J. (1959) *The Problems of Perception*, London: George Allen & Unwin.
Hume, D. (1962) *Dialogues Concerning Natural Religion* (ed. Smith, N.K.), Indianapolis and New York: Bobbs-Merrill.
Jackson, F. (1977) *Perception: A Representative Theory*, Cambridge: Cambridge University Press.
Jaki, S.L. (1978) *The Road of Science and the Ways to God*, Edinburgh: Scottish Academic Press.
Jantzen, G.M. (1984) *God's World, God's Body*, London: Darton, Longman & Todd.
Jerison, H.L. (1973) *Evolution of the Brain and Intelligence*, New York: Academic Press.
—— (1976) 'Paleoneurology and the evolution of man', *Scientific American* 234, 1: 90–101.
Kant, I. (1963) *The Critique of Pure Reason*, (trans. Smith, N.K.), London: Macmillan.
Kenny, A. (1987) *Reason and Religion: Essays in Philosophical Theology*, Oxford: Basil Blackwell.
Kneale, W.C. (1974),'The demarcation of science', in Schilpp, A. (ed.) *The Philosophy of Karl Popper*, La Salle, Ill.: Open Court.

Knight, M. (1952) 'Consciousness and the brain', *Science News* 25: 97–104.
Lack, D. (1947) *Darwin's Finches*, Cambridge: Cambridge University Press.
—— (1957) *Evolutionary Theory and Christian Belief*, London: Methuen.
Le Guin, U. (1968) *A Wizard of Earthsea*, Harmondsworth: Penguin Books
Leibniz, G. (1973) *Philosophical Writings* (ed. Parkinson, G.H.R., trans. Morris, M. and Parkinson, G.H.R.), London: J.M. Dent & Sons.
Lenneberg, E.H. (1967) *Biological Foundation of Language*, New York: John Wiley & Sons.
Lewis, D. (1986) *On the Plurality of Worlds*, Oxford: Basil Blackwell.
Lewis, J. (1974) *The Uniqueness of Man*, London: Lawrence & Wishart.
Lewontin, R. (1972) 'Testing the theory of natural selection', *Nature* 236, 5343: 181–2.
Locke, J. (1964) *An Essay Concerning Human Understanding*, London: Collins.
Lorenz, K. (1975) 'Kant's doctrine of the a priori in the light of contemporary biology', in Evans, R.J. (ed.) *Konrad Lorenz: The Man and His Ideas*, New York: Harcourt Brace Jovanovich.
—— (1977) *Behind the Mirror*, London: Methuen.
Lovell, B. (1975) *In the Centre of Immensities*, London: Book Club Associates.
Lucretius (1951) *The Nature of the Universe* (trans. Latham, R.E.), Harmondsworth: Penguin Books.
McGinn, C. (1982) *The Character of Mind*, Oxford: Oxford University Press.
Mackie, J.L. (1974) *The Cement of the Universe*, Oxford: Oxford University Press.
McMullin, E. (1972) 'The dialectics of reduction', *Idealistic Studies* 2, 2: 95–115.
Malcolm, N. (1960) 'Anselm's ontological arguments', *Philosophical Review* 69: 41–62.
Manser, A.R. (1965) 'The concept of evolution', *Philosophy* 40, 151: 18–34.
Margulis, L. (1971) 'Symbiosis and evolution', *Scientific American* 235, 7: 48–57.
Marsden G.M. (1984) 'Understanding fundamentalist views of science', in Montagu, A. (ed.) *Science and Creationism*, Oxford: Oxford University Press.
Mason, R.V. (1988) 'Logical possibility', *Metaphilosophy* 19, 1: 11–24.
Mayr, E. (1978) 'Evolution', *Scientific American* 239, 3: 38–47.
Maze, J.R. (1983) *The Meaning of Behaviour*, London: Allen & Unwin.
Midgley, M. (1985) *Evolution as a Religion: Strange Hopes and Stranger Fears*, London: Methuen.
Miller, K.R. (1984) 'Scientific creationism versus evolution: the mislabelled debate', in Montagu, A. (ed.) *Science and Creationism*, Oxford: Oxford University Press.
Miller, S.L. and Orgel, L.E. (1974) *The Origin of Life on Earth*, Englewood Cliffs, N.J.: Prentice Hall.
Monod, J. (1974) *Chance and Necessity*, London: Fontana.
Moore, J.N. and Schultz, H. (eds) (1974) *Biology: A Search for Order in Complexity*, Grand Rapids, Mich.: Zondervan Publishing House.
Nagel, E. (1961) *The Structure of Science*, London: Routledge & Kegan Paul.
Nagel, T. (1974) 'What is it like to be a bat', *Philosophical Review* 83: 435–50.
Nicolai, J. (1974) 'Mimicry in parasitic birds', *Scientific American* 231, 4: 92–8.
Olding, A. (1968) 'Armstrong, Smart and the ontological status of secondary qualities', *Australasian Journal of Philosophy* 46, 1: 52–64.
—— (1977) 'D.Z. Phillips and religious language', *Sophia* 16, 1: 23–8.

—— (1983) 'John Anderson and religion', *Philosophical Investigations* 6, 3: 200–13.
Oparin, A.I. (1953) *The Origin of Life* (trans. Morgulis, S.), New York: Dover Publications.
Paley, W. (1831) *The Works of William Paley, D.D.*, Edinburgh: Thomas Nelson & Peter Brown.
Partington, J.R. (1966) *General and Inorganic Chemistry*, London: Macmillan.
Partridge, P.H. (1934) 'Logic and evolution', *Australasian Journal of Psychology and Philosophy* 12, 3: 161–72.
Passmore, J. (1962) *Philosophical Reasoning*, London: Duckworth.
Perrault, C. (1680) *Essais de Physique*; quoted (p.37) in Gasking, E. (1967) *Investigations into Generation, 1651–1828*, London: Hutchinson.
Phillips, D.Z. (1976) *Religion Without Explanation*, Oxford: Basil Blackwell.
—— (1985) 'The friends of Cleanthes', *Modern Theology* 1, 2: 91–104.
Pitcher, G. (1971) *A Theory of Perception*, Princeton, NJ: Princeton University Press.
Plato (1954) *The Symposium* (trans. Hamilton, W.), Harmondsworth: Penguin Books.
Polanyi, M. (1962) *Personal Knowledge: Towards a Post-Critical Philosophy*, London: Routledge & Kegan Paul.
—— (1966) *The Tacit Dimension*, London: Routledge & Kegan Paul.
—— (1976) 'Life's irreducible structure', in Grene, M. and Mendelsohn, E. (eds) *Topics in the Philosophy of Biology*, Dordrecht: D. Reidel Publishing.
Popper, K.R. (1957) *The Open Society and its Enemies*, London: Routledge & Kegan Paul.
—— (1959) *The Logic of Scientific Discovery*, London: Hutchinson.
—— (1972) *Objective Knowledge*, Oxford: Oxford University Press.
—— (1974a) 'Reply to my critics', in Schilpp, P.A. (ed.) *The Philosophy of Karl Popper*, La Salle, Ill.: Open Court.
—— (1974b) 'Scientific reductionism and the essential incompleteness of all science', in Ayala, F.J. and Dobzhansky, T. (eds) *Studies in the Philosophy of Biology*, London: Macmillan.
Popper, K.R. and Eccles, J.C. (1977) *The Self and its Brain*, Berlin: Springer International.
Price, H.H. (1932) *Perception*, London: Methuen.
—— (1964) 'Appearing and appearances', *American Philosophical Quarterly* 1, 1: 3–19.
Priestley, J. (1965) 'Of the seat of the sentient principle in man', in Passmore, J.A. (ed.) *Priestley's Writings on Philosophy, Science and Politics*, New York: Macmillan.
Pringle-Pattison, A.S. (1920) *The Idea of God in the Light of Recent Philosophy*, Oxford: Oxford University Press.
Puccetti, R. (1968) *Persons: A Study of Possible Moral Agents in the Universe*, London: Macmillan.
Ray, J. (1691) *The Wisdom of God Manifested in the Works of the Creation*, London: Samuel Smith. Republished (1979) New York: Garland Publishing Co. Inc.
Root-Bernstein, R. (1984) 'On defining a scientific theory', in Montagu, A. (ed.) *Science and Creationism*, Oxford: Oxford University Press.

Rorty, R. (1970) 'Mind–body identity, privacy and categories', in Borst, C.Y. (ed.) *The Mind/Body Identity Theory*, London: Macmillan.
Rose, S. (1976) *The Conscious Brain*, Harmondsworth: Penguin Books.
Rosenberg, A. (1985) *The Structure of Biological Science*, Cambridge: Cambridge University Press.
Ruse, M. (1986a) *Taking Darwin Seriously*, Oxford: Basil Blackwell.
—— (1986b) 'Booknotes', *Biology and Philosophy* 1, 4: 477–81.
Schramm, D.N. and Clayton, R.N. (1978) 'Did a supernova trigger the formation of the solar system?' *Scientific American* 239, 3: 98–113.
Shimony, A. (1988) 'The reality of the quantum world', *Scientific American* 258, 1: 36–43.
Short, T.L. (1983) 'Teleology in nature', *American Philosophical Quarterly* 20, 4: 311–20.
Simon, M.A. (1971) *The Matter of Life*, New Haven, Conn.: Yale University Press.
Smart, J.J.C. (1963) *Philosophy and Scientific Realism*, London: Routledge & Kegan Paul.
—— (1970) 'Sensations and brain processes', in Borst, C.V. (ed.) *The Mind/Brain Identity Theory*, London: Macmillan.
—— (1987) 'Philosophical problems of cosmology', *Revue Internationale de Philosophie* 160: 112–26.
Smith, J.M. (1978) *The Evolution of Sex*, Cambridge: Cambridge University Press.
Smith, N.K. (1967) *The Credibility of Divine Existence*, London: Macmillan.
Sorsby, A. (1941) *Medicine and Mankind*, London: Faber & Faber.
Sperry, R.W. (1969) 'A modified concept of consciousness', *Psychological Review* 76, 6: 532–6
Stahl, B. (1974) *Vertebrate History: Problems in Evolution*, New York: McGraw-Hill.
Stent, G.S. (1974) 'Cellular communication', in Kennedy, D. (ed.) *Cellular and Organismal Biology*, San Francisco: W.H. Freeman.
Swinburne, R.G. (1968) 'The argument from design', *Philosophy* 43, 164: 199–212.
—— (1972) 'The argument from design – a defence', *Religious Studies* 8, 193–205.
—— (1977) *The Coherence of Theism*, Oxford: Oxford University Press.
—— (1979) *The Existence of God*, Oxford: Oxford University Press.
—— (1986) *The Evolution of the Soul*, Oxford: Oxford University Press.
Thorpe, W.H. (1974) *Animal Nature and Human Nature*, London: Methuen.
Torrance, T.F. (1981) *Divine and Contingent Order*, Oxford: Oxford University Press.
Toth, I. (1969) 'Non-Euclidean geometry before Euclid', *Scientific American* 221, 11: 87–98.
Trivers, R.L. (1976) 'Introduction', in Dawkins, R. *The Selfish Gene*, Oxford: Oxford University Press.
Vollmer, G. (1984) 'Mesocosm and objective knowledge', in Wuketits, M. (ed.) *Concept and Approaches in Evolutionary Epistemology: Towards an Evolutionary Theory of Knowledge*, Dordrecht: D. Reidel Publishing.
Wade, N. (1972) 'Creationists and evolutionists: confrontation in California', *Science* 176, 4062: 724–9.

Wassermann, G.D. (1974) *Brains and Reasoning*, London: Macmillan.
—— (1978) 'Testability of the role of natural selection within theories of population genetics and evolution', *British Journal for the Philosophy of Science* 29: 223–42.
—— (1981) 'On the nature of the theory of evolution', *Philosophy of Science* 48, 3: 416–37.
Weinberg, S. (1977) *The First Three Minutes*, New York: Basic Books.
Wheeler, J.A. (1982) 'Bohr, Einstein and the strange lesson of the quantum', in Elyee, B.Q. (ed.) *Mind in Nature*, San Francisco: Harper & Row.
Whitehead, A.N. (1978) *Process and Reality*, New York: The Free Press.
Whitrow, G.J. (1955–6) 'Why physical space has three dimensions', *British Journal for the Philosophy of Science* 6, 21: 13–31.
Whitteridge, G. (1971) *William Harvey and the Circulation of the Blood*, London: Macdonald.
Wilkes, K. (1978) *Physicalism*, London: Routledge & Kegan Paul.
Wilson, E. (1979) *The Mental and the Physical*, London: Routledge & Kegan Paul.
Wilson, J.C. (1926) *Statement and Inference with Other Philosophical Papers*, Oxford: Oxford University Press.
Wimsatt, W.C. (1976) 'Reductionism and levels of organisation', in Globus, G.G., Maxwell, G. and Savodnik, I. (eds) *Consciousness and the Brain: A Scientific and Philosophic Inquiry*, New York: Plenum Press.
Woese, C.R. (1981) 'Archaeobacteria', *Scientific American* 244, 6: 94–106.
Woodfield, A. (1976) *Teleology*, Cambridge: Cambridge University Press.
Woolley, G. (1988) 'Must a molecule have shape', *New Scientist* 120, 1635: 53–7.
Wright, L. (1976) 'Functions', in Grene, M. and Mendelsohn, E. (eds), *Topics in the Philosophy of Biology*, Dordrecht: D. Reidel Publishing.

Index

abstract types 27, 28
accidents v. functions 16–17, 18, 20–1
actions, basic v. mediated 131–2, 133–5
Adair, Robert K. 119, 161
adaptations, complex 85–6
aetiologies, functional 12–15
Alexander, Samuel 65
Alland, Alexander 88
Anderson, John xviii–xix, xxi–xxii, 7, 64, 153, 160, 169
'anthropic principle' 120–3, 124
applied science 38
Aquinas, Thomas 10
archaeobacteria 38
Aristotle 3, 49, 77, 89
Armstrong, D. M. xx, 78–9, 102, 108, 109–10, 129
'aspects' of the world 35–6
atomic theory 50–3, 59

Barrow, J. D. 36–7, 124
behaviour, importance for survival xvii, 102
behaviourism 48, 102
belief, perception as 106–12
Bergson, Henri 26–7, 75, 90, 166
Berkeley, Bishop George xv, 36, 153, 160
Bernoulli, Daniel 160
'big bang' theory 119–20, 168
birds 45–6, 81–2, 86
Bohm, David 59
Bohr, Niels 42–3
Boyle, Sir Robert 47–8, 52, 159

brain; and consciousness 112–14; and vision 76–8, 79; evolution of 80–92; predispositions of 75–9; v. mind xx–xxi, 81–3, 94, 96, 127–9, 141–2
Brierley, C. L. 38
Bugs Bunny 156–8
Burt, Cyril 167

Cairns-Smith, A. G. xiii
Canfield, J. 20–2
Carter, Brandon 121, 122
causality in universe 141–53
Charlesworth, B. 45
chloroplasts 43
Christianity 3, 4, *see also* creationism
Clark, A. J. xviii
Clark, R. E. D. 6
Cohen, M. L. 56
colour vision 79, 90–1, 110–12
combustion of stuffs 35
'common-sense philosophers' 105–6
complexity 85–6, 118
computers 95–101
consciousness xix–xx, 81, 82, 94–114, 117
consequence-selection, conscious 13–15
Copleston, F. C. 10
cosmological argument 147, 148–53
'CP (charge-parity) symmetry' 119–20
creation; accidental v. willed 135–7; and intention 141–4; and knowledge 138–40; and order 144–6

creationism 31–5, 165
Crick, Francis 61
critical capacity 92–3
Crombie, A. C. 94
Cummins, Robert 14

Darwin, Charles xi–xii, 6, 9–10, 25, 36, 165
Darwinism xv, xvi–xvii, xviii, xix, 22–3, 25, 30, 71–4, 80–93, 117, *see also* natural selection, evolution by
Davies, Paul 122
Dawkins, Richard xi–xii, xv, xvi, 73, 88–9
deism 146, 147–8, 151–2, 154–62
Descartes, René xi, 23, 80, 92, 151
design argument; analogy with humans 130–5, 141–4; and 'anthropic principle' xx, 120–2, 124; and biological functions 10–15; and brain evolution 82–3; and deism v. theism 146–62; and improbability of evolution 117–20, 123; and mind v. brain xxi–xxii, 125, 133; and problem of evil 163–4; origins of x–xi, 6–8
Deutscher, Max 54–5
Dewdney, A. K. 96
Dirac, Paul 121
disease 19
DNA 60–2, 65–6, 73–4
'downward causation' 58
dualism, mind–body xxi–xxi, 66, 94–5, 104, 113, 125, 126, 129–31, 133, 135, 141
Dyson, Freeman xiii–xiv

Eccles, J. C. 57–8
Eddington, Sir Arthur 161
elements 42–3, 48–50
'eliminative materialism' 104–5
emergent evolution 53–4, 64–7
environments, pressure of 21
epiphenomenalism 81
Euclidean geometry 77–8
Everett, H. 168
evil, problem of 155, 163–4
evolution *see* emergent evolution; natural selection, evolution by

existential statements 42–3
experience xvii–xix
eye, human 6–7

falsifiability of scientific theories 40–2, 89
Farrer, Austin 152
fideism x, 164
'final causes' 11, 27–9, 30
fitness v. survival 22–3
Flew, Antony 129
Fodor, Jerry A. 104
'force of selection' 72, 73, 117
Ford, Adam 147
form v. matter 3, 4
Forrest, Peter 118–19, 125
Foster, M. B. 3
functional accounts 10–15
functions; and accidents 15–18, 20–1; biological 10–15

Galloway, John 30
Gardner, Martin x
gases/gas laws 29–30, 158–61
Geach, Peter xii, 25, 26, 27
Ghiselin, Michael T. xvii, 165
Gibson, James J. 54
Glashow, Sheldon Lee 4–5
goal-directed activity 16
God, analogy with humans 130–5; and complexity of universe 119; as creator of order 144–6; as creator of universe 135–40, 141–4, 146; as 'sustainer' of universe 147–54; embodied 125–30; interaction with universe 143–4, 145–6; will of 135–40, 141–4;
gravitational 'constant' 121
Greek thought 3
Grene, Marjorie 11, 60–1

hafnium 42–3
Haldane, J. B. S. 51, 96
Hardy, Sir Alister 81–3
Harrison, R. G. 39
Harvey, William xi, 5, 19, 165–6
Hawking, Stephen W. 55
heart, understanding of xi, 5, 19, 20, 21, 165–6

Henderson, L. J. 118
Heracleitus 166–7
'hierarchical reductionism' xv
Hirst, R. J. 105
historical account 87–8
human evolution 82, 84, 85–91
Hume, David xxi–xxii, 8, 75, 125–6
'hypothetical realism' xviii–xix

'identity theory' xx
intellect, unreliability of xvi, xvii, 75–9, 80–1, 83–4, 87–93
interaction between God and universe 143–4, 145–6

Jackson, Frank 108–9
Jaki, Stanley L. 4
Jantzen, Grace M. 126–30
Jerison, Harry L. 75–6, 89
John Paul II, Pope 35

Kant, Immanuel xvii–xviii, 51, 75, 153
Kenny, Anthony xiii
Kierkegaard, Søren Aabye 152
Kimura, M. 41
Kneale, W. C. 39, 41, 42
Knight, Margaret 96–7
knowledge, and creation 138–40

Lack, David 80, 83, 84, 85, 86, 87
language 56–7, 92–3, 106
Lavoisier, Antoine Laurent 35
'laws of nature' 148, 149–51
Le Guin, Ursula 169
Leibniz, Gottfried 95, 96, 107
Lenneberg, E. H. 92
Leonardo da Vinci 161
levels, notion of 53–5; contradiction in 64–7; ontological 56–9; Polanyi's 60–4;
Lewis, David 158–9
Lewis, John, 65–6
Lewontin, R. C. 44–5
Locke, John 52–3, 153, 161
logic 97–8, 101–2
logical positivism 36–7
Lorenz, Konrad xvii–xix
Lovell, Bernard 145

Lucretius 51, 166–7

McGinn, Colin 103
machines, comparisons with organisms 6–8, 18, 19–20; principles of 62–3; thinking 95–101
Malcolm, N. 95
Malthus, Thomas Robert 7, 165
Manser, A. R. 22
'marks of contrivance' 6–7, 8
Marsden, George M. 31
materialism xii, xiv, xx, 94, *see also* reductionist materialism
matter 3, *see also* elements; particles, fundamental
Maze, J. R. 12–13
mechanical causes 26–7, 28–30
'methodological issues' in religion/science debate 32, 33
Midgley, Mary 166
Miller, Kenneth 31–2
Miller, S. L. xiv
mind v. brain xx–xxi, 81–3, 94, 96, 127–9, 141–2
misogyny, pseudo-scientific 48
Monod, Jacques 30, 47
Montefiore, Canon Hugh xii
morality, biological basis of xvii
Morris, Henry 31, 32
Muller-Lyer illusion 108, 109
mutation 15–16, 73

Nagel, Thomas 91
'naked ape' types of theory 47–9
National Academy of Sciences in America 32
natural selection, evolution by, and biological functions 11, 16–18, 20–2; and brain evolution xvi–xvii, 80–93; and conscious consequence-selection 13–15; and consciousness 117; and 'fitness for survival' 22–3; and statistical mechanics 27–9; arguments against xii–xiii; as complete explanation 9–10; case histories of 25, 38–9, 44–6; creationist objections to 30–1, 165; nastiness of 30; v. reductionism 68, 71–4

Newtonian physics 71
Nicolai, J. 46

ontological levels 56–9
order, creation of 144–6
organisms; chain of 8–9; comparisons with machines 6–8, 18, 19–20; complexity of x–xi, 6–7, 10–15
organs, functions of 5, 6–7, 13–15, 16–18, 19, 20–1
Osteostraci 5

pain, reality of 104–5
palaeontologists 5
Paley, William xii, 6–10, 25
particles, fundamental 4–5, 53, 59, 67, 94, 157
Partridge, P. H. 64–5
Passmore, John 64
Peirce, C. S. 27
perception, and god 129; and reductionist materialism 95, 103–6; and self 112–14; as belief 106–12; survival value of 89–91; truth/reality of xvi, 76–9, 92
Perrault, C. 168–9
Phillips, D. Z. 126, 166
physics 3–5
Pitcher, G. 109
Plato 141, 169
Polanyi, Michael 60, 61–4, 67
Popper, Sir Karl 35, 37–9, 41–3, 44, 55, 57–8, 89, 97
'possible worlds' 155–62
premisses, truth of 87
Price, H. H. xix, 103–4, 105–6
Priestley, Joseph 35, 114
primitive peoples 18–19
Pringle-Pattison, A. Seth 34
probability of evolution 85–6, 118, 119–20
'propositional attitudes' 102–3, 108
Puccetti, Roland 99
purposive explanations, decline 3–24

quantum mechanical theorists 55–6

radiometric dating techniques 31–2
Ray, John x–xi, xii, xx

reductionist materialism xiv–xv, xix, xx, 24; and atomic theory 50–3, 54–7, 67–8 and consciousness 94, 95, 96, 102, 104–6, 111–12, 113–14, 117; and elements 49–50; and 'naked ape' theories 47–9; and notion of levels 56–9, 60–3; v. Darwinism 71–4
relativism 31, *see also* scepticism
religion; and natural selection 30–1; v. science 31–6
replicators xiii, 73, *see also* DNA
reproductive system xii–xiii
RNA xiii
Root-Bernstein, Robert 32–3
Rorty, Richard 104
Rose, Steven 56
Rosenberg, A. 18
Ruse, Michael xvii, 35
Russell, Bertrand 103

scepticism 37, 75–6, 79–93
Schaffer, Jerome 11
science xi, xiv; and theism 152–3; origin of 3–4; philosophy of 36–46; v. religion 31–6
Scientific American x, 4, 104
'scientific creationists' 31–2, 33
'selection effect' 122–3
self, perceiving 112–14
sex, origin of 39
Short, T. L. 27–9
Simon, Michael A. 11
Smart, J. J. C. 79, 91, 104, 110, 120
Smith, Norman Kemp 10
social Darwinists 21
sociobiology 76; ideological motivations of 48
solidity, idea of 52–3
Sorsby, Arnold 18–19
Sperry, R. W. 112–13, 167
Stahl, Barbara 5
stars *see* sun/stars
statistical mechanics 27, 28
Stent, Gunther S. 76–8
sun/stars 39–40, 122
Super-Self-Directing Automatic Drivers (Super-SDADs) 99–100
'supersimilarity fallacy' 126, 131

survival; and brain functioning 75–6, 78–9, 80, 83–4, 87, 91; v. fitness 22–3
'sustaining' of universe 147–54
Swinburne, R. G. xxii, 10, 110, 126, 131–2, 134, 135, 147–52, 168
'systems-analysis' account 16

teleological thinking 3–24; and biological functions 10–18; and 'fitness for survival' 22–3; in physics and biology 3–10; reasons for 18–22
'teleonomy' 23
Thales 49–50
theism 119, 146, 147–8, 149–51, 152–4
'thinking' 97–102, 103
Tipler, F. J. 36–7, 124
Torrance, Thomas F. 155–6
Trivers, Robert L. 79
truth/reality, perception of xvi–xix, 76–8, 80, 81, 83–4, 88–91, 92–3
'two worlds argument' 64

universe; and 'big bang' theory 119–20; anthropic explanations for 120–3, 124; as body of God 127–30; creation of 135–40, 141–4, 146; independence of 146, 147–8, 155; multiple 122–3, 163; possible 155–62; sustaining of 147–54

Van der Waals, J. D. 159, 160
'veridical perception' 108, 109
vestigal organs 20
vision 76–8, 79, 90–1, 103–4, 105, 106, 110–12
vitalism, theory of 26, 67
Vollmer, Gerhard xx

Wallace, A. R. xi–xii
Wassermann, G. D. 38–9, 40–1, 44
water hypothesis 49–50
welfare state 21
Whitehead, A. N. 93
Whitrow, G. J. 120–1
widow birds 45–6
Wilkes, Kathleen 56–7
will, action of 135–40, 141–4
Wilson, Edgar 128
Wilson, John Cook 163
Wimsatt, William C. 71–2
Woese, C. R. 38
Woodfield, Andrew 20
'world-ensemble' theory 123
Wright, Larry 11–15, 16–18, 20–2